The Waite Group's

C++
Programming

The Waite Group's
C++
Programming

John Thomas Berry

SAMS

A Division of Macmillan Computer Publishing
11711 North College. Carmel. Indiana 46032 USA

International Standard Book Number: 0-672-22619-7
Library of Congress Catalog Card Number: 88-61754

From The Waite Group, Inc.
Development Editors: *Mitchell Waite* and *James Stockford*
Content Editor: *Harry Henderson*
Technical Reviewers: *John Carolan*
Managing Editor: *Scott Calamar*

From SAMS
Acquisitions Editor: *James S. Hill*
Development Editor: *James Rounds*
Editor: *Gary Masters*
Production Coordinator: *Katherine Stuart Ewing*
Word Processor: *David Ann Gregson*
Cover Artist: *Ron Troxell*
Illustrator: *Wm. D. Basham*
Indexer: *Ted Laux*
Compositor: *Impressions, Inc.*

Printed in the United States of America

*To my wife Nancy and my daughter Rebecca
for their patience, help, and, above all, love.*

*To my students at Foothill College
who understood if their projects
were sometimes a little bit late.*

Overview

Contents

Preface

Even in the short time that this book has been under development, C++ has gone from a relatively unknown programming language, primarily used under UNIX, to a widely discussed software development tool. Rumors abound about its ultimate domination of software development under its original UNIX, as well as in MS-DOS and the developing OS/2. As this book goes to press, some professional programmers are even predicting that C++ will supplant C as the dominant language in the software industry.

With all the interest in C++ and its migration to the MS-DOS and OS/2 environments, it soon became obvious that there was a great need for a straightforward tutorial book to serve as an introduction to this programming language. Experienced C programmers, especially those who concentrate on the IBM-PC and its clones, need an introduction to C++ that emphasizes the practical aspects of the language. They need something to show how the complex—but powerful—new syntax of this programming environment offers efficient solutions to the everyday problems of the professional programmer. These needs were my motivation for writing this book.

Although C++ is a more powerful tool than C, moving from the older language to the newer one is a simpler transition than you might at first expect. C++ is more of an "evolutionary" movement from C. The basic kernel of statements and operators are the same, including such things as function definition, separate compilation, and other tools of modularity commonly used by the professional C programmer. Most C programs are also legal C++ programs. What C++ adds to this basic syntax is the ability to create *classes*; these complete structures create enhanced modularity within a program. They also are the foundation for implementing many of the concepts of object-oriented programming. C++ also contains many additional improvements to the original C syntax; many—but not all—are mirrored in the new ANSI standard for C.

It's important to see these new and complex features used within a context of programming and design, not just as theoretical discussions that force the reader to apply this new knowledge as trial-and-error exercises. In this book, we have tried to temper discussions with examples that show the highlighted feature in the context in which it should be used; this is particularly important with such a new and evolving programming tool as C++. Note that the programs in this book were designed to illustrate specific points about the language. Although they eschew the "bells and whistles" that tend to obscure the point at hand, they stand as firm foundations for solid C++ applications.

As you will see, context is extremely important, because not everything that is possible in C++ is usable. As with any software, traps await the unwary. The author has already fallen into most of them—so this book may make your journey a little smoother.

John Thomas Berry
San Francisco

Acknowledgments

The enormity of even considering such a project as writing a book on a topic like C++ is overwhelming, even now that it's finished. It certainly would not have been possible without the assistance of many people who devoted more time than could possibly have been expected; they helped to keep the errors to a minimum.

Mitch Waite, Scott Calamar, and especially Jim Stockford from The Waite Group.

Harry Henderson and Gary Masters, my editors.

Takanori Adachi, Ivar Von Elsnitz, and especially John Carolan of Glockenspiel Limited, who provided technical support.

In addition, I would like to thank the following companies for their co-operation and help:

Glockenspiel Limited
Lifeboat Associates
Guidelines
Miwa Systems Consulting Company, Ltd.
Oasys

John Berry

The Waite Group extends thanks to the following people. Harry Henderson did a wonderful job as content editor and rewrite artist. Gary Masters did the most thorough copy-editing job we could have hoped for. Thanks to John Carolan for taking time to give us a careful technical review. Thanks also to Joseph McIsaac at Zortech, Ivar von Elsnitz, Craig Hubley, and Bob McIlree for their support.

The Waite Group

Trademarks

All terms mentioned in this book that are known to be
trademarks or service marks have been appropriately
capitalized. Neither The Waite Group nor SAMS can attest
to the accuracy of this information. Use of a term in this
book should not be regarded as affecting the validity of
any trademark or service mark.

UNIX is a registered trademark of AT&T Bell Laboratories
AT&T is a registered trademark of American Telephone and
    Telegraph
MS-DOS is a registered trademark of Microsoft Corp.
QuickC is a trademark of Microsoft Corp.
IBM-PC is a registered trademark of International Business
    Machines
OS/2 is a trademark of International Business Machines
Turbo C is a registered trademark of Borland International

Writing Your First C++ Program

1

Writing Your First
C++ Program

This chapter highlights the features of C++ and demonstrates how to use them in your programs. Starting with familiar concepts of C, it shows how C++ provides both minor enhancements and major new facilities that support a new model for program development. The chapter concludes with an overview of C++ program development in the UNIX and MS-DOS environments. Succeeding chapters provide in-depth discussions of each of the features presented here, together with numerous programming examples.

C++ Is Derived from C

One of the strengths of C++ is that it derives directly from the C programming language, and thus it is based on familiar ground. Indeed, C is a subset of C++. Because C++ is usually implemented as a translator that produces regular C code from C++ source statements, C++ is not a completely new programming language that requires a long learning curve. If you already know how to program in C, you know most of the basic syntax of C++. You have little to unlearn, so you can concentrate on the wealth of features that C++ adds to the previous language.

It is impossible to include in this book a discussion of the complete syntax of C, so we assume you have a basic familiarity with that language. However, the following brief summary highlights some important programming elements and points out some of the differences introduced by C++.

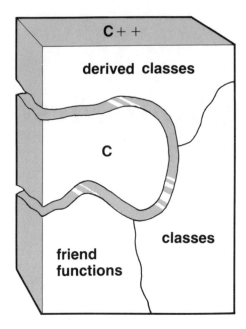

Figure 1-1.   The relationship between C and C++

The Form of a C++ Program

A C++ program consists of a series of one or more functions. These functions can be combined in a single file or be spread throughout several disk files. There must be one—and only one—function called *main()*. Although *main()* is where execution of the program officially begins, this is not an absolute, and later discussions show that it's possible to execute code both before *main()* is called and after it finishes executing.

C++ also permits greater modularity in programming through several interesting additions to the usual C syntax. One feature—class—integrates functions into data structures; another permits the "overloading" of function names, enabling two or more functions to share a common calling sequence.

Overall Similarity of C and C++

C++ is closely linked to C: it contains the same programming statements and constructions; it has essentially the same scope and storage class rules; and even the operators are identical. Of course, C++ offers more, but it's important for you to recognize the similarities. These similarities are best demonstrated by an example program that clearly shows the *superset-subset* relationship. To drive the point home, *day.c* (Listing 1-1) is both a good C program and a legal C++ program.

Listing 1-1.   A legal C and C++ program: *day.c*

```
#include <stdio.h>

char* days[] = { "Thursday", /* set up day names */
                 "Friday",
                 "Saturday",
                 "Sunday",
                 "Monday",
                 "Tuesday",
                 "Wednesday"};

main(argc,argv)
int argc;
char* argv[];
{
 int jdate;
 char* day;

 if(argc == 1)  { /* check for command line arguments */
   printf("format: list1 <julian date>\n");
   exit(1);
  }
jdate = atoi(argv[1]); /* convert argument to an integer */
day = days[ (jdate % 7) ];  /* find the right day name */
printf("day = %s\n",day);
}
```

This simple program accepts a Julian calendar date (defined here as the number of days since January 1) and returns the appropriate day of the week. The key to this program is the external character string array, *days[]*, containing the days of the week. The Julian date is divided modulo 7; this returns a number between 0 and 6, the remainder after dividing by 7. This remainder is used as an index into the array. The arrangement of the days of the week in the array is not random but is set for the current year. The second cell in the array—

index 1—is set for the day of the week upon which the first of the year falls; counting proceeds from there. Another interesting feature of the program is the command line interface. If you run the program without the required argument, it displays the correct command line format and exits.

Although *day.c* is a legitimate C and C++ program that compiles with either language translator, if you were to write this program purely in C++, you would do some things differently. Consequently, when you compile this program using a commercial C++ translator, the program generates some warning messages. Nonetheless, it is a good illustration of the close relationship between these two programming languages.

Basic features and syntax that are shared by C and C++ include:

- ► the *main()* function
- ► use of function arguments
- ► arithmetic and logical operators
- ► control and looping statements
- ► bitwise manipulation
- ► basic data types

However, keep in mind that even these similar areas have distinctive C++ characteristics. The power that's packed into C++ makes it more than just another version of C, and, as you will learn in this book, this power dictates a new approach to programming. Thus, the example in Listing 1-1 is legal C++ but not good C++.

C++ Is Not *Only* C

Do not overestimate the similarities between C and C++; they have significant differences, some of which are easy to overlook. Also, any comparison of the two languages is complicated by the fact that C is in a transition period. The industry-wide standard for C differs in some respects from traditional C syntax, and this standard often mirrors some of the changes introduced by C++. Therefore, this book concentrates on C++ and does not compare it to any great extent with the C standard; this way, you gain a feeling for the spirit of C++ without having to spend time reconciling different programming constructions and styles. At the same time, let's briefly look at similarities to the ANSI standard for the benefit of those programmers who are already using it.

Declarations in C++

One of the most obvious differences in the two languages is in the declaration of variables. Although an integer is still declared *int x* in C++, the order of the declaration within the program is more flexible. Recall that in C, all declarations must occur at the top of a function block or a block created by a pair of braces ({ and }). You must declare all variables not only before they are used, but before any executable statement. For example, a function that calculates the mean of a set of numbers might look like *mean.c* in Listing 1-2.

Listing 1-2.   A function to illustrate declarations: *mean.c*

```
double mean(num,size)
double num[];
int size;
{
int loop;
double total = 0;

for(loop = 0 ; loop < size ; loop++ )
    total += num[loop];

return total/size;
}
```

Inside the braces, the function is divided into two parts—a declaration section and an action section.

In C++, declarations can be placed anywhere in the program. In fact, as a matter of C++ style, you should keep declarations as close to their point of use as possible; this underscores their relationship to the statements that use them, and it reminds the programmer of their scope. A revision of the example function *mean()* into C++ as *mean2.c* (Listing 1-3) illustrates this point.

Listing 1-3.   A rewrite of the *mean()* function: *mean2.c*

```
double mean(double num, int size)
{
double total = 0;
for( int loop = 0 ; loop < size ; loop++ )
    total += num[loop];
```

continued

```
return total/size;
}
```

In *mean2.c* the integer variable loop occurs only inside the *for* statement. Therefore, you can delay declaring it until you initialize the *for* statement. Note that the format of the parameter declarations is also new; a later section in this chapter discusses that change.

The Scope of a Variable

The scope rules of C++ are similar to those of C. There are three possible scopes for a variable or other data object: *local*, *file*, and *class*. The discussion of the C++ *class* occurs later in this chapter. For now, let's examine the other two scopes.

A local variable is used exclusively within a block. Blocks are defined by a pair of braces. For example, in

```
example()
{
int x,y;
    .
    .
}
```

the variables *x* and *y* are local to the function *example()*.

A block can also be defined within another block, as follows:

```
example2()
{
    int x,y;
    {
    int p;
        .
        .
    }
    .
    .
}
```

In this example, *x* and *y* are local to *example2()*, but the variable *p* is local to the inner block defined by the second set of braces; this is the same in C++ as it is in C. However, this form is rarely used in either language.

The main issue with scope is the *visibility* or *accessibility* of the variable. A local variable is known only within its block. In the last example, *p* can be accessed only inside the inner block; it is invisible to other blocks. The variable *y*, however, illustrates another aspect of the visibility rules—its relativity. The *y* object is available both inside the outer block and the inner one as well.

In contrast to a local variable, a variable of *file* scope is declared outside any function or class. The availability of this kind of data object extends from the point of declaration to the end of the source file in which it is declared, regardless of the number of blocks involved. For example, the following code:

```
int count;
example()
{
     .
     .
}


example2()
{
     .
     .
}
```

defines an integer variable, *count*, which can be accessed in both *example()* and *example2()*. This corresponds to the *global* variable of other programming languages.

One important aspect of the scope of variables concerns the notion of data or variable hiding. Consider the following code fragment:

```
int count = 5

example()
{
int count = 10
     .
     .
}
```

There appears to be a conflict between two objects with the same scope. Which version of *count* does the function use? The answer is simple and it's the same in both C and C++. The most local name takes precedence. Here, the *count* that is declared within *example()* is used inside the function. What's new in C++ is the ability to bypass this restriction and to refer to a variable or other name outside the current scope, even if a local name hides that object. You can do this by using the scope resolution operator (*::*).

The scope resolution operator changes the reference of a name from a local variable to one of file scope. The *scope.c* example (Listing 1-4) demonstrates the use of this operator.

Listing 1-4.   The scope resolution operator: *scope.c*

```
int count = 5;


int example ()
{
int count =10;


cout << "inner count = " << count;
cout << "outer count = " << ::count;
}
```

By placing the *::* in front of the variable, you force it to refer outside the defined scope to the file. Of course, if no variable by that name exists in the global scope, an error occurs. (The *cout* statement is a simple output statement that displays text and variable values.)

Storage Classes in C++

Scope is only one of the factors that a designer must be aware of when creating an application. The *storage class* of a variable also affects the way a program uses the variable. Basically, the storage class of a variable or other data object determines the length of time that that object exists. Although the four C++ storages classes are the same as those in C, C++ adds some nuances to their use.

A variable of *automatic* storage class exists only when the program executes the block in which the variable is defined. For example, in

```
example()
{
int i = 0;
    .

    .

}
```

i is an automatic variable. Space is allocated for it while the function *example()* is executing. However, that space is deallocated as soon as control returns to the function that called *example()*. You can declare an automatic variable by using the designator *auto* in the declaration, but because this is the default for a local variable, the explicit declaration is almost never used.

You can also declare a variable as *static*. A static variable comes into existence when the program begins execution and lasts until the program ends; this permits the variable to retain its value even though program execution has passed beyond its scope. Consider the following code fragment:

```
example()
{
static int x = 0;

x++;
    .

    .

}
```

In this case, *static* modifies the declaration of a variable local to a function. Note that the scope of the variable *x* hasn't changed; it is still accessible only while the program is executing *example()*. However, because it is static, its memory locations are maintained from function call to function call, and the value stored in *x* is retained indefinitely.

You can also declare a variable of file scope as *static*:

```
static int i;
example()
{
    .

    .

}
```

This declaration restricts the scope of the variable *i* to the file in which it is declared. In C++, as in C, large applications often encompass several files. A static declaration restricts the scope of a global variable to its file of origin.

Note that the *int* in the two previous examples is redundant. A declaration of *static x* assumes the data type to be *int*. However, a static declaration of any other data type must be declared explicitly. For example, you must declare a real number value as *static double x*.

You declare a variable or function name in a program as *extern* to reference a definition or declaration that is found in another file. This was originally designed to facilitate the separate compilation of files; however, in C++, any variable or function name that you do not explicitly declare static is of type *extern* implicitly.

A *register* declaration works the same way as it does in C. It is, after all, only a suggestion to the compiler—one that is ignored if no registers are available. A register value must be an integer type—*char*, *int*, *long*, and so on—whose size fits into the register. (The maximum size is, of course, hardware dependent.)

Free Store Objects—A Fifth Storage Class

C++ actually has a fifth storage class—objects created using the C++ *new* operator. This operator dynamically allocates specified memory locations. Once allocated, these objects remain in existence until you use the *delete* operator to specifically deallocate them.

Objects manipulated by the *new* and *delete* operators are not automatic because they are not destroyed when the program leaves their scope; however, they also are not static. A static data object exists for the full term of the program's execution. A variable created by *new* can be destroyed and its memory allocation returned to the pool of available locations at any point in the program. This capability gives the programmer complete control over dynamic memory use.

Declaring a Constant Value in C++

In traditional—but not ANSI standard—C, the preprocessor macro facility creates a kind of *constant* value. The statement #*define RATE 1.5* on a line replaces the character string *RATE* with the value 1.5 throughout the program. This is done at the preprocessor stage before the compiler is called, and the replacement is purely a textual substitution.

C++ offers a true constant object. By prefixing a declaration with the *const* specifier, you can create a data object that has variable-like scope and visibility, but also has a value that the program cannot change. Thus, in the code fragment

```
const x = 1.2;

example()
{
    .
    .
int y = x * 23;
    .
    .
}
```

x is a constant integer value that you can use anywhere you can use a variable, except on the left-hand side of an assignment statement.

The chief advantage that the *const* modifier has over the more traditional *#define* construction is that the constant is a memory location like a variable and is not merely a substitute identifier. This distinction is an important consideration when using pointers, because you can combine this modifier with a pointer variable declaration.

Pointers in C++

Pointer variables—variables that contain the address of another variable—operate in analogous ways in C and C++. You must declare a pointer variable as a pointer to a built-in or user-created type. The most commonly used pointer variable in C++ is the character pointer, which is the base type to the character string. Almost as common are pointer variables to the complex data types that dominate a C++ program; these include structures, arrays, and (in C++ only) classes.

The syntax of a pointer is the same in both languages. The * operator in a declaration designates a pointer variable. For example, the declaration *char *x* creates a character string variable. The * operator causes the declaration of the variable *x* to allocate space not for the character value, but for the address of the memory location that holds such a value. Remember, the declaration of a pointer variable doesn't create the space needed to store a value, only the place to store an address. To store that value, you must use the *new* operator or assign the value of some preexisting variable to the variable.

The same two operators that manipulate pointer variables in C— & and *—are also available in C++. The *address-of* operator (&) puts the address of an existing variable into a pointer, as follows:

```
int x = 123;
int *y = &x;
```

After this code executes, the variable *y* contains the address of the variable *x*. The *dereferencing* operator (*) performs the complementary operation of obtaining the value at the location whose address is stored in the pointer. The following code:

```
int x, y = 123;
int *z = &y;

x = *z;
```

copies the value in *y* into *x* by way of the pointer z. The * operator performs an indirect memory access: It reads the value at location z and then uses this value as an address to find a location that contains another value. This last value is the one the assignment operator uses.

Pointer access to functions is the same in C++ as it is in C. An extra set of parentheses performs the necessary indirection. For example, the declaration of a pointer to a function might look as follows:

```
int (*f)();
```

You must use parentheses around the variable name to ensure that the correct indirection is performed. Note that the declaration *int *f()* specifies a function that returns a pointer to an integer—not the same operation shown in the preceding example. The *address-of* operator (&) assigns a value to the pointer as follows:

```
int (*f)();
f = &example();
(*f)();
```

This code fragment assigns the address of the function *example()* to the variable *f*, which has been declared as a pointer to a function. The third statement calls the function through the pointer variable by using the *indirection* operator enclosed in parentheses. As with the declaration, you must use the parentheses to generate the correct dereferencing operation. Of course, if *example()* has any parameters, you must also include them in the function call.

void **Pointers in C++**

One new development in C++ is the *void pointer*. The *void* data type, which specifies functions that don't return a value to the calling function, is common to both C and C++. However, C++ also lets you declare pointer variables to this type. Although you can't dereference these pointer variables, you can assign other pointer variables to them. In fact, they are most useful because they are compatible with all types of pointer variables and therefore can serve as generic pointer variables in situations where code must handle several different data types. Then you can use a type cast or merely assign them back to variables of the original types to return accessibility.

Declare a *void pointer* as you would any other pointer variable—*void *x*—and use it in an assignment statement as you would a normal pointer. Although you can't use the & and * pointer operators on it, you can assign it another *void* pointer variable or a pointer of any other type. For example, in the following code fragment:

```
int y = 123;
int *p = &y, *q;
void *vp;


vp = p;
q = vp;
```

the pointer *p* contains the address of an integer value, in this case *y*. The pointer *vp* accepts the value of this address and then passes it to the third pointer variable *q*.

The *void* pointer type gives you an important advantage—the capability of writing more general programs. Now you can create code that handles a variety of different data types without having to "wire in" this information early in the development process.

Pointers and *const*

Another important difference in C++ is the interaction between pointers and the *const* modifier. This relationship permits programming possibilities not found in C. For example, you can declare a pointer to a *const* object to give the program another access path to this unchanging value. More interestingly, you can declare a constant pointer or even create a constant pointer to a constant variable. Each of the above examples is a unique construction that you can add to your repertoire of programming tools. Let's explore these combinations further.

To declare a pointer to a constant value, merely add the *const* modifier to the declaration. For example, in

```
const char *x
```

const modifies *char* and not the * operator. The variable *x* points to an object of type *char*, which is constant when accessed through this particular variable—but which may be variable through some other name! In

```
const char *x = "This is only a test";
```

the variable *x* is initialized with the literal value of the character string.

A constant pointer declaration has a slightly different syntax and a different meaning. The declaration:

```
char *const x = "this string is frozen";
```

creates a constant that contains the address of the specified character string; its value cannot change because the pointer itself is a constant. The character string, however, does not need to be a constant.

You can also create a constant reference to a constant value by invoking the *const* modifier twice, as follows:

```
const char *const x = "This is also an example";
```

This example declares a constant *x* that points to another constant. Constant pointers are valuable in a variety of situations. They give you the convenience of the pointer notation, while protecting program values from being inadvertently changed.

What's Unique About C++

So far, this chapter has focused on the many similarities between C and C++ to help the beginning C++ programmer learn the language. However, there are many elements that are unique to C++, elements that are not found in the traditional C syntax, even in a modified form. These include an enhanced input/output system, function overloading, and, above all, the central concept of C++—the class. Now, let's look at these unique aspects of the language.

Simple I/O in C++

C++ doesn't have any built-in I/O operations. It maintains maximum flexibility by using functions in the standard library to support all such activities. C++ was designed to be upwardly compatible to C, and, therefore, it contains all of the familiar I/O functions, including *getchar()*, *putchar()*, *scanf()*, and *printf()*. In fact, a C program that depends heavily on these capabilities compiles as well under C++ as it does with an ordinary C compiler.

However, C++ greatly enhances the input and output of values. This enhancement includes a great improvement in convenience and a more streamlined interface to the outside world that eliminates the need for using large functions, such as *scanf()* and *printf()*, which carry a lot of extra baggage. The object-oriented nature of C++ led to the creation of routines for getting values from the keyboard and putting them on the display screen that are as general as their C counterparts yet are much more efficient and simpler to use. The details of the implementation of this subsystem are covered in a later chapter, but, basically, C++ gives you access to a series of small general-purpose input and output routines that can be tailored to the specific values you need to use. In addition, their convenience rivals that of the *printf()* and *scanf()* routines because the system automatically chooses the proper routine for the desired operation.

The basic I/O declarations are in the standard header file *stream.h*, which you must include in any program that uses the routines. This header file defines an interface to the I/O subsystem that consists of the three standard files—*cin*, *cout*, and *cerr*. When a program begins execution, it automatically opens these files and initially attaches the first to the keyboard and the others to the display screen, although all can be redirected like any of the standard files in C. Coupled with these files is a set of I/O operators that are truly unique to C++. Two operators connect the specified output values with the appropriate file: ≪ sends values to *cout* or *cerr* and ≫ retrieves values from *cin*.

In both cases, the operator acts as a mediator between a variable or expression and the outside world. The code fragment

```
#include <stream.h>

main()
{
char x;

cin >> x;
    .
    .
}
```

reads a character value from the keyboard and puts it in the variable *x*. The following code:

```
#include <stream.h>

main()
{
char x = 'a';

cout << x;
    .
    .
}
```

performs the complementary operation—it takes the value of *x* and displays it on the screen.

There is a twofold advantage in using operators instead of the function call syntax found in C. First, this notation is more natural to write and thus easier to read. The double *greater than* signs compel you to see the direction of the flow of characters; this is not available with the C-style function call. More importantly, the operators give I/O statements a more fluid style, enabling them to be combined into complex I/O expressions. Thus, C++ offers two new operators with the same economy of style and power as the increment operator (++) and makes them part of I/O notation.

These specialized operators are an integral part of the C++ programming philosophy. Later chapters show how C++ gives the program designer an almost unlimited capability for redefining the operator symbols available in the language. You can use this capability to create code that is both exact and concise; as a result of this, your code is also easier to maintain.

Another important aspect of these I/O operators is that they do data conversion. This results from their flexibility in using only two operations to get and put data. The two previous examples used declarations of the most basic character data type, but, as a matter of fact, you can retrieve or display any type of value with complete confidence that the program will make the appropriate conversion. Consider the lines in *io.c* (Listing 1-5).

Listing 1-5.   Using the I/O operators: *io.c*

```
#include <stream.h>

main()
{
double x = 1.23, y;

cin >> y;

cout << "the answer is " << x * y << "\n";
}
```

This is actually a complete—if uninteresting—program that compiles. It defines two real number variables—one with an initial value and one that receives a value from the keyboard. The latter operation is accomplished by using the input operator >> with the file *cin*. The operator implementation performs the necessary conversion to a *double*. Note that in an earlier example this same operator handled a character value. The output also illustrates more of the capabilities of this input/output subsystem. The output operator << lets you group together several values and send them to the screen as part of a single operation. These pieces need not be the same data type because each use of the operator represents a separate call to the operator code. For example, *io.c* displays a character string, a *double* value, and a special character string. The special character string is merely a new line character that you should recognize from the C *printf()* function. (C++ understands all of the carriage control characters.)

This brief introduction should help you get started writing C++ programs that communicate with the outside world. However, there is much more you can do with *cin, cout, cerr, <<,* and *>>.* Chapter 7 contains a complete discussion of these important C++ elements.

Function Definition in C++

Although the main design module in C++ is the yet-to-be discussed *class,* the *function* is still an important tool for organizing program code. Functions permit the program designer to create local *regions* within a program and then to carefully control the entrance to and exit from the code in these regions. More importantly, the programmer can create libraries of compiled general-purpose routines and then use them in many different programs.

The syntax of C++ function definition follows the *prototyping* format of the new ANSI C standard. A function definition starts with a header line that contains a declaration of the return value of the function and a list of declarations for any of the parameters, as follows:

```
int example(int x, int y)
```

In this declaration, the function returns an integer value and takes two integer values—*x* and *y*—as arguments. Note that the parameter declarations are done in a single step within one set of parentheses.

The declaration of parameters in the header line differs from traditional C, which requires that you use a separate line. However, that is only half of the new prototyping syntax. You can also declare a function and its parameters at the same time. The following example demonstrates this declaration syntax:

```
main()
{
int example(int,int);
    .

    .

}
```

In contrast to the definition header, here you do not need to explicitly mention the parameter name, only the data type, although you can include parameter names if you want to use them. However, C++ requires that you declare each function in the calling program. This procedure differs from normal C programming style, which doesn't explicitly declare integer data objects or functions.

Function Overloading

Function overloading is a unique part of C++ function syntax that lets you create a family of similar functions. All functions in the created family share the same name, but each has an independent code definition. Each overloaded function must have at least one parameter that differs from the other functions; that is, the data type of at least one parameter must be unique to each version of the function. When the function is called, the parameter list that is passed to it causes the system to choose the proper body of code. Thus, you don't need to add program statements that choose the correct function. Function overloading also eliminates the need for devising strange names to indicate the differences and the similarities of several related functions.

The *overload* keyword declares overloaded operators. Use it as part of the declaration of the function, as follows:

```
overload cube;
int cube(int);
double cube(double);
```

This example declares a group of two overloaded functions called *cube()*. These functions differ in both the value they return and the data type of their single parameter. It is this parameter that determines which *cube()* is used by any particular function call.

An important caution must be added before leaving the subject of function overloading. As useful and powerful as it seems, this feature can easily be abused and can quickly lead to incorrect and misleading code. Many C++ programmers feel that this part of C++ has not been as well documented as it should be. In any case, function overloading should be used sparingly and with caution, especially by those programmers who are new to the C++ language!

The *class* Data Type

The focus of the C++ programming language is the *class*, a data type that supports both modular design and the exciting new notions of object-oriented programming. It is the *class* data type that defines the functionality of the C++ programming language and marks it as a significant improvement over C.

The advantage offered by the *class* is manifest in its most basic form. Consider the following declaration:

```
struct square  {
     int side;
     int area();
}
```

This is a declaration of a simple class. Obviously, the basic form of this data type derives from the familiar notion of a structure, or a heterogeneous collection of contiguous variables. Like a C structure, the C++ class has a variable part that stores a value. However, unlike the C *struct* type, the class also has an associated function. In the example, the declared function returns an integer value. This is the difference in a nutshell. A class is complete: It contains both a storage location to contain values and the functions that manipulate those values. This format is a necessary condition for the creation of object-oriented programs.

Much of this book is devoted to exploring the ramifications of the class definition. It shows how to create and then use these classes to solve common, yet complex, programming problems. The C++ *class* is not limited to this first basic definition; indeed, you can use it to create arbitrarily complex objects. From the process of exploring this exciting new territory, you will discover the practical side of this abstract concept.

Simple and Not So Simple Classes

So far, you have seen only the simplest kind of class definition—a declaration. However, even this simple form can be enhanced and expanded. Now, let's talk about implementation, such as how to create an object that reflects a defined class.

Let's expand the previous class declaration into a complete definition of a new data type. With such a simple construction, this is a straightforward matter. Consider the *struct.h* definition (Listing 1-6).

Listing 1-6.   An expanded *struct* definition: *struct.h*

```
struct square  {
     int side;
```

```
    void set(int);
    int area();
};

void square::set(int x)
{
    side = x;
}

int square::area()
{
    return side * side;
}
```

A complete definition must include not only the declaration but a definition of the functions that are members of the class. In this case the only member functions are the easily implemented *set()* and *area()*. The former initializes the variable part of the class, and the latter returns the area of a figure. Note that in this context the scope resolution operator (*::*) associates a function definition with the function name declared in the structure.

One important advantage of the class becomes apparent when you use the definition in some code:

```
main()
{
    .
    .
    .
square x,y;

x.set(2);
cout << "area of figure x = " << x.area << "\n";
y.set(3);
cout << "area of figure y = " << y.area  << "\n";
    .
    .
    .
}
```

Each object that you create by declaring a class variable (often called an *instance* of the class) is an independent region of the program. For example, when the function *set()* is invoked, it alters only the values in the object that calls it. This frees the program designer from worrying about passing variables back and forth to a function. The function *belongs* to the variable; it's a *member* function.

Another advantage of the class is that it eliminates the need to use the awkward *struct square x* notation in the declaration of a variable. C++ is smart enough to find the definition of the class variable.

Classes as Objects

The class defined by the keyword *struct* is only the most basic of such objects; it lacks one of the most important advantages of the class— privacy. A more complete object uses the class declaration, as in *class.h* (Listing 1-7).

Listing 1-7.   A complete class declaration: *class.h*

```
class  precord  {
     char *name,
          *id;
     long salary;
public:
     precord(char*,char*);
     void set_sal(long);
     char* display();
};

precord::precord(char* nm, char* i)
{
     name = new char[strlen(nm)+1];
     strcpy(name,nm);
     id = new char[strlen(i)]+1;
     strcpy(id,i);
}

void precord::set_sal(long s);
{
     salary = s;
}

char* precord::display()
{
```

```
    temp = new char[strlen(name) + strlen(id) + 36];

    sprintf(temp,"name=%s\nid number = %s\nsalary = %ld\n",name,id,salary);

    return temp;
}
```

This example is still a simple class, but, unlike the previous examples, it has all the elements of this data type. The most important thing to notice is that it is divided into two sections—a public part that contains the member functions and a private section. In the example, the private section contains only variable members. Note that only the members that are declared in the public part of the class definition are known to other parts of the program; the members in the private part are hidden. Also, the only way to access the variable members in this example is through the member functions, which form a kind of *interface* to the class.

A member function of a class can serve as an interface because it has special access to the private part of the class. The simple member function *set_sal()* can take its parameter and store that value directly into the member variable *salary*. The members in the public part of a class serve as a bridge between the rest of the program and the hidden part of the class object. The simple class created by a *struct* declaration lacks this private part—all of it is public. The members of such a object are freely available to be set and unset by any part of the program.

The private part of a class adds a new dimension of modularity to a C++ program. Now you can hide from the rest of the program not only data items but also the functions that serve them. Thus, you can create programs that more fully approach the ideal of a series of independent objects—the goal of object-oriented design.

Although the code in this example is straightforward and easy to understand, it contains another concept that you should be aware of before moving on to other topics. The function *precord()* might seem a little strange to the traditional C programmer. That's because *precord()* is a special member function called a *constructor*. You can call a constructor—primarily through a declaration—each time you create an object of this class. It represents a kind of initialization routine in which the designer supplies the code to put the values into the multifaceted class. A complementary *destructor* function should be called as soon as a class object is destroyed. Neither constructors nor destructors are required for a class definition.

Changing the Meaning of Operators Through Overloading

Another important capability made manifest by the class definition is the ability to overload operators. This very simple concept is used frequently in programming languages; C++ merely extends its scope. The basic idea behind operator overloading is to redefine a commonly used symbol so that it applies to a new set of values. For example, the + operator represents the addition operation. Furthermore, this simple operator can be used with any type of numeric data. You can add two integer values, or you can add doubles or longs. (In C++, you can even add two character values together if the operation makes sense in the context of the program!) The C code that adds two double values is quite different from that which adds integer values. Thus, C uses an overloaded + sign with its built-in data types. If you define a *class* data type, you also can overload any of the common operators so that they will apply to the new class. Therefore, C++ gives you the same capability with user-defined types that C offers with the built-in data types.

The key to redefining an operator is to associate the appropriate *operator* function with a class object. (One important restriction on operator overloading is that it must involve an object of type *class*.) You can accomplish this association by defining an operator function and passing it a *class* as a parameter, however, the simplest method is to make the operator function a member of the class itself. Once declared, the operator function can be defined like any other function. For example, suppose you have defined a class with three components—*x*, *y*, and *z*. Furthermore, you want to define the addition of two objects of this type as the sum of their corresponding parts; the *x* values are added, then *y* values, and so on. Although this can be accomplished by definition and the *addition* function, it is more convenient to use a traditional symbol for addition and expand it to embrace this new definition. This is easily accomplished in *overload.h* (Listing 1-8).

Listing 1-8.   A class with an overloaded operator: *overload.h*

```
class triad  {
     long x, y, z;
public:
     void operator+(triad);
};
void triad::operator+(triad p)
```

```
{
    x += p.x;
    y += p.y;
    z += p.z;
}
```

For clarity, this example defines only an operator function. The function *operator+()* redefines the + operator—but only in the context of this class. Note the format of the function redefinition. There is a corresponding operator function for each of the symbols available in C++. Once you understand that symbol, the redefinition is no more exotic than writing a function to handle its details. This example brings in one object of type *triad* as a parameter and changes the object that calls the +. This calling sequence is the same as if you were adding two integers:

```
    .
    .
triad a,b;
    .
    .
a + b;
```

This similarity to traditional uses of the symbol is what makes operator overloading a convenient tool for program design.

As with function overloading, operator overloading is fraught with potential dangers. It is an easy facility to abuse, particularly through overuse. Its inherent dangers are compounded by the fact that it is too easy for you to overload an operator in one context and then try to use its older meaning in another context. Always approach the use of operator overloading with care and caution.

Derived Classes

Another important feature of C++ is that it gives you the ability to create hierarchies of class objects. In other words, you can define a class A and a class B in such a way so that everything that is in A is also in B, yet B contains some additional elements. The advantage of this is obvious to anyone who has had to solve programming problems in database design or in similar fields, such as expert systems. However, this capability offers advantages for even the most mundane programming tasks. For one thing, C++ lets you create a class and compile it. Even if you distribute only the object form, another programmer can create a derived class based on your original definition without having any access to your source code; this increases the flexibility of the programming language enormously.

The mechanism for creating a derived class is easy to use. First, you create an ordinary C++ class, as in *base.h* (Listing 1-9).

Listing 1-9.   A base class: *base.h*

```
class new_rec  {
     char *name,
          *id;
public:
     new_rec(char*, char*);
     char* display();
};
```

This class becomes your *base*. A derived class must specify this as its base; however, you then can add anything to the derived class to supplement this base, as in *derived.h* (Listing 1-10).

Listing 1-10.   A derived class: *derived.h*

```
class rec : new_rec   {
     char *address,
          *city,
          *state;
public:
     new_rec(char*,char*,char*,char*,char*);
     char* show();
};
```

In the class definition header in Listing 1-10, the phrase *: new_rec* marks this class as one derived from the earlier defined *new_rec*. Although the declared *rec* object is also a *new_rec* object, there are limitations to the access that the *rec* object has to its parent class. Specifically, it can't access the private part of *new_rec*. However, its members *can* access the member functions of the base class without any further dereferencings.

Creating a C++ Program

Now that you have had an overview of what C++ has to offer, the rest of the book is devoted to helping you master the practical techniques and considerations involved in C++ programming. First, let's look at the mechanics of writing C++ programs and how you get from source code to executable file.

C++ is available in a variety of implementations for UNIX, MS-DOS, and other operating systems. Obviously, the operating system affects such things as how files are named and what physical I/O services, graphics, and so on are available. Because C++ is still relatively new, you may have to use many services from the underlying library of the C compiler with which you compile the C++ translator output. Thus, the C compiler support of a given C++ implementation is also an important consideration. Finally, each implementation differs in its mechanics for creating, editing, compiling, linking, and debugging source files. Some implementations use menu-driven interfaces, while others rely heavily on batch files (MS-DOS) or shell scripts (UNIX). Your ultimate resource in these matters is your C++ product documentation. Following are some general considerations and helpful hints for creating C++ programs.

The Source File and Naming Conventions

All programs start as ordinary ASCII text files called source files. The text of these files consists of statements in the C++ language that are arranged in a logical order to produce useful programs. Thus, you generate the first stage of a C++ program with a text editor. Which editor you use depends both on your temperament and your software development environment.

The naming conventions of the various types of files in a C++ program are usually determined by which C++ implementation you use. Under the UNIX operating system, both traditional C and C++ programs share a common naming convention—they both end in the extension ".c". Other programming environments, however, distinguish between these two kinds of programs. The two most popular choices for C++ extensions are ".cpp" (Guidelines C++) and ".cxx" (Advantage C++ and Oasys C++). The specification of an extension is the only file-naming requirement for the C++ translator. Beyond this, your choice of filenames should follow local custom—14 characters for UNIX names and eight characters for MS-DOS names, to name the two most common operating system choices. This book adopts the UNIX convention of using the *.c* extension for both C and C++ programs.

Developing an Example Program

Because the focus of this section is the practical matter of producing executable code from a C++ source file, let's develop an example program to work with. The *averager.cpp* program (Listing 1-11) illustrates a simple example.

Listing 1-11.   A program that calculates the mean of a set of numbers: *averager.cpp*

```
#include <stream.h>

main(int argc, char *argv[])  // pick up command line arguments.
{
 double total = 0 ;  // set up an accumulator variable

 for(int i = 1 ; i < argc ; i++ )
   total += atof(argv[i]);   //use the stdlib to convert arguments

 cout << "mean=" <<  total/(argc-1);
}
```

The *averager.cpp* program accepts a series of numbers on the command line, totals these numbers, and then calculates their average value. The code is straightforward and represents a simple C++ program that uses the file extension specified for Guidelines C++. Note that because *argc* is always at least one, the program does not need to check for division by zero. An identical program, *averager.cxx*, (Listing 1-12) is set up for Advantage C++. Note the different extension for the stream header file as well as the new filename extension.

Listing 1-12.   A program that calculates the mean of a set of numbers: *averager.cpp*

```
#include <stream.hxx>

main(int argc, char *argv[])  // pick up command line arguments.
```

```
{
 double total = 0  // set up an accumulator variable

 for(int i = 1 ; i < argc ; i++ )
   total += atof(argv[i]);   //use the stdlib to convert arguments

 cout << "mean=" << total/(argc-1);
}
```

Compiling the Program

It's important to realize that most current implementations of C++ are translators rather than true compilers. That is, they take a C++ source file and produce a file of C code that then must be fed into an existing C compiler. For C++ translators licensed from AT&T, this translation is a two stage process:

► A program called *cpre* takes the C++ source file and executes all the preprocessor commands, thus producing an intermediate C++ source file.

► A program called *cfront* accepts the intermediate file and produces legal C code.

Note that the output from *cfront* must still be processed by a C compiler and a linker to produce an executable program.

Most software designers do not directly execute these translator programs. Instead, they use a *front-end* program to call each stage in turn. The formats of the front-end interfaces of the various C++ implementations vary greatly. Figure 1-2 shows a "generic" diagram of the steps involved in developing a C++ program.

Under UNIX, you compile a C++ program much like you compile an ordinary C program. To compile the example program, you execute the following line:

```
CC  averager.c
```

This produces an executable file named *a.out*. (Note that in UNIX the C++ processor front end is *CC*, which distinguishes it from the regular UNIX C compiler, *cc*.)

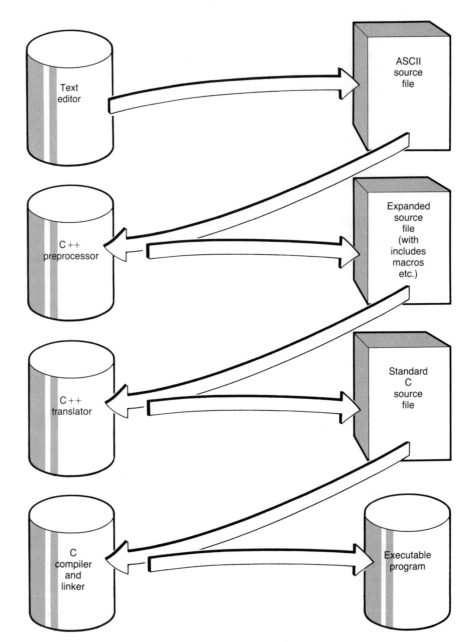

Figure 1-2. Developing a C++ program

At the time of publication, the most popular MS-DOS implementations of C++ are Guidelines, Advantage, and Oasys. You compile the
example program under Guidelines with the following command:

```
cppexe averager.cpp
```

Both Advantage and Oasys require the following command:

```
ccxx averager.cxx
```

to produce an executable file. In both cases the supported C compiler automatically compiles the final C code produced by the C++ translator. Future developments probably will lead to integrated C++ environments that are as easy to use as the *QuickC* and *Turbo* C products are for C programmers.

The example compilations in this section are only three of many variations and involve only the simplest program. In real-world situations you also must configure and control the C compiler and linker and maintain *make* files for projects with multiple source files. For details of these matters, you must consult the manual of your specific C++ implementation.

Review questions

1. The central notion that makes C++ unique from C is the _____.

2. Function declaration syntax in C++ is similar to the _____ standard, which is increasingly being used in C.

3. The use of several definitions for the same function or operator is called _____.

4. Most C++ implementations do not directly produce machine code; instead, they produce _____, which then must be fed to a _____.

Programming problem

1. Using the proper procedures for your C++ implementation, type in and compile the *averager* program.

Summary

This chapter presented highlights of C++ and offered a variety of examples of C++ code. You have seen where C++ is similar to C, where it expands on some everyday C concepts, and where it strikes out on its own to be quite different from C. Although the discussions and examples give only a brief idea of the power of this programming language and the details of its use, they should be sufficient to get you started "thinking C++." Succeeding chapters offer detailed discussions of the unique features of C++, including function overloading, classes, operator overloading, and derived classes, and many practical and complete examples.

Using Functions in C++

- ► Enhanced Function Syntax in C++
- ► Providing Parameters with Default Values
- ► Call By Reference
- ► *inline* Expanded Functions
- ► Creating Versatile Functions with Overloading
- ► Functions with a Variable Number of Parameters
- ► Pointers and the *const* Modifier
- ► Summary

2

Using Functions in C++

Functions are the basic building blocks of program design. As with C, programmer-defined functions are central to C++. In C++, however, the function syntax familiar to C programmers has been expanded to offer important new capabilities. This chapter shows you how to declare and define functions and how to use the following powerful new features:

- ▶ an improved interface between functions
- ▶ optional default values for function parameters
- ▶ a reference pointer parameter type
- ▶ *inline* functions
- ▶ the overloading (multiple definitions) of function names
- ▶ the capability of using a variable number of function arguments

If you are familiar with the new proposed ANSI standard for C, you might recognize some of these features of C++; however, C++ takes a more comprehensive and integrated approach to implementing them. Nevertheless, the proposed C standard is philosophically in tune with the basic principles of C++: It supports both the general concept of structured design and specific C++ features such as function overloading and parameter prototyping.

This chapter also compares C++ function definitions to traditional C techniques. Although it's important to realize that C++ is derived from C—it is C, in a sense—it's equally important to explore the differences.

Enhanced Function Syntax in C++

Functions are the heart of any C++ program. In fact, programs are merely collections of functions; even *main()*—where execution officially begins—is nothing more than a function. Therefore, the creation and connection of functions must always remain the focus of the C++ program designer. Carefully constructed functions let you modularize programs into subprograms that are short, readable, easy to debug, and easy to maintain. Furthermore, C++ is even better suited than C for collecting functions in libraries that can be used many times in different applications. Thus, the time you spend designing and redesigning functions in C++ is time well spent.

Function Declarations

In C++, you declare *all* functions within the scope of the program in which they operate; this includes functions that return an integer value. Thus the declaration

```
int example();
```

replaces the pre-ANSI C form *example()*. Indeed, not only do you declare the function itself, you must also include the type and number of the parameters in the declaration. In C++, a complete function declaration might look like the following:

```
int example(int);
```

The *int* inside the parentheses represents the data type of the parameter that this function takes—a syntax essentially the same as *function prototyping* in the new ANSI C standard.

When a function has multiple parameters, you must specify the type for *each* parameter separately. For example:

```
int example(int, char);
```

represents the declaration of an integer function that accepts two parameters—an integer and a character. Even if all of the parameters have the same data type, you must specify the type name for each argument, as follows:

```
int example(int,int,int);
```

This declares a function that accepts three integer parameters and returns an integer value. Note that you also can include parameter identifiers in a declaration:

```
int example(int x, char ch);
```

Such an inclusion is not required and offers no particular advantage.

Function Return Values and the *void* Type

The first item you specify in a function declaration is the type of data the function returns. The return value of a function in C++ can be any of the following simple data types: *char*, *short*, *int*, *long*, *float*, or *double*. Although a function cannot directly return an array type, it *can* return a structure or a class type. Of course, a pointer to any structured type—even an array—is always a legal return value.

In C++ (and ANSI C), the special data type *void* explicitly indicates the *absence* of a return value. You specify a *void* return value for a function that is used for its side effects, such as one that writes to a file or controls a peripheral device. For example, the following function might position the cursor at a given line and column:

```
void cursor (int, int);
```

In C++, unlike pre-ANSI C, you must explicitly use the *void* declaration for functions that do not return a value. If you do not, the compiler issues a warning message; however, future implementations might treat the absence of *void* as an actual error condition. Another reason for using the *void* return type is that it permits you to use the enhanced type-checking capabilities of C++.

What about functions that take no parameters? Traditional C practice uses empty parentheses following the function name to indicate the absence of parameters. ANSI C requires you to use the *void* parameter. For example,

```
example (void);
```

indicates that *example* takes no parameters. The preferred C++ practice, however, is to use the empty parentheses:

```
example()
```

Function Definitions

The previous function declaration format is also the format of the header for the definition of a function. The only differences are that you must include the names for the parameters and that you don't use a semi-colon at the end of the header. The following schematic shows an example of a function definition header:

```
int example(int x, int y)
{
    int z;
    .
    .
    return z;
}
```

(Lines with a single dot represent the code that implements the function.) Note the use of identifiers (x and y in this example) for the parameters. You no longer declare parameters on separate lines following the definition header. The new syntax is more compact and easier to read.

A Complete C++ Program

The *calc.c* program (Listing 2-1) illustrates proper C++ syntax in a simple four-function calculator program. To use the calculator, enter an expression in the form:

> *<number> <operator> <number>*

at the keyboard. This input is captured by the *cin* operator (see Chapter 7 for further details) in three variables—a numeric variable, a character variable (for the operation), and another numeric variable. A *switch* statement driven by the character variable chooses the proper operation to be performed, and the program displays the result on the screen.

Listing 2-1. A simple calculator program that illustrates the format of function declaration and definition: *calc.c*

```
#include <stream.h>

// define some useful substitutions

#define BLANK ' '
#define STOP 0

main()
{
double x,y,
        radd(double,double),  // declare a simple add function,
        rsub(double,double),  //...a subtraction function,
        rmul(double,double),  //...multiplication,...
        rdiv(double,double);  //...and finally, a division function.
char opr = BLANK;             // declare a variable for the operator

while ( opr != STOP ) {             // continue until the user says "exit"
  cout << "enter expression ";      // prompt...
  cin >> x >> opr >> y;             // ...read...

  switch (opr) {                    //...and evaluate
    case '+' : cout << "=" << radd(x,y);  // create a clause for each
               break;                      // operation.
    case '-' : cout << "=" << rsub(x,y);
               break;
    case '*' : cout << "=" << rmul(x,y);
               break;
    case '/' : cout << "=" << rdiv(x,y);
               break;
    case 'x' : opr = STOP;                 //...a cheap trick, "x" is the
               break;                      // second letter in "exit"
    default  : cout << "not yet implemented!\n";  // unbounded optimism!
    }

  cout << "\n\n";

  }
}
```
continued

```
//////////////////////////////////////////////////////////////

double radd(double a, double b)    // a function to add doubles
{
 return( a + b);
}

//////////////////////////////////////////////////////////////

double rsub(double a, double b)    //...one to subtract them
{
 return a - b;
}

//////////////////////////////////////////////////////////////

double rmul(double a, double b)    //...multiply...
{
 return a * b;
}

//////////////////////////////////////////////////////////////

double rdiv(double a, double b)    //...and divide
{
 if(b == 0)        // don't forget to check for division by zero.
  return 0;
 return a / b;
}
```

Program design includes a separate function for each possible operation. In most cases, these functions are single-line constructions, using only a *return* statement to contain the appropriate expression. (*rdiv()* is an exception because it must check for division by zero before it performs any calculation.) This kind of modularization is justified here because it makes the program more readable. In larger programs, using separate functions enables you to decrease development time and to give yourself room to expand or customize each operation—for example, to accommodate a new numeric representation such as BCD (Binary Coded Decimal).

Note that each operation's function is declared within the *main()* function. Consistent with C++ syntax, both the return type and the type of each parameter is specified. Note also that in each function definition the parameter list is declared within the parentheses of the function header—not outside, as is common in traditional C programming practice.

Let's examine this program a little more closely to see how these new features are used. The section before the *main()* function performs three useful initializations: It includes the standard output declarations found in *stream.h* and defines two identifiers—*BLANK* and *STOP*. The identifiers enhance the readability of the listing. Note that the program uses the older preprocessor syntax—the *#define* directive; this is appropriate because only simple textual substitution is required. (Later, this chapter shows how *inline* functions are superior to *#define* macros in many circumstances.)

The first section in *main()* contains the required declarations:

```
double x,y,
      radd(double,double),
      rsub(double,double),
      rmul(double,double),
      rdiv(double,double);
char opr = BLANK;
```

Although C++ no longer requires you to do all declarations at the beginning of a block or function, in this particular case, it seems appropriate. Notice that the functions that do the work of the program—*radd()*, *rsub()*, *rmul()*, and *div()*—are declared in the prototype format, which specifies both the return value and the parameters that each accepts.

The *while* loop, which controls the overall flow of the program, defines a simple *enter-and-act* loop. Within it, the program issues a prompt, accepts values from the keyboard, performs the appropriate operation, and displays the results on the screen. The program also uses the flexibility of the input operator >> to concatenate three values on a single input line. Thus, users have the illusion that they are typing in a single expression. The *while* statement

```
while ( opr != STOP )  {
    cout << "enter expression ";
    cin >> x >> opr >> y;
    .
    .
```

continues as long as the operator in an expression is not the *STOP* character defined at the beginning of the program.

The core of the *while* loop is the following *switch* statement:

```
switch (opr)  {
    case '+' : cout << "=" << radd(x,y);
        break;
    case '-' : cout << "=" << rsub(x,y);
        break;
    case '*' : cout << "=" << rmul(x,y);
        break;
    case '/' : cout << "=" << rdiv(x,y);
        break;
    case 'x' : opr = STOP;
        break;
default  : cout << "not yet implemented!\n";
}
cout << "\n\n";
```

Each legitimate operator is assigned a clause in this *switch*. In most cases, one line of code calls the appropriate function and displays the result. The program also uses a trick to develop an easy user interface. Recall that a character is actually an integer value. Because implicit type conversion is easy and unregulated in C++, the program can accept as input the value *exit*. The *e* is converted from its integer representation into a real number. The same thing happens to the *i*. However, the value *x* is stored in the character variable *opr*. This value then triggers the exit clause of the *switch*. Thus, the special operator *STOP* isn't actually needed to exit the loop; it merely helps improve program read-ability.

Finally, the service functions are almost identical, differing only in the operation that's performed. For example, *radd()*:

```
double radd(double a, double b)
{
    return( a + b);
}
```

accepts two double values as parameters and immediately returns their sum. Only *rdiv()* differs significantly:

```
double rdiv(double a, double b)
{
    if(b == 0)
```

```
        return 0;
    return a / b;
}
```

Notice the error checking. The program checks *b* to ensure that its value is not zero; this procedure is necessary for any expression that involves division.

Providing Parameters with Default Values

Many programs contain definitions of general-purpose functions that usually work with one set of values but occasionally must handle another set. For example, a function that raises a number to a power can be defined as a general-purpose subprogram, but many times it will be called merely to square a number. In C, you can handle these different operations in two ways: You can define a series of specialized functions to handle each occurrence, or you can explicitly pass the function a parameter that indicates the specified power. The obvious problem with the former solution is that it leads to a proliferation of functions that might be too small for efficient design; in these functions, the overhead of a function call is more than that of the statements executed. The latter solution, which is more commonly chosen, leads to programs whose readability can suffer from a lack of clear focus, especially if the general-purpose function must handle many special cases.

C++ offers a third alternative. In C++, you can call a function without providing a value for some of its parameters. To do this, the function definition provides default values that are used for these parameters when the calling function does not supply a value. For example, consider the following code fragment:

```
int example(int, int =12),
x=23;
example(x);
```

Because the call to *example()* does not specify a value for the second parameter, the value of the second parameter is set to 12 (the default value specified in the declaration). If the function call had been *example(x, 4)*, then the second parameter would have been set to four, as specified in the call.

The example clearly shows the syntax of the default argument specification. In the declaration for each parameter with a default value, you must include an expression of the following form:

```
<type> = <value>;
```

You can set any or all of the arguments of a function this way. Note that the default specification appears in the declaration of the function *example()* and not in the definition itself. In fact, it's not clear in this definition that there *is* a defined default value; this is evident only when you examine the declaration. The *calc2.c* program (Listing 2-2) is an example of how to define a general-purpose function and provide defaults for the most commonly used values.

**Listing 2-2.   A simple calculator program with a function
                that uses a default parameter value: *calc2.c***

```
#include <stream.h>

// define some useful substitutions

#define BLANK ' '
#define STOP 0

main()
{
 double x,y,
         radd(double,double),   // declare a simple add function,
         rsub(double,double),   //...a subtraction function,
         rmul(double,double),   //...multiplication,...
         rdiv(double,double),   //...and finally, a division function.
         rpow(double, double =2); //...create a power operation--defaulting
                                  // to power of two--square.
 char opr = BLANK;               // declare a variable for the operator

 while ( opr != STOP ) {          // continue until the user says "exit"
   cout << "enter expression ";   // prompt...
   cin >> x >> opr >> y;          // ...read...

   switch (opr) {                           //...and evaluate
     case '+' : cout << "=" << radd(x,y);   // create a clause for each
                break;                       // operation.
```

```
        case '-' : cout << "=" << rsub(x,y);
                    break;
        case '*' : cout << "=" << rmul(x,y);
                    break;
        case '/' : cout << "=" << rdiv(x,y);
                    break;
        case '^' : if(y == 2)  // check for default case (2)
                        cout << "=" << rpow(x);   // call power with one parameter
                    else
                        cout << "=" << rpow(x,y); // call it with both specified
                    break;
        case 'x' : opr = STOP;                    //...a cheap trick, "x" is the
                    break;                         // second letter in "exit"
        default  : cout << "not yet implemented!\n";  // unbounded optimism!
        }

    cout << "\n\n";


   }
}


/////////////////////////////////////////////////////////////////////////

double radd(double a, double b)     // a function to add doubles
{
 return( a + b);
}


/////////////////////////////////////////////////////////////////////////

double rsub(double a, double b)     //...one to subtract them
{
 return a - b;
}


/////////////////////////////////////////////////////////////////////////

double rmul(double a, double b)     //...multiply...
{
 return a * b;
}
```

continued

//

```
double rdiv(double a, double b)     //...and divide
{
 if(b == 0)         // don't forget to check for division by zero.
  return 0;
 return a / b;
}
```

//

```
double rpow(double a, double e)                 // a power of function.
{
 double t = a;  // create a temporary holding variable

 if(e == 0)        // test for special "0 power" situation
   return 1;

 for(double i = 1 ; i < e ; i++)       // a simple algorithm for finding
   t*=a;                               // the power--it doesn't work for any
 return t;                             // exotic cases.
}
```

This program uses the earlier calculator program and adds a new operator (^) to handle exponentiation. The function that manipulates the operator—*rpow()*—is declared in the same list as the other functions. However, the parameter list for the declaration of *rpow()* not only lists each parameter, it also includes a default value for the last parameter. Examine the *switch* clause that handles the input for this function. If the specified power is two, *rpow()* is called with only one parameter, even though two are specified in the definition of the function. The default value of two is automatically assigned to the second parameter. If you specify a number other than two, both parameters are included in the call, and the function does not use the default value.

There are some commonsense restrictions for using default arguments. The values you specify must either match the parameter in type or be reasonably compatible—that is to say, the implicit conversion from one to the other must make sense. Converting a *char* value to an *int* makes sense, because a *char* is in essence a small integer number. On the other hand, a conversion from a *double* to an *int* usually generates an incorrect or unreasonable value.

Furthermore, C++ does not provide for defaulting parameters in the middle of an argument list. When you call a function, you can omit all of the arguments (as long as the declaration specifies all of the defaults), but you cannot eliminate only the middle arguments and expect them to assume default values. For example, in the following function declaration:

```
double example(int =123, char ='a', double =1.2);
```

you can call the function with the *int* and *char* parameters (using the default of the *double*); you can call the function with only the *int* parameter (using the default for both the *char* and the *double*); or you can call the function with no parameters (using the defaults for all of the parameters). However, you can't call *example()* by supplying the only *int* and the *double* arguments, because the C++ preprocessor can't tell whether you intended to omit the second value or the third value.

Review questions

1. In C++, the practice of declaring a function with its parameters—in the form *example(int)*—is called _____.

2. You must declare a function as returning a specified type. Therefore you must use the _____ type to declare a function that doesn't return a value.

3. If the programmer supplies a set of _____ values as the parameters of a function, then these values are used if none are supplied in the function call.

Programming projects

1. Expand the program *calc.c* to include operations that find a remainder and perform square roots and cubes.

2. Add a display operation to *calc.c*; this should just show values and not return any value.

Call By Reference

Another C++ feature that expands the versatility of functions and function calls is its provision for *call by reference*. Although this term might be foreign to many practical C++ programmers, the action that it implies is used every day. When a function with an associated list of parameters is called from another function, the variables represented by the parameters must be supplied with values. Ordinarily, you do this by calling the function with a set of variables, expressions, or other values—one per formal parameter—although C++ also lets you specify a default value that doesn't need to be supplied explicitly. Often, these *formal arguments* are in the form of variables. When you invoke the following function:

```
x = example(x,y);
```

the variable *x* is associated with the first parameter of *example()* and *y* with the second.

Parameters that are declared in the function definition have a scope that restricts them to the function. In the following example:

```
int example(int x, int y)
{
    int z;
        .
        .
    return z;
}
```

x, y, and *z* are local variables. Using a variable in the calling sequence is identical to initializing a variable in the declaration statement within the function being called. The values that are passed to the parameter are *copies* of the formal arguments. For example, if you call the *example()* function with the following set-up:

```
int p = 2, q = 4, w;
w = example(p,q);
```

the value in *p* is copied into *x* and, similarly, *q* is copied into *y*. These two sets of variables are connected only in that they share the same values. Values move in only one direction—from the calling function to the called function. Any changes that occur in the variables in the function are not passed back to the caller. This syntax is known as a *call by value.*

In C, the call by value is the default operation, but you can achieve a *call by reference* by using a pointer as a parameter. In a call by reference, you pass the actual variable (in other words, the memory storage address) to the function. When you use a pointer, which represents an address, the address of the actual argument—not its value—is sent to the function. In the following example:

```
int example(int *x);
{
    int z;
        .
        .
    *x = 2*z;
}
```

a change in the parameter *x has a permanent effect in the calling function because it changes the value of the variable *x*. This is one way to retrieve values from a function without using the *return* statement. It also is a common alternative to using global variables when two functions must share data.

Declaring Reference Variables

C++ provides a form of call by reference that is easier to use than pointers. First, let's examine the use of *reference* variables in C++. As with C, C++ enables you to declare regular variables or pointer variables. In the former case, memory is actually allocated for the data object; in the latter, a memory location is set aside to hold an address for an object that will be allocated at another time. C++ has a third kind of declaration—the *reference* type. Like a pointer variable, it refers to another variable location, but like a regular variable, it requires no special dereferencing operators.

The syntax of the reference variable is straightforward:

```
int x;
int& y = x;
```

This example sets up the reference variable *y* and assigns it to the existing variable *x*. At this point, the referenced location has two names associated with it—*x* and *y*. Because both variables point to the same location in memory, they are, in fact, the same variable. Any assignment made to *y* is reflected through *x*; the inverse is also true, and changes to *x* occur through any access to *y*. Therefore, with the *reference* data type, you can create an alias for a variable.

The *reference* type has a restriction that serves to distinguish it from a pointer variable, which, after all, does something very similar. The value of the *reference* type must be set at declaration, and it cannot be changed during the run of the program. After you initialize this type in the declaration, it always refers to the same memory location. Thus, any assignments you make to a reference variable change only the data in memory, not the address of the variable itself. In other words, you can think of a reference variable as a pointer to a constant location.

Call By Reference in C++

Why use references? Consider the declaration of function parameters. By using a *reference* type in a parameter declaration, you can create a call by reference without using the cumbersome pointer mechanism discussed earlier. The advantage of using a reference variable inside a function is that the assignment and manipulation of its values are straightforward—they don't need to be constantly dereferenced with the * pointer operator, a situation fertile for accidental misreferencing. The following example:

```
      .
      .
      .
int value = 123;
example(value);
      .
      .
void example(int x&)
{
    x = 2 * x;
}
```

doubles the value currently in *x* and returns that value to the calling function. Reference parameters eliminate the need for declaring pointer variables with their attendant dereferencing syntax—*x* or *rate*—in order to perform a call by reference.

The *mean.c* program (Listing 2-3) demonstrates the use of a *reference* data type in the parameter list of a function. This simple program calculates the mean of any set of real numbers; it consists of three functions—*get_value()*, *mean()*, and *main()*. The *get_value()* function accepts values from the keyboard and accumulates them in the variable *acum*; the function's parameter is defined as a reference type in the parameter list and is incremented through the *for* loop. The special input value of *stop* ends the operation of this function and returns control to the calling function. The *mean()* function checks for division by zero and then calculates the value. The *main()* function ties the two functions together by calling each one and displaying the results.

Listing 2-3. **A program that calculates the mean of a set of numbers and uses a reference parameter:** *mean.c*

```
#include <stream.h>
#include <string.h>


main()
{
 int temp;
 double get_value(int&),      // declare an input function.
        mean(double,int),     //...and an average calculator.
        accum;
 accum = get_value(temp);     // get the input.
 cout << "mean =" << mean(accum, temp) << "\n";  // display the results
}



/////////////////////////////////////////////////////////////////


double get_value(int& t)      // an input function
{
 char x[50];         // define an input buffer
 double accum = 0; //...and an accumulator variable

 cout << "enter values below:\n";

 for(t = 0;;t++) {            // set up a loop that increments a counter
   cin >> x;                  // fill input buffer
   if(!strcmp(x,"stop"))      // stop?
     break;
   accum += atof(x);          // convert buffer to number and accumulate
 }
 return accum;
}
```
continued

//

```
double mean(double x, int total)   // calculate the mean
{
  if(total == 0)  {                         // check for error condition
    cout << "error--attempted division by zero!\n";
    return 0;
  }
  return x / total;                    //return the calculated value.
}
```

The first few lines of *mean.c* perform the necessary initialization by including the header files *string.h* and *stream.h* from the standard directory. The following declarations:

```
int temp;
double get_value(int&t),
mean(double,int),
accum;
```

set up the functions that get the numbers and calculate the mean. The *int&t* parameter in *get_value()* is a reference parameter; therefore, changes in the *get_value()* function are reflected in *main()*. The *accum* variable is an ordinary real variable that holds the current total of entered numbers, and *temp* counts the number of values that are entered.

The heart of *main()* consists of two function calls. The first:

```
accum = get_value(temp);
```

retrieves the numeric values from the user through the input function. The second:

```
cout << "mean =" << mean(accum, temp) << "\n";
```

displays the result of the calculations based on the two values in *mean()*. Because the parameter of *get_value()* was declared as a *reference* type, you do not need to use the *address-of* operator &.

The definition of *get_val()* echoes the reference declaration:

```
double get_value(int& t)
```

This declares the variable *t* equivalent to any formal argument that calls it and passes all changes to the calling function. The rest of the program is straightforward. After the declarations, the function prompts the user to enter data and uses a loop to accept values from the keyboard:

```
for(t = 0;;t++) {
cin >> x;
if(!strcmp(x,"stop"))
    break;
accum += atof(x);
}
```

The program handles keyboard values as character strings—through the standard input stream *cin* and the input operator >>—because they are the most convenient form of input to test. Here, the function tests only for the special string *stop*, but you also could add more thorough error checking. If the loop doesn't encounter the exit condition, *get_value()* uses the standard library function *atof()* to convert the character string into its numeric value. It adds this value to the current total and sends the accumulated value to *main()* through the *return* statement. Because the counter *t* is a reference variable, all of the changes that occur in the loop also occur in the originating function. Notice that this function is much more readable than an orthodox C program because it doesn't require pointer dereferencing.

The *mean()* function does calculations based on the two values supplied by *get_val()*. After it tests for division by zero, it performs a simple division and returns the result.

This example is particularly interesting because of the interaction between the parameter *t* in *get_value()* and the variable *temp*, which invokes it from *main()*. Because *t* is a variable parameter, the calling sequence initializes it to the value of *temp*—that is, both variable names are set to point to the same location in memory. Any changes to *t*—in this case, incrementing by one—are permanent changes.

There are several reasons why you should use a reference variable as a parameter rather than a pointer variable. Assignments are direct and need not be mediated by an indirection operator. Even more importantly, the calling function does not need to use the & address operator with the parameter; it directly uses the variable name. *Reference* types present fewer chances for errors—particularly the mistake of invoking a function with a variable when a pointer variable is expected.

inline Expanded Functions

Let's shift the focus of this discussion from improvements in the function call mechanism to the question of whether you should use a function call at all. In traditional C, you can use macros to conveniently insert code into a program. Anywhere a macro name occurs in the code, the preprocessor replaces the name with the defined statements. This is a useful device because it improves readability and sometimes helps you avoid the overhead of function calls. The problem with the macro preprocessor is the way it simple-mindedly interprets a macro definition—it performs a straight textual substitution. For example:

```
#define RATE 1.5
```

causes the character string *1.5* to be substituted for the string *RATE*. This works fine, but what happens when you use a *#define* with parameters to produce a function-like syntax? This kind of macro is more powerful because it can generate program code for a variety of situations; but it also can often lead to problems. The following definition:

```
#define tax(x) x*RATE;
```

works for some substitutions but not for others. For example, if you call the macro with an expression rather than a single variable:

```
tax(p+2);
```

the macro expansion generates the following code:

```
p + 2 * RATE;
```

instead of the correct *(p + 2) * RATE*. C programmers must be extremely careful when using the *#define* in this way. Other problems with the construction focus on the fact that a macro is not a function: It doesn't have local variables; it doesn't even define a block. Macros also do not permit parameter checking when prototypes are used. In short, a *#define* macro is a series of statements masquerading as a function.

inline Functions in C++

C++ solves the drawbacks of the C macro with a feature called the *inline expanded function*. Inline expanded code gives a programmer the opportunity to use a macro-like facility without any of the problems associated with the *#define* preprocessor statement.

The *inline* modifier lets you mark a particular function to be expanded rather than compiled as an ordinary function. Thus, whenever the function is called, it is replaced literally with the statements found in the function definition. (Actually, inline expansion is merely a request to the C++ translator; it can be ignored if your function is too complicated or too long, in which case it becomes an ordinary function.) The big advantage that an *inline* function offers is that it maintains all of the attributes of a true function: It defines a block; it can have local variables; and it permits the same kind of error checking as an ordinary function. Creating multiline inline functions also presents no special problems.

Another important advantage of using *inline* functions is that they can help you write well-designed, modular programs that remain efficient at the code level. For convenience, most programmers divide a program into small, individual functions. When many modules are defined, the program is usually easier to follow and understand and, thus, better designed. Ideally, each module should perform a single task. A well-structured program is also much easier to update or change because side effects caused by data objects with wide-ranging scope are eliminated and any errors created by new program code can easily be isolated.

However, small functions can also create a problem—they can be inefficient. A function containing only a single line can require more time and resources to set up than to actually run. This overhead includes such operations as saving the status of the calling function, copying parameter values to the function, and calling the function. Reloading the original function after the called function executes involves the inverse of this procedure. Thus, the overhead of the function dominates its execution time. Often, the designer can ignore these factors, but, occasionally, a program requires high performance, especially if it must perform many repetitive operations. C++ lets you eliminate this type of overhead. Merely use the *inline* modifier to declare small functions as inline expanded.

Defining an *inline* Function

When you use the *inline* modifier as the first element of the function definition line, as follows:

```
inline example(int x);
{
    .
    .
    .
}
```

it requests the compiler to place the following function in the program whenever the program calls the function. With ordinary function calls, value objects are saved and control is passed to a subprogram; with the *inline* modifier set, the function code is copied into the program at the point of every call. At compilation, there are as many copies as there are calls in the program, and none of them require overhead. However, because the code is reproduced many times—thus increasing the size of the object code—only very small functions benefit from this modification.

The *mean2.h* function contains the *mean()* function of the previous example program (Listing 2-4) declared *inline*. Nothing else in the definition has changed. Actually, the function is a borderline case for inline expansion, and it is almost too long to benefit from the treatment. Loading a file with code created from *inline* functions can cause its own overhead problems.

Listing 2-4.   A function declared as *inline*: *mean2.h*

```
inline double mean(double x, int total)  // calculate the mean
{
 if(total == 0) {                        // check for error condition
   cout << "error--attempted division by zero!\n";
   return 0;
  }
 return x / total;             //return the calculated value.
}
```

Review questions

1. A reference variable contains the ———— of a memory location and not its ————.

2. A reference variable is commonly used as a function parameter to create a call by ———— situation.

3. A function that is declared ———— is similar to the preprocessor macro command.

Programming projects

1. Redefine *mean.c* so that all the functions are inline expanded.

2. Redo *mean.c* using pointer variables in place of the reference parameters.

Creating Versatile Functions with Overloading

Often, two functions within a program perform the same operation but on different data types. For example, one function might perform a series of calculations on a set of real numbers while another handles integers. C programs usually differentiate between these functions with special switching code. For example, in the following:

```
if( real_flag)
      x = f_std(z);
else
      i = i_std(z);
```

the function *f_std()* performs calculations on real value parameters, and *i_std()* performs the same calculations on integers. You must create a separate, unique function for each one.

C++ provides a better solution—it lets you create a single function name that serves both purposes. The *overloading* feature handles the differences.

You must approach the technique of function name overloading with a great deal of caution. When you first begin to program in C++, you should restrict yourself to a few carefully considered and obvious examples. During the process of reusing a name, you can easily lose track of which version is being used in any specific context. It is even more difficult for someone reading the program to keep these different contexts straight. Proceed with care!

Declaring an Overloaded Function

When you declare a function name with the following form:

```
overload example;
double example(double);
long example(int);
```

you alert the compiler that the program contains more than one set of code referenced by the name *example()*. In this case, *example()* returns a *double* or *long*, depending on the data type of the parameter used when it is called. Note that a specific declaration of each form must follow the *overload* declaration. The only requirement for an over-loaded function is that the parameter lists must differ by at least one argument; this is how the compiler selects the proper set of code to honor a function call. The total number of function parameters involved and the type of the return value, if any, are unimportant as long as at least one parameter differs in each function definition.

The "uniqueness" requirement for an overloaded function list of arguments includes some additional restrictions. There must be a clear-cut, unambiguous difference between the parameter lists of overloaded functions. You cannot always rely on the flexible data conversion that C++ does implicitly. In order to resolve the call of an overloaded function, C++ first tries to exactly match the type of the actual arguments with the type of the appropriate parameters. For example:

```
int example(int,int)
```

matches

```
x = example(1,2);
```

If C++ doesn't find an exact match, it applies a built-in conversion to try to reconcile the actual argument with the formal argument. However, those conversions don't always make sense—*double* to *int*, for example, is not carried out by the overloading mechanism, even though C++ generally permits such operations to take place. As a last resort, C++ attempts user-defined conversion operations to choose the proper function. (This kind of conversion is discussed in connection with operator overloading in the *class* data type.)

The *mean2.c* program (Listing 2-5) is an example of an overloaded function name. This program lets the user enter a series of numbers on the command line in the following form:

```
mean 1.2 3.4 6.3 7
```

and it returns the average of these numbers. You may specify either real or integer values; the answer always matches the entered numbers—*double* for real numbers, *long* for integer numbers.

Listing 2-5.   A program that calculates the mean of a set of numbers and uses function overloading: *mean3.c*

```
#include <stream.h>
#include <string.h>


overload mean;    // declare the name "mean" overloaded
double mean(double, char*[], int);  // declare a double version
long mean(long, char*[], int);      //...and a one returning long


main(int argc, char* argv[])    // set up to take command line arguments
{
  if(argc == 1)  {    // check to see if any values have been entered
    cout << "Enter values on command line\n";
    exit(1);
  }


  if(strchr(argv[1],'.') == 0)  {   // is the first number a real?
    long i = atol(argv[1]),         // call the long mean()
    long x = mean(i,argv,argc);
    cout << "mean = " << x << "\n";
  }
  else  {                           // call the double mean()
    double j = atof(argv[1]),
    double x = mean(j, argv, argc);
    cout << "mean = " << x << "\n";
  }
}
```

continued

//

```
long mean(long x, char* buffer[], int len)    // a mean() for long values
{
  long temp = x;                              // initialize to the first value
  for(int i = 2 ; i < len ; i++)              // extract all the others
    temp += atol(buffer[i]);
  return temp / (len - 1);      //return the mean
}
```

//

```
double mean(double x, char* buffer[], int len)  // a mean() for doubles
{
  double temp = x;                            // the initial value is already figured
  for(int i = 2 ; i < len ; i++)
    temp += atof(buffer[i]);        // get the rest
  return temp / (len - 1);          // return the result
}
```

Following the *#include* statements, the program declares the nature of the function *mean()*:

```
overload mean;
double mean(double, char*[], int);
long mean(long, char*[], int);
```

The declarations of the two versions of the function must follow the *overload* statement. Note that only the first parameter in each one differs; the rest of the parameter lists are the same. The overloading mechanism uses this first parameter to decide which version to use throughout the course of the program. (The second parameter in each function, *char* buffer[]*, might seem unusual; it passes an array of pointers to character strings.)

Notice that the code in *main()* that manipulates the arguments is passed through *argv[]* from the command line; this is a common C convention that carries over to C++. If the user runs the program without supplying additional arguments, the program prints an error message and ends. This is accomplished by the following code:

```
if(argc == 1)  {
    cout << "Enter values on command line\n";
```

```
    exit(1);
}
```

(Remember, a program always has one command-line argument—the program name itself. Thus, if *argc* is 1, the user entered no number on the command line.) Another method of handling incorrect input would be to rewrite the function to prompt the user for the missing values.

In normal execution, the program checks the first argument to see if it contains a period; if it does, it is a real number. The first argument is converted into a number, and the rest of the arguments—still in the form of character strings—are sent to *mean()*. The the program displays the return value. If the function doesn't detect a period, it assumes the value is an integer and converts the first character into a *long* value. This value and the rest of *argv[]* are sent to *mean()*; however, because this is a *long* value, the second definition of *mean()* is called. Again, the program displays the value. The two mean functions differ only in the manner in which they handle the string-to-number conversion.

Let's examine the mechanics of the program in more detail. Once the program confirms that the command line contains some arguments, it must decide which function to call. First, it converts the first argument to the proper numeric value. This is accomplished by sending the first argument in the parameter list to the standard library function *strchr()*, which checks the digit string for an embedded period. A real number will have a decimal point and *strchr()* tests for this. If no decimal point is found, the program converts the first value into a *long* value with the standard library function *atol()*. Otherwise, the program calls *atof()* to convert the value into a *double*. In both cases, the resulting value is passed to *mean()*, and the calculated value is displayed. Note that the variable *x* is declared as an automatic variable and is initialized by a call to *mean()*. This declaration is restricted to one of the inner blocks of the *if* statement. Thus, using the same variables helps make the code more symmetrical.

Both *mean()* functions have nearly identical code. After execution passes to the appropriate definition header:

```
long mean(long x, char* buffer[], int len)
```

or:

```
double mean(double x, char* buffer[], int len)
```

the function handles the command line arguments by converting each one into a number while simultaneously adding it to the current total. The only difference between the two headers is in the data type of the function. The first parameter makes the choice of the correct definition unambiguous—if it is a *double* value, then double *mean()* is called; if it is a *long* value, long *mean()* is called.

Functions with a Variable Number of Parameters

The same flexibility that permits function overloading also lets you specify a variable number of parameters. This feature is needed because the parameter values in a function might not be set until run time; sometimes even the number of parameters is not known until then.

A good example of this kind of function is *printf()*, which occurs in most C programs. Before the ANSI standard, you could use functions with a variable number of parameters in C, primarily because that language did no parameter checking. You could leave out arguments of a function, and, as long as you supplied code to recognize this situation in the function definition, the program would still run. Also, C contains a set of macros that help support functions with no set parameters—the *varargs* macro set—although *printf()* is not implemented with them.

However, when function prototyping—as in ANSI C—was established, this simple C solution became impossible. Now, if you declare a function and an attendant argument list, such a declaration checks for proper argument passing, thus preventing you from sending extra variables or failing to supply some arguments. Flexibility was discarded for safety.

However, C++ offers an easy-to-understand syntax for this kind of unspecified function call—without sacrificing the benefits of parameter type checking. You need only to use an ellipsis (. . .) to indicate a variable number of parameters.

Specifying a Variable Number of Parameters

A typical use of the ellipsis syntax involves a function declaration in which some set parameters are followed by the variable parameter specifier. For example, the following:

```
int example(int,int,double ...)
```

specifies a function that requires two integer arguments, a *double*, and an unknown—at compile time—number of further parameters. This is a proper declaration of a C++ function, yet it preserves the freedom that C programmers take for granted—a fluidity of parameter passing. C++ also has an associated set of macros (found in the header file *stdarg.h*) that collect any actual parameters that you might send to the function. This syntax allows the full C++ parameter checking for those parameters that are specified.

The *prntvals.c* example (Listing 2-6) is a simple program that uses these macros to call a function.

Listing 2-6.   A program that illustrates a function that uses a variable number or arguments: *prntvals.c*

```
#include <stream.h>
#include <string.h>

// include the macros for extracting function parameters

#include <stdarg.h>

main()
{
 void print_many(int ...); // declare a function with only one set parameter

 print_many(3,1,2,3);        // call it with 3 arguments.
}


void print_many(int n ...)    // define the function
{
 va_list ap;              // call the set up macros
 va_start(ap,n);

 for(int i = 0; i < n; i++)  {
   int temp = va_arg(ap,int);  //extract each parameter
   if(temp != 0)
     cout << temp << "\n";
   else
     break;
```

continued

```
    }
  va_end(ap);    // call the closing macro.
}
```

In this example, *main()* declares a function called *print_many()*, which takes a variable number of parameters. Note that the header file, *stdarg.h*, appears at the beginning of the program file. This file contains the macros that support the use of variable numbers of arguments. Because *print_many()* always takes an integer as its first parameter, the program first passes it the argument *3*, which indicates the number of items to be printed. Next, the program passes the value to be printed—*1*, *2*, and *3*.

The first statement in *print_many()*

```
va_list ap;
```

declares the argument list *ap*. The startup macro *va_start()* uses this argument list as its first parameter and the name of the last parameter specified before the ellipsis as its second argument (the integer *n* in this example). After *va_list* is set up, the macro *va_arg()* strips off each argument that is passed to the function. The macro

```
va_arg(<va_list object> , <data type>);
```

returns a variable of the same type that it receives as a parameter. In the example, it returns an integer type and assigns the value to the variable *temp*. After *cout* displays this value, the last line in the function calls the macro *va_end()* to clean up the *val_list* object.

Pointers and the *const* Modifier

Pointers have always been a central part of the C programming language, and they retain their importance in C++. Although C++ adds the *reference* data type that lets you create parameters that can return values (*call by reference*), you still need to use pointers to create this kind of reference situation for character strings and other arrays. Recall that one of the benefits of the call by reference is that the compiler makes no copy of a function argument because only the address is passed. With a large data object, that can represent a big savings in memory.

One vital new possibility is created by combining the C++ *const* modifier with a pointer variable. When you use the resulting constant pointer in a parameter declaration, you gain the memory efficiency of a call by reference while retaining the safety of a call by value. Let's examine the details of this procedure.

When most programmers design a function that uses one or more character string parameters, they usually define them as pointers to a character. For example:

```
void example(char *s1,char *s2)
```

represents the header line of such a function. The only other way to declare character string parameters is to declare the parameters as character arrays. However, this is inefficient—even in traditional C— because the compiler merely converts them into memory address references, or, in other words, a pointer. Thus, the only real way to handle a character string parameter is by a call by reference. This is equally true for other arrays; however, character strings represent the most common case.

In C++, you can create what is effectively a call by value for a character string type by modifying the parameter declaration with *const*. This is not a true *call by value* parameter—it's not local to the calling function, and only a pointer is passed—but, unlike a call by reference, the program cannot change the value of the parameter variable. This lets you use pointer syntax without having to worry about inadvertently modifying what must be a constant value.

The *compare.c* function (Listing 2-7) demonstrates a simple comparison of two character strings. A return value of zero indicates that the strings are equal, a positive number indicates the first position in which they differ, and a negative number indicates that the second string is longer. (This function duplicates most of the features of the standard library function *strcmp().)

Listing 2-7. A function that compares two character strings and uses parameters of type const pointer: *compare.c*

```
#include <string.h>

int compare(const char *p1, const char *p2);
{
  int l1 = strlen(p1),      // note the length of each string        continued
```

```
      l2 = strlen(p2);

   if(l1 == l2)   {                      // strings are the same length
     for(int cnt = 0 ; *p1 != '\0' ; cnt++)   {  // look for where they differ
       if( *p1++ != *p2++)
          return cnt;
       cnt++;              // increment the counter
     }
     return 0;  // no difference detected. They must be equal.
   }
   else if(l1 < l2)   {
     for(int cnt = 0 ; *p1 != '\0' ; cnt++)   {  // look for a difference
       if( *p1++ != *p2++)
          return cnt;
       cnt++;
     }
     return l1;  // the end of l1 is the difference since its shorter
   }
   else   {
     for(int cnt = 0 ; *p2 != '\0' ; cnt++)   {  // look some more
       if( *p2++ != *p1++)
          return -cnt;
     }
     return -l2;  // the end of l2 marks the difference.
   }
}
```

This function receives two character string parameters. These parameters, however, are defined as *const* because the values in the character strings never need to be altered. The function needs only to examine them and make some comparisons. Because the function uses some standard library functions, you must use the following line at the beginning of the program:

```
#include <string.h>
```

The following statements:

```
int l1 = strlen(p1),
    l2 = strlen(p2);
```

store the respective lengths of each parameter; this efficiently sets up the parameters for later comparisons. These comparisons occupy the rest of the code.

If the strings are equal, then a simple *for* loop checks for character positions that differ in the two strings. The variable *cnt* maintains the current character position, the value of which is returned if the pointers have different values at any position (indicating that a difference exists between the strings). The test ends when the first character pointer reaches the *end of string* marker '\0'; at this point, the function returns a value of 0 to indicate that there is no difference. Note that in this example the failure to find a difference indicates equality.

If the first string is shorter than the second, the function continues to test the strings for differences. The code for this is identical to that which is used when the strings are equal. The only difference is that if the function reaches the end of the first string without finding a difference, it returns the end position as the first place that the two strings differ.

Finally, the function tests for the situation in which the second string is longer than the first one. Here, the loop continues until the end of the second character string. This is accomplished with the following code:

```
else {
    for(int cnt = 0 ; *p2 != '\0' ; cnt++) {
    if( *p2++ != *p1++)
        return -cnt;
}
return -l2;
```

If a difference is found, the function returns the position via *cnt*. If the end of the string is reached without any difference being found, the function returns the length and generates a negative value to indicate that this position refers to the second string.

Review questions

1. A _____ function uses the same name for two or more similar functions.

2. A function declared as *example(int . . .)* indicates a function with a _____ number of parameters.

3. The declaration *const char* p* produces a _____ pointer variable.

Programming projects

1. Rewrite *calc.c* so that it works for both long and double values. Use function overloading.

2. Design an addition function that can total any number of values. Declare the function with a variable number of parameters.

Summary

This chapter explored the function-related improvements in C++. Some—but not all—of these improvements are also found in the emerging ANSI C standard; all, however, are compatible with the C++ programming philosophy. Included in this group are function prototyping and the ellipsis parameter specification. The former lets the programmer specify not only the return value of a function but also the number and type of its parameters. The latter reconciles the time-honored C practice of deferring parameter specifications until run time with the new, stricter type specification. Default values for parameters are another improvement noted here.

The biggest advance discussed in this chapter concerns function name overloading. With this improved function definition syntax, C++ lets a designer create more than one function with the same name. An important use for this capability arises when the same set of operations must be performed on data of differing types. With an overloaded function, the system automatically calls the correct function based on the differences in the parameters that are passed to the function name.

The *inline* modifier is another important improvement in function definition. This request to the compiler tries to replace a function call with the actual code specified by the function definition. This is a safe alternative to the macro facility created by the preprocessor command *#define*.

3

Defining and Using Classes

3

Defining and
Using Classes

The last chapter discussed how a C++ program is organized into separate functions and showed how C++ adds new versatility to the definition and use of functions. Now, let's examine how you can combine functions and data declarations into new data types. These data types offer a programmer the tools to create internal data objects that more closely match the behavior of the real-world objects and systems that the program must manipulate. Whether the work involves nuclear physics or sales records, the software designer's main task is to create ever more accurate ways of representing the real world within the architecture of the computer.

C provides basic mechanisms—header files and separately compiled functions—that help programmers divide a program into functionally related, yet separately maintainable, parts or modules. However, truly modular program design requires more than this. The programmer also needs to control how the modules are accessed and to determine which parts are private (internal) and which are public (external). Through the mechanism of the *class*, C++ provides a new degree of control for specifying the relationship between and the access to the various objects in a program.

The C++ *class* represents an improvement over C; it combines flexible data representation with fully controllable modularity, thus establishing a new concept—the object—which honors both issues. After a discussion of the existing facilities in C, this chapter introduces the structure and design of the class in C++, focusing first on issues of data representation, then on the subject of modularity.

Data Representation

When most programmers think of data types, they tend to think of the built-in ways that C and C++ represent such things as integers, floating-point numbers, or characters. However, often one must take into account objects that consist of many different, yet related, kinds of data. A simple example of this is a client record, which might include character data (name and address), integers (inventory), and financial data (dollar amounts). Although the computer must use different methods to manage these different basic types of data, the programmer needs to have a way of handling the data record as a single entity, as well as by individual data items.

Structures in C represent a first step toward this higher level of data organization. C's structure definition facility lets you combine many different variables into a kind of "super" data object that has two aspects. On one hand, the entire object can be manipulated: You can send it as a parameter to a function, for example. On the other hand, you can also access the individual components of such a structure data type. Thus, the ability of structures to mirror the complex "real-world" entities that they represent makes them an indispensable part of a C programmer's repertoire.

However, a structure definition in C refers only to value storage, and a structure data type is merely a collection of variables. For each set of data, the programmer must provide a set of tools to manipulate the data—for example, to allocate memory for a new data record, to move data into and out of the record, to perform operations on the various fields, and to free memory when the record is no longer needed. Traditional C has no organic way of relating the data to the tools that work with the data. The best it can do is to permit you to put both structures and related functions into one header file or a separately compiled module.

C++ takes this notion of a structure data type and expands it to include not only the members that store values but also the member functions that operate on those variables. The result—a complete object called a *class*—is the basis for calling C++ an "object-oriented" programming language. Thus, C++ can be seen as a quantum advance to the more commonly used "functional" or "procedural" languages—like C—in which data and algorithms are strictly separated.

The Problem of Data Representation in C

The problem of data representation is central to all programming languages. Much of the problem-solving effort that goes into program design involves finding the proper format, or representation, for the internal values that the program must handle. Sometimes, this representation is obvious; for example, a program that does statistical analysis must translate its values into floating point numbers. Often, however, the choice of an internal format is a little surprising; for example, you might decide to use integer values to represent currency in a program in order to avoid the round-off errors associated with real numbers. Most problems are so complex that the programmer must declare a general-purpose data type, such as a C structure, to combine variables of different types into a cohesive whole.

Let's examine a simplified example of a typical data processing application. Suppose you must write a general purpose program to manipulate a client's financial data. This data can be in many different forms—bank accounts, stocks, certificates of deposit, receipts, cash, and bonds. The problem is further complicated because information records are not homogeneous; some individuals have most of their money in savings accounts, some invest mainly in bonds, while others use a more diversified combination of financial vehicles. How do you represent this disparate information in a computer?

Before you experiment with different data types, stop and think about the information that the program must manipulate. First, you need to write a function that manipulates all of an individual's record—perhaps to report on someone's net worth. Other parts of the program, however, must handle the various components of this wealth individually, so you can't merely lump an amount in a simple variable. The dilemma revolves around maintaining the details of a record while retaining the ability to deal with the record as a whole.

The standard C solution is to create a new data type that contains as components the individual parts, or fields, that make up the information. This new type is called a *struct* (structure) type. The *finance.h* example (Listing 3-1) shows a simple structure definition that can hold the previously described financial data.

Listing 3-1.   A financial record structure in C: *finance.h*

```
struct precord {
    char id[9];          /* some way to identify the owner  */        continued
```

```
long savings,        /* savings account total */
      checking,      /* demand deposit */
      cd,            /* certificate of deposit */
      stocks;        /* what's tied up in the stock */
      bonds;         /* ...and bond market */
};
```

The definition of the *precord* structure contains one entry (called a *member* of the structure) for each possible category. A character string member might contain code for identifying the individual that owns the record. One member contains the total amount in a bank account, another contains the total worth of the individual's stock portfolio, and so on. For more complex situations, you could expand this data type to include, for example, the account numbers of the certificates of deposit and even the checking and savings accounts.

In C, once you define a structure, you can declare a variable of that type, as in the following example:

```
struct precord new_client;
```

You access individual parts, or "members," of the structure variable *new_client* through the variable and the member name. For example, *new_client.id* accesses the *id* member, *new_client.cd* the member variable containing the *cd* value, and so on.

A pointer to a structure requires a special syntax, as in the following example:

```
struct precord *p;
```

Also, with a pointer, the "arrow" notation refers to the parts of the structure being pointed to. *p->cd*, for example, refers to the *cd* member of the structure. Note that both methods carry over to the C++ class type.

Now, let's use the syntax of the structure type to manipulate values. A structure variable is the same as any other variable: It can take an assignment, or it can be sent as a parameter. Furthermore, like any other data object, it has a scope and a storage class. It can be either local or global; it can be *automatic*, *external*, or *static*. To use its values or modify them, you must access the structure and follow the usual rules for variables in C. Unfortunately, the two mechanisms provided by C for accessing structure members (the "dot" notation for individual members and the "arrow" notation for pointers) are rather unwieldy and often are the source of programming errors.

Representing Data with Objects

Let's develop an easy-to-use set of tools for working with the values in a structure. Ideally, these tools should access individual values in a straightforward manner. First, let's examine the characteristics of an internal computer "object." Clearly, it must consist of two parts:

► a value, or data, section

► the operations that manipulate those values

The value part is needed to maintain consistency from one use of the object to another. After all, there must be a storage scheme that saves the results of the transformations performed on the object. Then, there must be the operations that perform these transformations. Together, data and operations define the object.

This definition of an object shouldn't be particularly mysterious. Although you might not realize it, ordinary variables in C consist of the same bipartite structure. An integer value, for example, is stored as a single computer word—the value part—and a series of operators—such as '+' and '*'—that define how it is used. Let's extend this low-level construction up the ladder of complexity to more abstract programming concerns and to user-designed objects as well as to the built-in data types.

The *stack.c* example (Listing 3-2) shows how you might implement an "object" in C.

Listing 3-2. A *stack* data type implemented in a file: *stack.c*

```
#define MAXSIZE 15

static stack[MAXSIZE],top;

push(x)
int x;
{
 if(top == MAXSIZE)  {   /* check for stack overflow */
   err_rep(1);           /* print error message */
   return 0;             /* push failed */
 }
```
continued

```
  stack[ ++top ] = x;      /* set stack */
  return 1;                /* push succeeded */
}


pop(flag)
int *flag;
{
  if(top == 0)   {         /* check for stack underflow */
    err_rep(1);            /* print error message */
    *flag = 0;             /* send back an error signal */
    return 0;
  }
  return stack[ top-- ];
}


static err_rep(n)
int n;
{
  static char *msg={"stack overflow",
                "stack underflow"};  /* error message list */

  printf("%s\n", msg[n]);            /* display message */
}
```

The *stack.c* example consists of a file of function definitions that create a *stack* type. The key concept here is that the data type is an amalgam of both functions and static storage strategies. Recall that a stack is a data structure with a *last-in, first-out* access scheme. The last value you send to the stack is the first value to be returned. This data type is defined by the two operations that are performed on it—*push* and *pop*. Push is the operation that puts a value onto the stack. Pop, its complement, returns a value from the stack. Because the push and pop operations are central to the definition of the data type, this is an ideal example for explaining the new notion of an "object." You can easily implement these operations as functions, but they must have a static data structure on which to work.

The *stack.c* example contains a typical C solution to this problem. This file declares a data array, *stack*, and defines three functions for manipulating this stack. The *push()* function adds an integer item to the stack, while the *pop()* function removes the top item. The function *err_rep()* prints messages if the stack overflows or underflows. Together, the array and functions provide both a data representation and a collection of tools for manipulating the data.

Another design factor (not apparent from the listing) is a key element to the definition of the stack—these items are separately compiled into an object file. Therefore, this binary file is available to any program that requires the services of this *stack* data type. The rules of scope restrict the "visibility" of variables and functions and create a separate space, or module, which contains the implementation of this type and strictly controls external access to its parts. The array *stack* and the variable *top* are declared *static* in order to limit their visibility to the file. No statement from outside—for example, in another part of the program—can directly manipulate these two variables. The same is true of the function *err_rep()*; it too is declared static and restricted to the file. The functions *push()* and *pop()*, in contrast, represent the entrance and exit of values from this module. They are the lines of communication between the module and the rest of the program, and they are the only means by which values can enter or leave.

The *stack* data type defined in *stack.c* is a good example of several important design techniques available to the C programmer. Data abstraction (or data hiding) is certainly a key element; another is the notion that a data type can be more than a static strategy to store data in memory—it can be a dynamic combination of values and operations on those values. This example also dramatically shows the possibilities inherent in a unit, or module, of code that is self-contained. Modularity is certainly an important design technique, and in this example it grows from the solution of a problem rather than being externally imposed as an organizing principle.

Modularity and Data Hiding in C

The most obvious advantage of modularity is that it gives a programmer the ability to manage large programs. It's folly to create a thousand-line program without dividing it into smaller, more easily controlled pieces; this bit of programming wisdom is axiomatic. Because the most basic module is the function, C supports this aspect of modularity well. You can use functions to implement each part of your overall design, finishing one part before proceeding to the next.

Files as Modules in C

C offers some additional tools to support structured programming design through modularization. By manipulating the storage class declarations of both variables and functions and by using C's capability of separate compilation, you can create another module—the file—which is less than the entire program yet more than a single function. The previous *stack.c* listing is an example of a file module that contains multiple functions; it is a separately maintained unit of code stored in its own file. Note that the declarations control access to the internal data of the stack object. A global variable declared static (the array *stack*, for example) has a restricted scope. Instead of being visible to the entire program, its scope is restricted to the current file. Thus, the file becomes a "region" set off from the rest of the program with its only access through non-static functions and variables.

The array *stack* and the integer variable *top* are declared in *stack.c* as *static*. Both of them are global to the functions *push()* and *pop()* and therefore are accessible from these functions. However, because they are static, their scope is restricted to the file in which they are defined. Any program that uses this *stack* type knows only that it can push values onto it and pop values from the top of the stack (by calling *push()* and *pop()* respectively), but the actual implementation is completely hidden from view. In fact, a user program would require nothing more than the compiled file to use it effectively.

Thus, the practice of spreading function definitions among many different source files, compiling and debugging each file independently of the others, and combining them in the linking phase, is well known to accomplished C programmers. The independent files combine with C's complicated, but well-articulated, scope rules to create regions within the program that maintain their own internal variables and functions as well as links to the rest of the program. These linked functions and variables can be thought of as an interface that permits access to these regions, but an access that is limited and controlled by the designer. Separate compilation is based on the fact that a global variable or a function that is declared as *static* cannot be accessed outside its file. The ability to create these limited-access objects is sometimes known as *data hiding* or *data abstraction*, and it is a useful technique for controlling the inherent complexity of real-world programming projects.

Modules as Objects

It's easy to see how programmers use structuring tools such as static variables and static functions to modularize programs. What might not be so obvious is that something more subtle occurs when you define these regions. The *stack* data type, for example, is truly a new type, an equal in everything but convenience-of-use with the traditional types such as *integer*, *long*, or *double*. By representing a value and defining specific operations that manipulate it, you create a kind of "object" that mirrors the reality that you are trying to implement.

Even when programmers know the full reality of number storage and manipulation within a computer, they often see a "natural" connection between a whole number value and an *int* variable. This is not so much a naive view as an attempt to control the large number of details attendant upon programming—programmers can't worry about shifting bits right and left and moving values in memory in order to add two simple numbers. The same kind of "detail control" is necessary for other kinds of computer representation, particularly user-defined representations such as the *struct* data type definition. You need to see the same kind of "natural" connection between a stack and its representation or between a structure and the *real-world* entity that it models.

The key elements that define an "object" are:

► an object structure

► the operations that manipulate that structure.

Also, the details of representation need to be hidden from the user, who should know only that a specific type exists, or, as in the stack example (Listing 3-2), that there is a stack that either receives or returns a value. The ideal situation, unattainable in C but featured in C++, is the ability to declare object variables, which would, in turn, hide the details of their own implementation.

The first steps toward the implementation of this kind of "object-oriented" programming were outlined in *stack.c*. This example is by no means complete, but it does point in the proper direction. Thus, the creation of an object is merely a two stage process that involves:

► defining the implementation in terms of ordinary static data types and C programming construction and

► "packaging" this implementation in an easy-to-use form.

You combine both data abstraction and modularity to form a "unit" that you can plug into a program and use without paying any attention to how it works. If you write a program today using the previous stack objects, you could come back to it next week, change it—make *stack* a linked list, for example—and still use the program you created. In practical terms, you would have to recompile and link, but you wouldn't need to make actual changes to the program itself. The measure of this "object" is its faithfulness to the well-understood definition of a stack—not to the method by which you created it. The implementation details necessary for an object are still in the program. However, you need to address this design issue only once—when you create the definition of the object; once you do this you can forget about design and use it as if it were a built-in part of the language.

This kind of *design-it-once; use-it-many-times* approach is exactly what is meant by modular programming. Each object is a module, an independent part of the program. If there is any difference, it's in the following emphasis: A data object is more deliberately general-purpose than a module need be. There are other aspects to object-oriented programming that are not addressed here. A data object is, in essence, a module, but it's also much more. The issue of communication between objects is critical to the definition, as is the relationship between objects called *inheritance*. These two items are discussed in Chapter 4.

Although a stack is a non-tangible thing in the real world, still it is different from the representation created in the program. The *operations* of this entity, however, are mirrored by the computer representation. (See Figure 3-1 for an illustration of this relationship.)

The kind of abstraction supported by C is certainly a useful and effective technique, but not one without problems. One problem has already been stated: The new data types and other forms of data abstraction that you create within a program never have the same status as the built-in types. For example, it's never as easy to declare a *struct* variable as it is to declare a character string. And in this case, convenience means efficiency and, most importantly, clarity. Clarity, in turn, means fewer inadvertent mistakes and fewer bugs.

This issue of convenience may seem like nit-picking but it is not. You can do many things with a built-in data type that you cannot do with your own designs. For example, when you create an automatic integer variable, as soon as the program leaves its scope—perhaps returns from the function—the computer reclaims that memory. In contrast, consider what happens when you define a structure and the pointers that refer to it. What happens to the pointers when the structure they point to goes out of scope? The situation is ambiguous, and

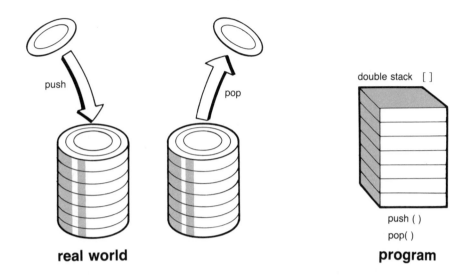

push

pop

double stack [ ]

push ( )

pop( )

real world   **program**

Figure 3-1.   The relationship between computer and real-world representations

the programmer must take care of this bit of housekeeping. In fact, the situation is just as ambiguous when the variable is declared. Those fields that are pointers require explicitly allocated space, which is tied up not only until the program leaves the variable's scope, but until it is explicitly deallocated by a call to the library function *free()*.

Finally, the use of a file to create a module is a good technique, one that is also used in C++. However, programmers still need something more intimate, something that lets them define a smaller controlled region in the file, something that is neither as large as a file, nor as small as a single function. They need to be able to create modules that both represent and encapsulate data—in other words, modular objects.

Review questions

1. Writing a program involves creating a _____ relationship between real world objects and computer representations.

2. A _____ programming style is the best tool for handling the complexity of large programs.

3. The two main tools for modularization in the C programming language are _____ and _____.

4. To use a new data type you must create a way to store _____ and _____ that work on them.

Programming problems

1. Redesign the structure definitions in Listing 3-1 so that they are complete and realistic.

2. Create a similar set of definitions for a simple data structure, such as statistics for a baseball player.

The Mechanics of the C++ Class

The class in C++ offers much of the modularity that separately compiled C files do when they use the data representation capabilities of the C structure. In C++, however, this modularity is only the initial advantage. You define a class much like you define a structure in C. In C++, however, the class not only has data members, it also has functional ones. The *circle.h* example (Listing 3-3) shows the simplest form of a class.

Listing 3-3. A simple C++ class: *circle.h*

```
const double pi=3.1415;        // define pi to any desired precision
struct circle {
    double rad;                // store the radius of a circle

    void set_radius(double);   // declare a function to initialize class
    double get_area();         // return area with current radius
    double get_circum();       // ...and circumference
};
```

```
void circle::set_radius(double r)
{
 rad=r;                     // simply set the radius to the parameter value
}


double circle::get_area()
{
 return pi*rad*rad;         // return the result of the usual calculation
}


double circle::get_circum()
{
 return pi*2*rad;           // return the circumference
}
```

Because the *circle.h* class refers to a geometric figure, *pi* is defined as a *double* constant with the appropriate value. The *struct* keyword indicates that the definition that follows is the class named by the *tag field* on the same line; in this case, the tag name is *circle*. The *double* variable *rad* is an ordinary static variable that contains the value of the circle's radius.

The C++ class definition is different than the C structure because it also contains function members. In *circle.h*, these members are:

```
void set_radius();
double get_area();
double get_circum();
```

The first function sets the radius variable *rad*. The second member function returns the value of the area of the circle, which is calculated from the current value of *rad*. Finally, the last member function returns the current circumference. The definitions of these members are straightforward. In each case, they are single-line functions that perform a calculation and then return the results.

Note that the evolutionary relationship between the C structure and the C++ class is explicit. The simplest class definition uses the keyword "struct". However, you must be careful when you use it; the class defined by *struct* in C++ is significantly different from the more primitive C structure. Not only does a class contain *function* members (a C structure has only static variable members), these member functions can directly access the variable part of the class—even though it has not been explicitly sent to them as a parameter. This feature is exploited in *set_rad()* to allow a parameter to be assigned to the member *rad*. The definitions of the functions themselves must include a reference to their class; you accomplish this by using the scoping operator (*::*).

Merely defining a class doesn't create any objects; you must still declare some class variables. For example, the current definition:

```
circle x;
```

accomplishes this task. Note that you do not need to use the keyword *struct* in the declaration. You access the members of the class with the dot notation. This is straightforward when you access variable members—*x.rad*, for example, uses the same form as it does in a C structure. However, at first, you might find it strange to use this notation with functions. For example,

```
x.set_rad(1.23)
```

initializes *circle* *x* to a radius of 1.23. Similarly, *x.get_area()* and *x.get_circum()* return the appropriate values. It's important to remember that these functions are no less members of the class than the data member *rad*, and, as fellow members, they have a special interlocking relationship—each one of them knows about and can access the data member implicitly. Furthermore, the scope of the class defines an autonomous region in the program that includes all of the members. The only entrance to this region is through the *dot* notation.

As with structures, you also can declare a pointer variable to a class, as in the following:

```
circle *p;
```

The arrow notation manipulates any of the members as it would in a C structure. Thus, *p->rad*, *p->set_rad()*, *p->get_area()*, and *p->get_circum()* are all legal expressions.

This brief overview of the basic syntax of the C++ class lets you access its powers, but it doesn't fully explain them. The rest of this chapter and the next discuss more of the features and limitations of this programming facility.

Comparing C and C++ Solutions to Data Representation

One continuing problem that every programmer faces is how to represent and manipulate time. The main problem in dealing with time is converting from the time of day (hour and minutes) into a duration. Often, you must answer the question: "How long has it been since 'Event A' occurred?" Even with simple "What time is it?" questions, you must deal with two clocks—the AM/PM clock and the 24-hour time system. The following sections show two solutions to the problem of representing time—one in C and the other in C++. In order to compare these two programming systems, the discussion also shows how to convert one representation to the other; this clearly points out the differences and similarities in these languages.

In C, you usually handle the disparity found in everyday notions such as time by creating what amounts to a "family" of related types. A good strategy in such a traditional programming language is to find some simple and easy system of data representation to serve as a base. In the case of time, one natural base is the number of seconds since midnight; this is effective because it always generates a positive integer, and, therefore, the program can easily perform duration comparisons. After you determine a base type, you can write a series of functions to transform the basic representation into various user forms—AM/PM, 24-hour clock, or even duration reports. Examine this strategy at work in *time.h* (Listing 3-4).

Listing 3-4. Time-of-day functions: *time.h*

```
static long secs;    /* the current time in seconds since midnight */


/*****************************************************************
* set_time() will accept the time in 24 hour format and will set   *
*            the sec counter.                                       *
*****************************************************************/


set_time(tod24)
char *tod24;
{
long hours,minutes;

 minutes=atol(&tod24[2]);        /* convert the last two digit to a number */
```

```
     tod24[2]='\0';                    /* erase them */
     hours=atol(tod24);                /* convert the first part of the string */
     secs=(hours*3600)+(minutes*60); /* set total seconds */
     }




/**********************************************************************/
* get_time() will return the current time--as stored in the secs counter--*
*              in a 12 hour am/pm format.                             *
**********************************************************************/


get_time(tod)
char* tod;
{
static char *tday[]={"MIDNIGHT","P.M.","NOON","A.M."};
int hours,minutes,amflag=0;


hours = secs/3600;                        /* calculate the total hours */
minutes= (secs % 3600)/60;                /* ...and total minutes */


if(hours == 24)  {                 /* end of one day--beginning of another */
   hours = 0;
   amflag = (minutes == 0) ? 0 : 3;       /* midnight or just after */
  }
else if(hours > 12)  {             /* the  time is pm */
   hours = hours - 12;
   amflag = 1;
  }
else if(hours == 12 )              /* the time is noon */
   amflag = 2;
else
   amflag = 3;                      /* if it's nothing else, it must be morning */


sprintf(tod,"%2d:%02d %s",hours,minutes,tday[amflag]);
}
```

In this file, the *seconds* variable is declared *static global* to restrict its scope to the file, thus providing some modularity. The C function *set_time()* takes a time in the 24-hour clock format and sets the *secs* variable accordingly. For example, if you use 0900 as a parameter, *secs* becomes 32,400; a time of day of 2200 yields 79,200. On the other hand, the function *get_time()* returns the time of day in a twelve-hour format, converting the value in the seconds variable to the more natural "hours and minutes" format. In this case, the value is returned as a reference parameter. An additional marker at the end of this character string indicates the time of day—four are recognized: *AM, PM, NOON,* and *MIDNIGHT.*

The *time.c* example is a perfectly reasonable way of handling the reporting of time, and it represents a good C language solution to the problem. You can easily extend its range by defining separate functions to calculate or to display whatever aspect of this quantity you want to manipulate. For example, you could create a function to convert a time of day into elapsed minutes.

Let's contrast this C solution to the problem with a *time* class defined in C++. The simplest form of a class, the structure, can implement this time object. The *time2.h* class (Listing 3-5) shows this re-implementation of the time object.

Listing 3-5.   A time-of-day class: *time2.h*

```
struct time  {
  long secs;              // the common denominator for all time formats

  void set_time(char *);  // setting the time of day

  void get_time(char *);  // retrieving the current time
};


// Define the class functions.

void time::set_time(char *tod24)
{
  long hours,minutes;

  minutes=atol(&tod24[2]);    // convert the last two digit to a number
  tod24[2]='\0';              // erase them
  hours=atol(tod24);          // convert the first part of the string
  secs=(hours*3600)+(minutes*60); // set total seconds
}                                               continued
```

```
void time::get_time(char *tod)
{
static char *tday[]={"MIDNIGHT","P.M.","NOON","A.M."};
int hours,minutes,amflag=0;

hours = secs/3600;                    // calculate the total hours
minutes= (secs % 3600)/60;            // ...and total minutes

if(hours == 24)  {                    // end of one day--beginning of another
   hours = 0;
   amflag = (minutes == 0) ? 0 : 3;   // midnight or just after
   }
else if(hours > 12)  {                // the  time is pm
   hours = hours - 12;
   amflag = 1;
   }
else if(hours == 12 )                 // the time is noon
   amflag = 2;
else
   amflag = 3;                        // if it's nothing else, it must be morning

sprintf(tod,"%2d:%02d %s",hours,minutes,tday[amflag]);
}
```

This package consists of three parts: a *long* variable that stores the number of *secs* since midnight and the two member functions *set_time()* and *get_time()*. The *set_time()* function initializes the *secs* variable; it converts the character string that contains the proposed time in a 24-hour format into seconds. The function *get_time()* returns the time as a character string and displays it in the familiar AM/PM format.

The code in both listings is identical. What's different is the packaging. In Listing 3-4, the common denominator is the *long* variable, *secs*. For this variable to be common to each time function, it must be global to both of them. Thus, it must be either global to the entire file—as it is here with the *static* declaration—or to the entire program. The only way to control the visibility of *secs* is to restrict these functions to a file and separately compile that file.

Now, contrast the definition of *time.h* to the C++ version in *time2.h*. The latter version fulfills the requirements for a class: It has a data part, the long value *secs*, and two associated functions. These functions have a special relationship to the object created by the definition; they can refer directly to the data part, another member of the structure, without requiring any further dereferencing expression. Each of these functions treats the *secs* member as a common storage location. Both know about it; both can access it either to read its current value or to change that value. Thus, *secs* performs the same function as the *static long* variable did in the earlier C example in Listing 3-4. Note also that this example is declared using the keyword *struct*. A structure in C++ is actually a simple type of class.

The scope of this *secs* variable is strictly limited to the two functions defined as members of the class. Because this variable is known outside the class only through its membership in it, you need to declare a variable of this type to access it. For example,

```
        .

        .

char tstring[40];
time x;
        .

        .

x.secs = 23;
x.set_time("2000");
x.get_time(tstring);
        .

        .
```

are the only ways you can access the members of this class.

You can declare as many objects of type *time* as you need in both programs. Each is a unique object, but it shares its format and functionality with other objects of the same type. For example, each time you declare a variable of the *time* class, a new copy or *instance* of the class is created with the specified structure. This means that the functions of the class act on the specific data part associated with that copy of the class. Calling *set_time()* for one *time* object changes the *secs* counter in that copy only. Calling this function for another copy changes values only for that copy.

Thus, each time you create a new object of the class type, you create new data members and allocate memory for the variables. Note, however, that if the member is a pointer, only enough space to hold the address is allocated; the system does not set aside room for the variable that is pointed to, a fact that is easy to forget when you are working with character strings. The member functions of a class object are a different story. Because it isn't efficient to copy the function code into each object as it is created, member functions are linked to each controlling object and keep track of the class for which they are working. Only one copy is maintained in memory. (The only exception to this rule is the *inline* member function, which is discussed in the next chapter.)

The *dtime.c* program (Listing 3-6) is a driver program that illustrates and tests the operation of the *time2.h* class defined in Listing 3-5.

Listing 3-6. A driver program that tests the time definitions: *dtime.c*

```
// use the appropriate includes.
// "time.h" contains the definition of the time class

#include <stream.h>
#include "time.h"

main(int argc,char *argv[])
{
   if(argc < 3)       // if not enough parameters, beat a hasty retreat
      exit(1);

   time t0,t1;        // we need two time objects

   t0.set_time(argv[1]);       //set the current time
   t1.set_time(argv[2]);

   char tod0[15], tod1[15];    // declare two character strings

   t0.get_time(tod0);          // retrieve the time
   t1.get_time(tod1);

   cout << form("time t0 = %s\ntime t1 = %s\n",tod0,tod1);  // ...and display
}
```

A set of command-line parameters call the program. If the user does not supply two parameters, the program stops. With the correct input, the program declares two objects of type *time—t0* and *t1—*and initializes them with the command-line arguments *argv[1]* and *argv[2]*, respectively. The initialization is accomplished by calling the appropriate member function:

```
t0.set_time(argv[1]);
t1.set_time(argv[2]);
```

The two command-line arguments are character strings that contain the number of seconds with which the *secs* variable is set. The program does no real error checking; it merely assumes that the entered value is a number in the proper range.

After each time object has a value, the *get_time()* member displays the current value of the time. This member function converts the current time (measured in seconds) into the more familiar format of *hours:minutes*. Then, the formatted output function *form()* is used with *cout* to display the time and the appropriate designator—"AM", "PM", "NOON", or "MIDNIGHT."

Although the structure is the simplest class that can be defined in C++, it is not the most useful one. Although the data part has a special relationship to the member functions, it is, in fact, available to any function within its scope. Thus, if you create a program in a single file and declare a global structure at the beginning of the file, any variables in that structure can be changed by functions that are not members of the structure. This is not an adequate degree of modularity. Thus, a structure does not fully benefit from the mechanism of class.

Complete Classes in C++

With C++, you can create a more complete class structure by using the keyword "class" rather than "struct." The *time3.h* example (Listing 3-7) shows the preceding *time* class declaration transformed into a *true* class.

Listing 3-7.   A true *time* class: *time3.h*

```
class time  {
  long secs;        // the common denominator for all time formats
                    // private to the class object
public:
  void set_time(char *);  // setting the time of day

  void get_time(char *);  // retrieving the current time
  };
```

In addition to the use of the keyword *class* instead of *struct*, the primary difference between this version and the simpler class defined in Listing

3-5 is the word *public:*, which appears in the middle of the definition. This keyword divides the class into two parts—the public part, which is fully available to the rest of the program, and the rest of the definition, which is restricted to member functions of the class. See Figure 3-2.

Figure 3-2. The difference between public and private sections of a class

Access to the private part of a class is barred to any but the class' own member functions, which have the same special relationship as those in the structure type. Functions that are not members of the class can access the members of the private part only through the functions or variables in the public part. Thus, a program can only access a class through this public part—primarily through the functions there—and cannot rely in any way on the details of the implementation of the class, which are partly hidden. The *time* class represents a typical situation. The data part of the object is defined within the private part of a class, and the functions that operate on it are defined in the public section. These public functions form an interface to the rest of the program, thus allowing controlled access to its value sections.

Hiding the implementation details of a class lets a designer program maximum flexibility into programs and systems of programs. Because no other part of the program can access the private part of a class, the interface always remains the same. You can change the details of implementation in a class—even radically change them—without affecting all of the programs and systems that depend on that class. As long as you maintain the same access format, everything will continue to work. For example, in the *time* class, you might decide to store the current date as the number of minutes since midnight or even as the minutes and seconds since January first. In each case, as long as *get_time()* and *set_time()* use the same calling format, nothing else need change. However, without the privacy offered by the class, an element from somewhere else in the program might directly access the *secs* variable, in which case, any change to the storage structure would prove disastrous.

A secondary benefit of this controlled interface design results from the way a C++ classes are often used. General-purpose classes—ones that can be used in many different programs and systems—are very easy to write. Indeed, programmers often make a class the focus of a library of routines. This capability strongly supports structured design techniques.

As another example of a C++ class, consider *date.h* (Listing 3-8) which defines a simple *date* class. It holds the value for a complete date as a series of integer values that represent the day, the month, and the year; this constitutes the private part of the class. The *new_date()* function defined in *date.h* lets the programmer set the date, and *give_date()* displays the current value of the date. Note that the character string array *mname[]*, which contains the names of the months indexed by their number (January is 1, June is 6, and so on) is a constant because it never changes during program execution.

Listing 3-8. A simple *date* class: *date.h*

```
const char* mname[]={ "illegal month","January","February","March","April",
                "May","June","July","August","September","October",
                "November","December"};

class date  {
   int day,       // the internal storage scheme
       month,     // this is now private to the
       year;      // class and unknown outside

public:
  void new_date(int,int,int);  // a member function to change the date

  char* give_date();           // ...and one to report it
};

void date::new_date(int d,int m,int y) // take in the new values.
{
  day=d;        // assign the parameter values to the internal
  month=m;      // storage variables
  year=y;
}

char* date::give_date()
{
  char *buf=new char[80];

  sprintf(buf,"%s %d,%d",mname[month],day,year);
  return buf;
}
```

Review questions

1. A *class* data type contains both _____ and _____ members.

2. The simplest form of a class is the traditional _____ data type.

3. By combining _____ and _____ in the same object, you can create a more complete _____.

4. A class defines a _____ within the program.

Private vs. Public Members of a Class

The above examples demonstrate that the C++ class is a powerful tool for modularizing programs. In some ways, its operation is analogous to a C programmer's use of files and static variables. Although a class is much more than a substitute for these file structures, this is a good place to start exploring the practical issues of class design.

A class represents a part of a C++ program that is intentionally isolated from all other parts. This is often a point of confusion. The items in the private part of the class have a scope that extends to the entire class—private and public parts—but no further. You cannot access a variable in this private part, for example, from outside the class; this is similar to the relationship of a function to its local variables. Two important things, however, distinguish C++ classes from simple C structures. First, a class contains functions. Second, a class can appear anywhere within a program—even in the middle of a function. Remember, the primary function of a class is to modularize a program; this is the key to using it effectively.

What should you put into the private part of the class? This is sometimes one of the hardest design questions to answer. The general pattern for simple classes is to make the value part of the data type private and the access functions public. The previous class examples all have followed this policy. In the class defined in *time3.h* (Listing 3-7), the variable member that holds the current time in seconds (*secs*) is hidden from view, as are the three integer members in Listing 3-8. The functions that manipulate these variables, however, are public. Although this pattern is common, you should not view it as a rule. There are situations in which a private function member is best, and some classes even require a public value part. However, this typical arrangement often makes sense for practical reasons. Usually, the data section of any data type is likely to change. For example, porting a program to a different machine can make a difference in the size of a value. Or you might implement a high-level data structure as an array in one instance and a linked list in another. Functions are usually public for the simple reason that a program must have access to the data type if it's going to be useful at all.

The *stack2.h* example (Listing 3-9) is a definition of a *stack* data type as a C++ class. This class is more complicated than the previous examples, but it still represents a typical class definition. It implements the stack, which is a LIFO (last-in, first-out) data structure, as a small array (*stk[]*) and uses an integer variable (*top*) to indicate the current start of the array. When you push a value onto the stack, *top* is incremented. A call to the *pop()* function decrements *top*, which moves between 0 and a maximum value set by the constant MAX_STACK. The function *error_rep()* provides a simple error reporting facility. The *error_rep()* function and the two limit variables are hidden in the private section of the class. The public section consists of three stack access functions: *init()*, which initializes the class by setting *top* to an appropriate values; *push()*, which puts a value onto the stack; and *pop()*, which removes a value.

Listing 3-9.   A *stack* class: *stack2.h*

```
#include <stream.h>

const char* msg[] = {"stack overflow\n","stack underflow\n"};
const MAX_STACK = 5;      // set the maximum number of elements in the stack

class stack  {
    int top,              // the stack pointer
        stk[MAX_STACK];   // ...the elements

    void error_rep(int e_num) { cout << msg[e_num]; }  //report errors

public:
    void init() { top=0; }  // initialize the stack pointer
    void push(int,int&);        // put a new value on the stack
    int pop(int&);              // get the top value
    };
```

```
/////////////////////////////////////////////////////////////////
//  stack::push() will put a specified value onto the stack.
/////////////////////////////////////////////////////////////////

void stack::push(int x,&flag=1)
{
 if( top == MAX_STACK)  {    // check for overflow before incrementing
   error_rep(0);             // ...report error, if necessary
   flag=0;                   // set success flag
  }
 else
   stk[++top]=x;
}


/////////////////////////////////////////////////////////////////
//  stack::pop() will return the top item on the stack.
/////////////////////////////////////////////////////////////////

int stack::pop(int &flag=1)
{
 if( top == 0 )  {           // check for underflow before decrementing
   error_rep(1);             // report error, if necessary
   flag=0;                   // set success flag
   return 0;
  }
 return stk[top--];
}
```

Note the similarity of this listing to the C code that implemented the stack in *stack.c*. The basic algorithms for both *push()* and *pop()* are the same. First, *push* checks for an overflow condition, then it increments the *top* variable. Finally, it uses this value as an index into *stack*, in which it assigns the value passed from the member. The *pop()* function checks for underflow and passes the current value of the array back to the caller. Then, *top* is decremented. These descriptions apply to both versions. The *stack* class does some additional error reporting and uses a different format, but these are superficial changes.

The big distinction between the stack as defined in C and as defined in C++ is that with the former, you can have only one stack in the program. To create multiple stacks you would have to make multiple copies of the file that contained the code and then rename each function. With the *stack* class defined in C++, you can declare as many stacks as you need:

```
stack x, y, z;
```

Each is unique and each has access to all of the powers and capabilities of the stack. No extra selection code is necessary. You push values onto them simply by specifying the stack object you want to work with, as follows:

```
x.push(2);
y.push(3);
z.push(4);
```

You pop values from them in a similar manner:

```
int flagx, flagy, flagz;
cout << x.pop(flagx) << "\n";
cout << y.pop(flagy) << "\n";
cout << z.pop(flagz) << "\n";
```

In both cases, the same functions and the same syntax apply to each object.

Note that the data section and one function reside in the private part of the class, and all the other functions are located in the public part. The design criteria for the public part is obvious—the programmer needs to have access to the stack. There must at least be some kind of push and pop operation, or it's not a stack at all. These two functions represent the "interface" to the rest of the program. Almost as clearly, the rest of the program must be kept at a distance from the implementation of the stack. This avoids code that directly manipulates the array *stk[]* for the sake of efficiency. Because you might later want to reimplement the stack as a linked list, for example, you must keep the rest of the program in the private part so that neither another programmer nor forgetfulness can destroy your work. But what about *error_rep()*? Why is it private and hidden from the rest of the program, even though it has no particularly important role in the basic operation of the stack? Only the member functions use the error reporting function in this *stack* data type; it is not directly called by any other part of the program. Therefore, as a purely internal member, it belongs in the private part of the class. You should always restrict the public section to only those members that control access to the class.

Note that both *error_rep()* and *init()* are *inline* functions. Because they are so small, you should make this declaration to save the overhead of a function call. You can define a member function as *inline* in two ways—in the usual way, by declaring it using the keyword *inline*, or by including the body of the function within the declaration, as in this example. In the latter case, you do not need to use the *inline* specifier.

Nested Classes

Although the *class* data type is powerful even when it is restricted to simple members, other classes can also be defined as members of a given class. Thus, you can create arbitrarily complex data types by nesting classes within classes; this enhances the modularity of the program even more. Some problems can arise in this kind of combination, but the result is so powerful that it's well worth the effort. The *phone.h* example (Listing 3-10) demonstrates nesting in a simple phone book.

Listing 3-10.   A nested class definition: *phone.h*

```
#include <string.h>

struct name   {
  char first[40],
       mid[40],
       last[80];
 };

struct phone   {
  char area[4],
       exch[4],
       number[5];
 };

class p_rec   {
  name name;
  phone phone;

public:
  void fill_rec(char *[]);
  void display_rec();
 };
```

continued

```
void p_rec::fill_rec(char *info[])
{
 strcpy(name.first,info[0]);
 strcpy(name.mid,info[1]);
 strcpy(name.last,info[2]);
 strcpy(phone.area,info[3]);
 strcpy(phone.exch,info[4]);
 strcpy(phone.number,info[5]);
}


void p_rec::display_rec()
{
   cout << form("%s %s %s\n",name.first,name.mid,name.last);
   cout << form("(%s) %s-%s\n",phone.area,phone.exch,phone.number);
}
```

This example defines the class *p_rec* to contain the name and phone number of an individual. The name is subdivided into a first, middle, and last name. The telephone number is also divided into an area code, exchange, and number. To simplify the design, the *name* member of the class is itself a class—the structure *name*. The *phone* member, too, is predefined in this way. In both cases, the subclasses are groups of character strings. The interface consists of the member functions *fill_rec()* and *display_rec()*. The latter function takes no parameters and simply displays the current values of the class. The *fill_rec()* function takes an array of character strings as its parameter and sets the private part of *p_rec* accordingly.

The use of a *struct* class as a component for another class is a fairly straightforward operation. The simplicity of the structure—particularly one without member functions—fits many common design situations. One danger inherent in the ability to define classes is the temptation to create intricate class structures. Often, the complexity that occurs with many nested and interlocking class structures defeats the advantages of using classes in the first place. An important element in the philosophy of C++ programming is that you should not overburden programs with intricate class constructions.

Another important point to note when you deal with nested structures involves the scope of the class definition. C++ is, at heart, still C, and the degree of data hiding that you can do is still restricted. To understand this restriction, consider the following alternative definition for the class *p_rec* in Listing 3-10:

```
class p_rec  {
    struct name  {
        char first[40],
              mid[40],
              last[80];
    } name;

    struct phone  {
        char area[4],
              exch[4],
              number[5];
    } phone;
public:
    void fill_rec(char *[]);
    void display_rec();
};
```

Although it might not appear so, this code is equivalent to the earlier definition. Even though the structures are defined in the private part of the class and the definitions seem profoundly nested, the class definitions actually are not hidden from the rest of the program. The structure *name* and the structure *phone* are, in fact, available anywhere else in the program as new data types. You could, for example, declare a variable to be of type *name* later in the program. Because you cannot hide definitions the same way you hide data, you have little motivation to use this form. The original definition is neater and easier to read. The important point to remember is that you have limits to what you can do with data abstraction.

Review questions

1. A complete class has two sections: a _____ and a _____.

2. The private section of a class object can contain _____ and _____ members.

3. The private part of a class lets the programmer hide the _____ of the *class* data type.

4. The public part of a class creates an _____ to the rest of the program.

Summary

This chapter explored many aspects of the C++ class facility. Classes let the programmer create small autonomous regions within a program—regions with their own local variables and functions. These regions support the kind of modularization necessary for modern software design. In addition, the C++ class is an ideal medium for implementing the notion of a data object, or a structured representation of a complex real-world entity. You can use data objects to further enhance the modularity and structure of a program.

A class represents a high-performance, user-defined data type that includes both data storage and data manipulation functions. Furthermore, a class contains a private and a public section. The private section contains variables and functions that can be accessed only by other members of the class. The public section represents the interface to the rest of the program.

4

Creating Complex Classes

4

Creating Complex
Classes

This chapter continues the discussion of classes in C++ and introduces some of the other features of this important C++ tool. Key among these features are:

▶ constructors and destructors

▶ *inline* member functions

▶ the overloading of member functions

▶ *friend* functions

▶ static members

These features are versatile tools that let the designer create ever more powerful object-oriented programming structures. The final discussion in this chapter concerns the use of C++ classes to create linked data structures and culminates with a definition of a kind of linked list *container* class.

Creating Class Objects:
Constructors and Destructors

To help you thoroughly understand the concept of class, let's examine how C++ actually allocates and manages memory for a class. First, recall how C allocates memory for variables in general. When you declare an integer or double variable, C allocates storage space for it somewhere in memory—sometimes on a stack or in a particular memory segment.

Where and when this space is allocated depends on the interaction of the storage class and the scope of the variable. For example, C might put *extern* and *static* variables in one location and *auto* (automatic) variables in another. This allocation is a straightforward operation because variables and other data objects in both C and C++ are not dynamic; the compiler creates them before any action is performed on them, whether they are at the beginning of the program (*static* and *extern* variables) or at the entry to a function (automatic values). C always knows the parameters of the allocation—sizes and so on—before it actually allocates memory. The same is true for arrays and structure classes that do not have any member functions.

C also performs the same kind of allocation for user-defined structure types. A *struct* definition specifies a set of variable locations in a particular order. These variables are contiguous in memory. C allocates the structure as a whole, with the important exception of member variables that are pointers. The only memory allocated for a pointer is for the storage of an address, and it does not include the location that the member variable points to. The following example:

```
struct info {
char *name,
      *address,
      *phone;
} x;
```

allocates three pointer variables, but it does not allocate the space for the character strings to which they point. If you want to assign a name to the *name* member, you must first call the allocation function *malloc()* or find some other way to fill *name* with the address of a character string.

Creating complete class objects is more involved, however, because they have an internal structure that includes both data storage members and functional members, as well as the further complication of having private and public sections. An even greater level of complication arises when a class contains pointer variables that need to be initialized.

Constructors

To handle the greater complexity of class allocation and to enhance its power, the class declaration mechanism includes the capability of executing a special, class-specific function known as a *constructor*. The syntax of the constructor function is simple—it always has the same name as the class. For example, if the class is named *link_node*, the constructor is *link_node()*. This function is always executed when you create an object of the *class* type. For a variable of storage class *extern*, the constructor is called once at the beginning of the program. In contrast, if the variable is automatic, the constructor is called each time the scope is entered.

A note on terminology

The terminology of object-oriented languages such as C++ can be confusing because it is not always standardized. When discussing C++ classes, this book uses the terms "object" and "variable" interchangeably to refer to a complete instance of a class, including all of its members. The term "member variable" or merely "member" refers to an individual data item or function member of a class.

Note that C++ automatically calls the *constructor* function without any explicit action by the program code; thus, you do not need to worry about where or when you should use it.

The programmer, however, determines the contents of the constructor function. No special restrictions apply, and it can perform a wide range of initial actions on both the class and its constituent members. Some typical initialization actions include:

▶ allocating internal pointer variables (for example, creating character string variables)

▶ assigning specific values to member variables

▶ executing machine- or device-specific start-up code.

This list by no means exhausts the possibilities. To better understand the use of constructors, consider *message.h* (Listing 4-1), the definition of a *message* class.

Listing 4-1.   A simple *message* class: *message.h*

```
#include <stream.h>
#include <string.h>

class message  {                                    continued
```

```
    char *s;                        // a pointer to the message contents
    int len;                        // the length of the message

public:
  message(char*);                   // declare a constructor

  void send(char*);                 // send message out to the destination
  void get(char*);                  // get one from it
  void clear() { *s='\0'; }         // start out with a fresh buffer
  char* read_buf() { return s; }    // get the contents of the message
};

message::message(char* msg)         // declare an object with a message
{
 len=strlen(msg);                   // allocate memory for the message
 s=new char[len+1];                 // ...and copy it over
 strcpy(s,msg);
}

void message::send(char* p)         // p points to the destination buffer
{
 char* x=s;
 for(int i=0 ; i <= len ; i++)      // copy it character by character
   *p++=*x++;
}

void message::get(char *p)          // here p is the sender
{
 char* x=s;
 while( (*x=*p) != '\0') {          // copy from the sender to the local buffer
   x++;
   p++;
 }
}
```

In this example, the class *message* creates an object that has a
string of characters as its contents. Often, characters are used as a
general-purpose data type (although you could replace the pointer *s*
with a *void* pointer to make it compatible with all data types). A message
object contains both this character content and a value indicating its
length. The example defines only four member functions:

▶ *send()* copies the contents, character by character, to the destination

▶ *get()* copies a reply from the destination

▶ *read_buf()* accesses the internal buffer containing the message

▶ *clear()* resets the buffer

The design of the message-passing model is a simple one: It is based on a memory location that is common to both sender and receiver. To pass a message, you need only to fill this location. You also can easily expand this model to include any system that supports character-by-character transmission. For example, the character in the *send()* function could just as easily be copied to a port.

Thus, you could use this message class as part of a data communications program. To do this, you need to replace the memory location with the address of the serial port and then add the appropriate code to send the message through the port. Data communication is the most obvious—but by no means the only—place where this kind of message passing occurs. This kind of organization is useful whenever you need to coordinate the activity of two or more subsystems—hardware or software—within a single computer. Even non-communication applications can benefit from this message-passing facility. For example, although you might think of a printer as an output-only device, it often returns status values to the computer issuing the printing order. A *message* class would be an ideal structured way to handle this inherently low-level information (often these values are in form of a bit map or a single computer word).

Now, let's examine the *message* class constructor function, *message()*. After you create the message object, it must be initialized with the contents of the message. This is the primary job of the constructor function, which allocates the memory, attaches it to the pointer variable *s*, and copies the contents. This example demonstrates the typical uses of a constructor.

The example also highlights an important characteristic of constructor functions. If a constructor requires an argument, you must supply that argument when you declare the class object. In the example, the message object can be declared only by supplying it with some value, as in the following:

```
message msg("this is only a test");
```

Of course, you must also supply any additional parameters that the constructor requires.

Destructors

The member function known as a *destructor* is the complement to the constructor. When a variable is no longer needed, a well-behaved program returns that variable's memory to the operating system to be reallocated at some other time. Of course, this operation depends on the variable's scope and storage class—for example, an automatic variable can be created and destroyed many times in a program, while a *static* or *extern* variable is eliminated only when the program ends. As it provides a constructor, C++ also offers a destructor with the *class* data type. When a program passes beyond the scope of a class object, it automatically calls a destructor if one has been defined. Thus, the destructor function is the ideal tool for tidying up any loose ends created by the operation of the class itself.

Often, destructor functions are the complement of constructors. If you had to allocate a member variable with the *new* operator, you should deallocate it with a corresponding destructor. You also can use the sequencing created by the execution of this function to shut down any devices or subsystems of the computer that were opened on behalf of the class. This important use can be effected by sending a deinitialization string to a printer or a port, for example. Even something as basic as logging off a user could profitably be executed by a class destructor.

The *message2.h* example (Listing 4-2) adds a destructor to the previously defined *message* class. Because the destructor is the complement of the constructor, it is labeled with the tilde (˜), which usually is reserved for the bitwise complement operation. Thus, the destructor for the *message* class is called *message::˜message()*. Aside from the striking symbolism of its name, this destructor is a simple function that deallocates the internal memory of the class. This is a very typical—and necessary—use of this function. Recall that memory allocated with the *new* operator exists until a subsequent call to *delete*. This memory could easily be lost if a class variable passes out of its scope without releasing it. The memory would still be allocated, but you couldn't access it because the class variable would be gone. The other member variable of this class, *len*, is a simple integer that is recaptured by the ordinary mechanism that handles built-in data types.

Listing 4-2.   A *message* class with a destructor: *message2.h*

```
class message  {
   char *s;                      // a pointer to the message contents
   int len;                      // the length of the message

public:
  message(char*);                // declare a constructor
 ~message();                     // return allocated memory to the o.s.

   void send(char*);            // send message out to the destination
   void get(char*);             // get one from it
   void clear();                // start out with a fresh buffer
   char* read_buf();            // get the contents of the message
};

message::~message()
{
 delete s;            // return allocated memory to the free memory store
}
```

Global Constructors and Destructors

The destructor function is another tool that facilitates the C++ goal of allowing you to create programmer-defined types that are fully as convenient and as powerful as the built-in types. But don't let this goal obscure the fact that this facility—along with the companion constructor—can be used for much more than recapturing spent memory resources. Just as the constructor function broadens the notion of initialization, so, too, the destructor permits a redefinition of de-initialization.

You can use constructors and destructors to create a module that will be the last code executed in a program. Recall that variables that are declared as *static* or as global to any function exist for the duration of the program run. They come into existence when they are declared, and they are returned to the operating system after the *main()* function finishes executing—in other words, at program termination. This procedure is the same for class variables as it is for variables of built-in types. If a class variable has a constructor, the constructor is called when the variable is declared, and a defined destructor is called at the end of the program. For example, if you make a declaration before the main() function, then the constructor code executes before the program begins. The destructor executes after *main()* exits and is the last code executed in the program.

This ability to run a function before the start of a program and after a program executes gives you a greater degree of control over the execution cycle of a program than is possible with C. What's more, you exert this control not with some low-level access to the machine or the operating system, but by a straightforward programming construction. This adds portability to the code you produce.

The *phone2.c* program (Listing 4-3) illustrates the previous discussion. The program begins by defining a simple class that uses both a constructor and a destructor. The constructor loads the class object with values supplied by the user. The destructor merely displays the current values before relinquishing the variables. The interesting part of the example focuses on the declaration of the class object—it's declared directly before *main()*. This makes the scope of an instance of the class the entire program. The constructor is called and loads the class object before *main()* executes. Similarly, the destructor is called after *main()* finishes executing.

Listing 4-3. A program that uses a global constructor and destructor: *phone2.c*

```
#include <stream.h>
#include <string.h>

// define an interesting class type with a constructor and destructor

struct name {
  char first[40],
       mid[40],
       last[80];
};

struct phone {
  char area[4],
       exch[4],
       number[5];
};

class p_rec {
  name name;
```

```
    phone phone;

public:
  p_rec();              // declare a constructor for the class
 ~p_rec();              // and a destructor
  void display_rec();   // declare a simple display function
};


p_rec::p_rec()
{
 cout << "constructor called:\n";   // to indicate that its been called
 cout << "first name:";             // gather values from the user
 cin >> name.first;
 cout << "middle name:";
 cin >> name.mid;
 cout << "last name:";
 cin >> name.last;
 cout << "area code:";
 cin >> phone.area;
 cout << "exchange:";
 cin >> phone.exch;
 cout << "number:";
 cin >> phone.number;
 cout << "\n\n\n";
}


p_rec::~p_rec()
{
 cout << "destructor called:\n";    // indicate the call and display values
 cout << form("%s %s %s\n",name.first,name.mid,name.last);
 cout << form("(%s) %s-%s\n",phone.area,phone.exch,phone.number);
 cout << "\n\n\n";
}


void p_rec::display_rec()  // show the current values
{
  cout << form("%s %s %s\n",name.first,name.mid,name.last);
  cout << form("(%s) %s-%s\n",phone.area,phone.exch,phone.number);
  cout << "\n\n\n";
}
```

continued

```
p_rec x;              // declare a class variable global to main

main()
{
 cout << "here it's displayed in the main() function:\n";
 x.display_rec();  // do something with the class in main
}
```

This simple program has limited value; it merely illustrates the interaction between the declaration of a variable—its scope and storage class—and the execution of the constructor and destructor code. However, you can replace the routines defined here with more useful ones. For example, the destructor might also write the class object to a file as part of its clean-up code. The important fact to remember is that you can use these two special functions for a variety of purposes beyond the mere initialization and deinitialization of variables.

The Action Part of a Class

Thus far, this discussion of classes has not really considered the implementation of the functional members. Let's focus on the functions that are defined to be part of these complex, programmer-defined data types. Everything in Chapter 2 about functions is equally true of functions that are members of a class. Now, let's examine the characteristics of *inline* definitions and function name overloading. Both of these capabilities are often used with member functions in a class, in which case, their syntax varies from ordinary, non-member functions.

inline Functions in Classes

Recall that you can specify a function definition as *inline*, so that any call to the function within a file is replaced not with a jump to a location that contains the function code but with the code itself. Thus, if a file contains three calls of an *inline* function, three copies of its statements are placed in the file. These *inline* functions provide the benefits of a macro definition—which in C is merely a textual substitution—with the full protection of a function call containing local variables and fully articulated parameters. Actually, the most common use of *inline* functions is as class member functions.

The *message3.h* example (Listing 4-4) illustrates two types of *inline* definitions. You use the standard, or explicit, *inline* definition with member functions the same way as you would with ordinary functions. Here, the destructor function ~*message()* is explicitly *inline*. Note that the member is declared in the class definition, but no reference to how the function is defined is included. Only at the actual definition of the function code itself is the *inline* member function specified as *inline*.

You also can implicitly define an *inline* member function. If you include a function definition with the member declaration in a class, then that function is implicitly *inline*. In the example, *clear()* and *read_buf()* are implicit *inline* functions. The implicit form of *inline* functions is more commonly used because of its compactness.

Listing 4-4. A *message* class with *inline* function members: *message3.h*

```
class message  {
    char *s;                       // a pointer to the message contents
    int len;                       // the length of the message

public:
  message(char*);                  // declare a constructor
 ~message();                       // return allocated memory to the o.s.

   void send(char*);               // send message out to the destination
   void get(char*);                // get one from it
   void clear() { *s='\0'; }       // implicit inline definition
   char* read_buf() { return s; }  // this, too, is implicitly inline
};


inline message::~message()    // explicit inline definition
{
 delete s;                 // return allocated memory to the free memory store
}
```

Note that the usage here conforms to good design practice as it applies to *inline* definitions; only very simple—and, above all, short—functions should be declared in this way. Because the code that defines an *inline* function becomes part of each instance of the class, large *inline* functions needlessly waste memory and can even slow access to the class. Longer or more complicated functions should be left as regular functions. This axiom is as true for member functions as it is for ordinary ones.

Overloading Member Function Names

Member function names share the overloading capability of ordinary functions, a topic that was discussed in Chapter 2. In fact, programmers use overloading extensively with classes because it can produce highly flexible interface members. You overload a member function implicitly—no special declaration is needed or allowed. To create an overloaded member function, merely declare more than one definition with the same name.

The *date3.h* example (Listing 4-5) shows an overloaded member function. This listing is a variation of the *date* class that was defined in the previous chapter (Listing 3-8). Now, however, the member function that lets the user reset the date, *new_date()*, is overloaded. The user supplies a date to this function by entering three integers—one each for the month, the day, and the year. The user also can call *new_date()* by passing it a character string with the name of the month first and the day separated from the year by a comma.

This example shows the flexibility of an overloaded constructor. Because it offers two different methods for initializing this class, it increases the class's generality so that it can be used in more programming contexts. This flexible constructor also makes it easier for the designer to write the rest of the program and to reuse previously created modules. The reusability of modules is an important design tool, and the overloading of member functions increases the likelihood that two classes that are not designed together nevertheless can be used together.

This example also uses a constructor with default values. When you declare a variable of type *date*, the same three integers required by *new_date()* must be supplied—in fact, the constructor calls this function to do its work—or the internal values of the class are set to zero.

Listing 4-5.   A new *date* class that uses an overloaded member function: *date3.h*

```
#include <stream.h>
#include <string.h>
#define COMMA ","
#define SPACE " "
```

```
const char* mname[]={ "illegal date","January","February","March","April",
                      "May","June","July","August","September","October",
                      "November","December"};


// an enhanced version of a date class

class date  {
   int day,        // the internal storage scheme
       month,      // this is now private to the
       year;       // class and unknown outside

public:
   date(int =0,int =0, int =0);  // a constructor for the date class
   void new_date(int,int,int);   // a member function to change the date
   void new_date(char *);        // a change function with a different format
   char* give_date();            // ...and one to report it
};


date::date(int d,int m, int y)    // integer format: eg. 12, 28, 1987
{
 new_date(d,m,y);
}


void date::new_date(int d,int m,int y) // take in the new values.
{

  if ( (d >= 1 && d <= 31) &&  (m >= 1 && m <= 12) )  { // check values
    day=d;          // assign the parameter values to the internal
    month=m;        // storage variables
    year=y;
  }
}


void date::new_date(char* dat)  // string format: eg. December 28, 1987
{
 char *mn,*dy,*yr;  // need some pointers to the tokens

 mn=strtok(dat,SPACE);  // use strtok() from the standard library to
 dy=strtok(0,COMMA);    // pull out the month, day, and year
 yr=strtok(0,COMMA);
```

continued

```
    for(int i=1 ; i <= 12 ; i++)
      if( ! strcmp(mn,mname[i]))
        break;    // jump out if we've got a match to one of month names
    if(i <= 12)   {
      month=i;         // set the internal values of the class
      day=atoi(dy);
      year=atoi(yr);
     }
    else                    // set to weird value for case where there is no match
      month=day=year=0;
  }




char* date::give_date()
{
 char *buf=new char[80];

 if(day==0 || month==0 || year==0)  // check for unset date
   sprintf(buf,"%s",mname[0]);
 else
   sprintf(buf,"%s %d,%d",mname[month],day,year);
 return buf;
}
```

Although this revised *date* class contains a good example of overloaded member functions, you can use overloading even more effectively in another situation. Constructor functions can be—and often
are—overloaded to accommodate differing formats for the same data
type. To demonstrate this usage, let's expand the *date* example. Sometimes it is convenient to store a date as a single, positive number; this
simplifies comparisons and calculations of time duration. You can store
a date as the number of days since some convenient—but not always
significant—event. A date of this kind is frequently called a Julian date.
The problem with these arbitrary dates is that they sometimes run
counter to the way people think of dates. The problem is one of conversion and how to conveniently move back and forth between two
kinds of time representation. The solution is to create a new *date* class
that accommodates different methods of setting the date. The *date4.h*
example (Listing 4-6) implements this solution.

Listing 4-6. **A *date* class that uses overloaded constructors: *date4.h***

```
#include <stream.h>
#include <string.h>

// define some useful constant values

const int months[]={0,31,59,90,120,151,181,212,243,273,304,334,365};
const char* mnames[]={"","January","February","March",
                      "April","May","June","July",
                      "August","September","October",
                      "November","December"};

class julian {
    int days;        // number of days since January 1.

public:
    julian(int =0,int =0);  // first constructor: eg. 12,3
    julian(char*,char*);    // alternative: eg. December, 3

    char *current_date();   // display the current date in month-day format
};


julian::julian(int mon,int day)
{
 days = months[mon-1] + day;
}

julian::julian(char* mon,char* dy)
{
 for(int i=1 ; i <= 13 ; i++)  // find the right month
   if(!strcmp(mnames[i],mon))
     break;

 if(i > 12)      // error condition
   days=0;
 else if(i == 1)   // its January, days and dy are the same
   days=atoi(dy);
 else
   days=months[i-1]+atoi(dy);  //calculate the number of days since Jan 1
```

continued

```
        }


        char* julian::current_date()
        {
         int mn,dy;

         if(days<=31)  {                // check to see if the month is in January
            mn=1;
            dy=days;                    // no need to calculate the julian date
          }
         else
            for(int i=2;i<=12;i++)
              if(days<=months[i])  {
                  mn=i;                      // set the month number
                  dy=days-months[i-1];       // calculate the day
                  break;
              }
          char *buffer = new char[20];

          sprintf(buffer,"%s %d",mnames[mn],dy);  // covert to string format
          return buffer;                          //return date string
        }
```

This example defines a new class called *julian*. Dates are stored internally in the integer member *days*. The program interprets a date as the number of days since January 1 of the current year (no provision is made for leap years). Two constructors offer you two ways to create an object of type *julian*. You can supply two integer values that represent the month and day, or you can pass the constructor a character string containing the name of the month and another one specifying the day. The only other member function defined is *current_date()*, which converts the days from January 1 into a character string that consists of the month and day.

The code for the constructor in the *julian* class is obscure enough to require some elucidation. The initial constructor:

```
julian(int =0, int =0);
```

converts its initial argument into the number of days since January first. The first parameter represents the number of the month (January is 1, February is 2, and so on). This month identifier then must be converted into the number of days since the beginning of the year. The array *months* contains this translation information. Each cell in this array contains the Julian day (from January 1) of the last day of each month. For example, the Julian day of January 31 is 31, but the value for June 30 is 181. The current date is calculated by taking the Julian date of the prior month and adding the current day. The Julian day for July 3, for example, is 181 + 4, or 185. The constructor function uses the *mon* parameter to index the array for the previous month and then adds the other parameter, *day*.

The other form of the constructor uses a similar array, but this one contains the names of the months in the proper order. Examine the character string array *mnames*. The string "January" occupies cell 1, "February" cell 2, and the rest of the names follow in the appropriate order. This constructor converts the month name to a month number and then uses this value to extract the Julian date in the same manner that the first, simpler constructor did. This matching is done by the following loop:

```
for(int i=1 ; i < 13 ; i++)
    if(!strcmp(mnames[i],mon))
        break;
```

The standard library *strcmp()* function returns a 0 if the strings match (are equal), so this test for "not *strcmp()*" is actually a test for equality. Note that the loop goes beyond the number 12 to permit a distinction between "December" and an illegal month name. Later in the code, the *if-then-else-if* construction tests for this error condition, and it sets the variable *days* to zero if the user enters an illegal month. Otherwise, the program calculates the Julian day in a way similar to the other constructor.

Being able to create as many constructors as there are conversion formats is obviously a very convenient tool for the programmer. However, the overloading capability offers another power that transcends this convenience. For example, you can use the class *julian* to act as a bridge between as many different date formats as you require. Once you add the proper member functions and debug their code, you never have to be concerned with explicit conversion again—the object does it for you. Conversion software is always tricky, often messy, and sometimes renders a program unreadable. This procedure gives you the means of keeping it under control.

Review questions

1. A class constructor is called whenever an object of the class is _____.

2. A destructor performs any necessary _____ tasks on behalf of a class object.

Programming project

1. Design a simple message passing system using the class in *message.h*.

Creating a *friend* Function

Until now, this discussion has emphasized the internal isolation of the class. However, the C++ syntax also contains a mechanism that allows a non-member function to access the private part of a class. By declaring a function as a *friend* to the class, it gains the same privileges as a member of that class. The integrity of the class is maintained because it still has a restricted and declared interface; however, now you can permit entry to selected outsiders. Of course, you always must be careful not to declare so many *friend* functions that you compromise the privacy of a class. Used sparingly, however, this capability provides an important programming tool for creating easy-to-access software.

The *timedat.c* example (Listing 4-7) shows the syntax of a *friend* declaration. This example defines two simple classes—*time* and *date*—and includes a simple driver function that lets you explore their use. Each class has a constructor and a single *friend* function—*gtime()* for *time* and *gdate()* for *date*. Each *friend* function formats and displays the values currently held by the class: *time* uses the *hours:minutes* format; date uses the *day/date/year* format. Note that both *friend* functions also require a parameter of the appropriate *class* type. Note also that even though a *friend* function is given a special status when it accesses a class, it is not part of that class, and it is not within the class's scope. Therefore, you must pass it the class object that it will work on.

Listing 4-7.   A program that illustrates the use of a *friend* function: *timedat.c*

```
#include <stream.h>
#include <string.h>
#define SEMICOLON ":"


/////////////////////////////////////////////////////
// define a simple time class with a friend function
/////////////////////////////////////////////////////

class time  {
  long secs;        // the common denominator for all time formats
                    // private to the class object
  friend char* gtime(time);  // declare an outside access function

public:
  time(char *);  // setting the time of day
  };

time::time(char* tm)
{
  char *hr,*mn;
  hr=strtok(tm,SEMICOLON); // strip off the hour
  mn=strtok(0,SEMICOLON);  // ...and the minute


  secs = atol(hr) * 3600 + atol(mn) * 60;  // calculate total seconds
}


/////////////////////////////////////////////////////
// define a simple date class with a friend function
/////////////////////////////////////////////////////
class date  {
  int month,  // store the date values
      day,
      year;
  friend char* gdate(date);  // declare an outside access function

public:
      // a simple constructor
  date(int m, int d, int y)  { month=m ; day=d ; year=y; }
```

continued

```
};

////////////////////////////////////////////////////
// a simple driver function
////////////////////////////////////////////////////

main()
{
 time x("10:30");      //  create a time object
 date d(12,29,1987);   // ...and a date one

 char *gtime(time),    // declare the friend functions
      *gdate(date);

 cout << gtime(x) << "\n";  // access the time class
 cout << gdate(d) << "\n";  // access the date class
}

////////////////////////////////////////////////////
// define the friend functions
////////////////////////////////////////////////////

char* gtime(time x)
{
 char *buffer;                      // create a buffer
 buffer=new char[10];
 int h=x.secs/3600,
     m=(x.secs % 3600)/60;
 sprintf(buffer,"%02d:%02d",h,m);  // fill it with the time values
 return buffer;
}

char* gdate(date x)
{
 char* buffer;       // create a buffer and fill it with the desired format
 buffer=new char[15];
 sprintf(buffer,"%2d-%2d-%4d",x.month,x.day,x.year);
 return buffer;
}
```

This example shows other differences between *friend* and member functions. Declaring a class declares all the members of that class. However, because *friend* functions are independent, you must declare them as you would any other function. In the example, both such functions return a character string and are declared together. Of course, the dot notation used by member functions is not available to friends, and you must explicitly pass them class objects. This simple example explores the syntax of a *friend* declaration and definition. However, in both classes, this formatting and display function could have been better handled by a member function. Let's look at some practical uses for *friend* functions.

Friends as Bridges Between Classes

One important function that a *friend* can perform is to act as bridge between two dissimilar classes. In this case, it serves as a link between classes that aren't nested. Although other methods for linking classes are available (later, you will see that derived classes permit the creation of class hierarchies), in many cases, *friend* functions offer a more secure and cleaner connection. A simple example of this kind of "friend bridge" is shown in *timedat2.c* (Listing 4-8).

Listing 4-8. **A program that illustrates a *friend* function used to bridge two classes: *timedat2.c***

```
#include <stream.h>
#include <string.h>
#define SEMICOLON ":"


class date;  // forward declare this so it can be recognized as a type

/////////////////////////////////////////////////
//define a simple time class
/////////////////////////////////////////////////

class time  {
  long secs;                 // the common denominator for all time formats
                                    // private to the class object
  friend char *time_date(time,date);  // declare a bridge function

public:
  time(char *);  // setting the time of day
```

continued

```
    };

    time::time(char* tm)
    {
     char *hr,*mn;
     hr=strtok(tm,SEMICOLON); // strip off the hour
     mn=strtok(0,SEMICOLON);  // ...and the minute
     secs = atol(hr) * 3600 + atol(mn) * 60;  // calculate total seconds
    }


    /////////////////////////////////////////////
    //defining a simple date class
    /////////////////////////////////////////////

    class date  {
      int month,                        // store the date values
          day,
          year;
      friend char *time_date(time,date);  // declare the bridge

    public:                     // setting the date-a simple constructor
      date(int m, int d, int y)  { month=m ; day=d ; year=y; }
    };



    /////////////////////////////////////////////
    // a simple driver function
    /////////////////////////////////////////////

    main()
    {
     time x("10:30");                   //create a time object
     date d(12,29,1987);                //...and a date object

     char *time_date(time,date);

     cout << time_date(x,d) <<  "\n";    //convert and display the values

    }
```

```
/////////////////////////////////////////////////
//define the friend function
/////////////////////////////////////////////////

char* time_date(time t,date d)
{
 int h=t.secs/3600,                  //calculate the time
m=(t.secs%3600)/60;
 char *buf;                          // build a buffer with the desired output
 buf=new char[50];
 sprintf(buf,"time: %02d:%02d\ndate: %2d-%2d-%4d",h,m,d.month,d.day,d.year);
 return buf;
}
```

This example declares the function *time_date()* as a *friend* both to the *time* class and the *date* class. This "super friend" function formats a display string that contains both time of day and date information and returns it for display. The only way it can do this is to access the private parts of both classes. Although each class operates independently from the other and uses its own constructor and internal storage strategy, this *friend* function temporarily bridges them for a single purpose. You also could accomplish this task by creating a regular function that has a time and a date parameter. In that case, however, you would need to pass two class objects to the function and access to their internal values would require the overhead of a call to a member function. Clearly, the *friend* function approach is more efficient.

This example has another interesting facet. Note that you must declare the name *date* as a class before you actually define it. If you fail to do this, the declaration of *time_date()* in the *time* class will fail because one of its parameters—namely *date*—is undefined. This kind of predeclaration of *class* types is a relatively obscure concept and one that is easy to overlook. However, there is another way to avoid this problem—use the *void** data type. Recall that this type is compatible with a pointer to any data type. The *timedat3.h* example (Listing 4-9) illustrates this approach. It has no undefined reference problem because the parameter is declared as a pointer to a *void*. Later, in the definition of the *time_date()* function, the parameter is cast back to *date**; however, by then the *date* class has been defined and is no longer an unknown quantity.

Listing 4-9. A bridge function without a forward declaration: *timedat3.h*

```
#include <stream.h>
#include <string.h>

#define SEMICOLON ":"

/////////////////////////////////////////////
//define a simple time class
/////////////////////////////////////////////

class time  {
  long secs;                  // the common denominator for all time formats
                                      // private to the class object
  friend char *time_date(time*,void*);  // declare a bridge function

public:
  time(char *);  // setting the time of day
 };

time::time(char* tm)
{
 char *hr,*mn;
 hr=strtok(tm,SEMICOLON); // strip off the hour
 mn=strtok(0,SEMICOLON);  // ...and the minute

 secs = atol(hr) * 3600 + atol(mn) * 60;  // calculate total seconds
 }


/////////////////////////////////////////////
//...and a simple date class
/////////////////////////////////////////////

class date  {
  int month,                      // store the date values
      day,
      year;
  friend char *time_date(time*,void*);  // declare the bridge

public:                          // setting the date-a simple constructor
  date(int m, int d, int y)  { month=m ; day=d ; year=y; }
```

```
};
```

```
///////////////////////////////////////////////////
//define the friend function
///////////////////////////////////////////////////

char* time_date(time* t,void* v)
{
  date *d=(date *)v;              //convert to a date pointer
  int h=t->secs/3600,            //calculate the time
      m=(t->secs%3600)/60;
  char *buf;                     // build a buffer with the desired output
  buf=new char[50];
  sprintf(buf,"time: %02d:%02d\ndate:
  %2d-%2d-%4d",h,m,d->month,d->day,d->year);
  return buf;
}
```

Member Functions as Friends
to Other Functions

All of the previous examples declared independent functions as friends to one or more classes, thus offering outside links to the internal structure of these classes. However, friends are not restricted to these ordinary functions. The member functions of one class can also become the friends of another. In fact, you can even declare all of the functions of one class to be friends to another. In this case, just as with the more ordinary case of an independently defined function, the special access is granted to the member functions. The difference is, of course, that these functions also have access to the private part of their own class.

The *timedat4.c* program (Listing 4-10) demonstrates the usefulness of this procedure. Here, both *gdate()*, which gives the current date, and *gtime()*, which returns the current hour and minute, are members of the *date* class, even though there is a separate *time* class. By defining the entire *date* class to be a *friend* to the *time* class, you guarantee that *gtime()* has adequate access to the private part of the needed *time* class. Of course, you also could include an entire set of member functions in one class to stand in the *friend* relation to another class; you are not restricted to only one such function.

Listing 4-10.   A program that illustrates the use of *friend* classes: *timedat4.c*

```
#include <stream.h>
#include <string.h>
#define SEMICOLON ":"


class date;          // don't forget to forward declare the date class.

/////////////////////////////////////////////////////
// define a simple time class with a friend class
/////////////////////////////////////////////////////

class time  {
  long secs;          // the common denominator for all time formats
                      // private to the class object
  friend class date; // all member functions in date are friends to time

public:
  time(char *);  // setting the time of day
 };

time::time(char* tm)
{
 char *hr,*mn;
 hr=strtok(tm,SEMICOLON); // strip off the hour
 mn=strtok(0,SEMICOLON);  // ...and the minute

 secs = atol(hr) * 3600 + atol(mn) * 60;  // calculate total seconds
}


/////////////////////////////////////////////////////
// define a simple date class with a friend function
/////////////////////////////////////////////////////
class date  {
  int month,  // store the date values
      day,
      year;

public:
      // a simple constructor
```

```
  date(int m, int d, int y)  { month=m ; day=d ; year=y; }
  char* gdate();         // a member access to the date class
  char* gtime(time);     // a member that is a friend function to the time class
};
```

```
///////////////////////////////////////////////////////
// define the member functions for the date class
///////////////////////////////////////////////////////
```

```
char* date::gtime(time x)
{
 char *buffer;              // create a buffer
 buffer=new char[10];
 int h=x.secs/3600,
     m=(x.secs % 3600)/60;
 sprintf(buffer,"%02d:%02d",h,m);  // fill it with the time values
 return buffer;
}
```

```
char* date::gdate()
{
 char* buffer;         // create a buffer and fill it with the desired format
 buffer=new char[15];
 sprintf(buffer,"%2d-%2d-%4d",month,day,year);
 return buffer;
}
```

```
///////////////////////////////////////////////////////
// a simple driver function
///////////////////////////////////////////////////////
```

```
main()
{
 time x("10:30");     //  create a time object
 date d(12,29,1987);  // ...and a date one

 cout << d.gtime(x) << "\n";  // access the time class
 cout << d.gdate() << "\n";   // access the date class
}
```

Although *friend* functions are rarely essential to a C++ program, they do serve to produce code that is more efficient than that which is produced by relying solely on class member functions. This efficiency is particularly obvious when you consider the run-time overhead. Through their ability to directly access the private part of another class, *friend* functions often let you save the overhead that another member function would incur. This increased efficiency is particularly important if your program must continually change or update the private part of the class. Even with this advantage, you should use *friend* functions sparingly. From the standpoint of C++ philosophy, member functions that define the interface to a class are still to be preferred.

Review questions

1. Access to the private part of a class is restricted to member functions and _____ functions.

2. A *friend* function can serve as a _____ between two distinct classes.

3. An entire _____ can be declared as a friend to a class.

Programming project

1. Add a member function to the class in *date4.h* to measure duration.

Classes and Pointers

The relationship between pointers and classes (and the members of classes) is straightforward and derives directly from the relationship in C between pointers and structure objects. You can declare a pointer variable that contains the address of a class object. You initialize this variable either by using the *address-of* operator (&) or by calling the memory allocation operator, *new*. This latter method is more commonly used because it is more flexible.

After you initialize a pointer variable to a class object, you can employ the arrow notation to access the members of the class. For example, consider the *message* class defined earlier in Listing 4-1. You can declare a message and initialize it with the following statement:

```
message msg("this is a test");
```

Now that you have an object, you can declare and initialize a pointer to it, as follows:

```
message *ptr = &msg;
```

Now, you can access the member functions of the class through the pointer. To display the current contents of the message buffer, for example, include the following line:

```
cout << ptr->read_buf();
```

You can use the same method to access any other member in the public part of the class.

Linked Data Structures Using Classes

The ubiquitous linked data structure is an important challenge for the programmer because it taxes the resources of the implementing language. This data type ranges from common constructions such as binary trees to more exotic multilink networks. The C++ class has special features that simplify the creation of the code that manages these linked types.

The basic linked data structure, the linked list, is illustrated in Figure 4-1. The list consists of nodes that can be stored anywhere in the system's memory. Each node contains the data that is associated with the node and the address of the next node. The implementation is equally straightforward. Each node can be implemented as a class object, which is, of course, the same implementation commonly used in C. However, two features of C++ help simplify the creation of such nodes—static class members and the "this" pointer.

The variable members of a class have a scope that is restricted to objects of that class. The private members can only be accessed by member or *friend* functions. However, you can also declare these variable members as *static*, which makes them common to all objects of the class. A non-static member, in contrast, is unique to the particular object that is declared. This relationship is illustrated in Figure 4-2.

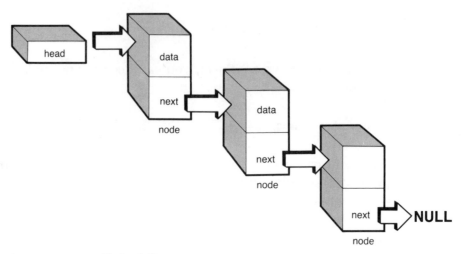

Figure 4-1.   A linked list structure

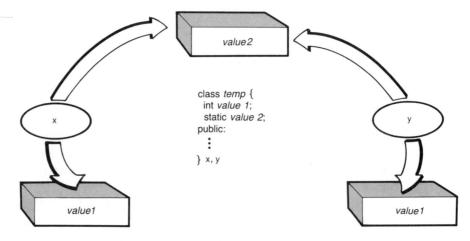

Figure 4-2.   Static and non-static class members

Any object of a class can invoke a member function of that class. The variable members of that object are, of course, also available to these functions. However, the object also has an associated self-reference pointer that contains the address of the object itself, not merely a reference to the internal member. The self-reference pointer is contained in a special variable called *this*.

The *list.h* example (Listing 4-11) uses these two features of the C++ class to implement a simple linked list. The heart of the list is a defined *node* class. Each time you must expand the list, merely create a new object of this class and attach it to the end of the existing list. The *static* pointer *head*, which is part of the private section, maintains the unity of the list. (There is only *one* copy of this member for all the class objects.)

Listing 4-11.   A simple linked list class: *list.h*

```
#include <string.h>

class node  {
   static node *head;   // a pointer to the chain of all class members
   node *next;          // the link to the next node
   char *info;          // the data part of the node
public:
   node(char* =0);      // declare the constructor
   void display_all();  // shows each node on the chain
};

node::node(char* ptr)              // the constructor
{

  if(ptr != 0) {                   //not the first node on the list
    info=new char[strlen(ptr)+1];  // make room for the value
    strcpy(info,ptr);              // ...and copy it.
    next=0;                        // set this up to be the last link
    node *cursor=head;             // create a cursor
    while(cursor->next != 0)       // find the end of the list
      cursor=cursor->next;

    cursor->next = this;           //assign the current node to the list
  }
  else {                           // the first node on the list
    info = new char[strlen("root")+1]; // set up the data part
    strcpy(info,"root");           // mark it as the first node
    next = 0;                      // set it up as the last link
    head = this;                   // assign the node to head
  }
}

void node::display_all()           // a simple display function
{
 node *cursor=head;                        //set up a temporary pointer variable
                                                          *continued*
```

```
while(cursor != 0)  {                    // walk through the list
  cout << form("*%s\n",cursor->info);    //...displaying each node
  cursor=cursor->next;
}
}
```

Each time you create a new *node* object, the class constructor starts at the member *head*. Because this member is static, its scope is common to the entire class of objects; therefore it points to the first node, not the currently created one. Any navigation of this list thus moves from the first member to the last member. Had you declared the member *head* as an ordinary member, its reference would be restricted to the current node, thus making the creation of the list impossible.

Figure 4-3 illustrates another important, yet subtle, feature of the C++ class. In the present context, you also need a way to refer to the newly created node—to the class object as a whole, not merely its members—in order to attach it to the end of the list. To do this you must use the *this* pointer. Recall that *this* always points to the current class object; therefore, it contains the address of the newly created node object.

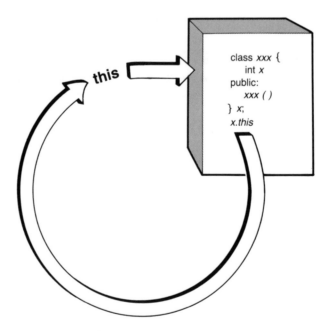

Figure 4-3. The *this* pointer

Container Classes

One important variation of the previously described linked list is the *container* class. Basically, a container class is a data type that consists of a dynamic collection of values—a traditional data table, for example. Although creating and using these types are important parts of all programming, the C++ *class* type makes their implementation particularly simple.

The *contain.c* example (Listing 4-12) defines a *token* class, or, more correctly, a "tokenizing" class. In creating an object of this type, the constructor accepts a character string as a parameter. The class *token* holds a linked list of the "tokens" that comprise its initializing character string. In this case, a token is defined as one or more contiguous characters separated by blank spaces. The primary interface is through the member function *nth_token()*. This function takes an ordinal number and returns the appropriate token in the list.

Listing 4-12.   An example of a container class: *contain.c*

```
// include the necessary header files

#include <stream.h>
#include <string.h>
#define SPA  " "


//////////////////////////////////////////////////////////////
// create a value class to hold a single token
//////////////////////////////////////////////////////////////

struct tvalue  {  // set up a token value class
  char *value;     // character string value
  tvalue *next;    // next token on the chain
 };


//////////////////////////////////////////////////////////////
// define a token class to contain the chain of tokens
//////////////////////////////////////////////////////////////

class token  {
  static tvalue *toke;  // pointer to linked list of tokens

 public:
```

continued

```
   token(char *);   // constructor
  ~token();          // destructor

   char *nth_token(int);  // access to individual tokens on the chain
  };

///////////////////////////////////////////////////////////
// define the constructor and destructor
///////////////////////////////////////////////////////////

token::token(char *x)
{
 char* temp;

 if((temp=strtok(x,SPA)) == 0)  {  // test for error condition: no tokens
   cout << "error condition\n";
   exit(1);
  }
  toke=new tvalue;                   // create and initialize the first token
  tvalue *cursor=toke;
  cursor->value=new char[strlen(temp)+1];
  strcpy(cursor->value,temp);
  cursor->next=0;

  while((temp=strtok(0,SPA)) != 0)  {  // use strtok() to strip off tokens
    cursor->next=new tvalue;           // create a new node and initialize it
    cursor=cursor->next;
    cursor->value=new char[strlen(temp)+1];
    strcpy(cursor->value,temp);
    cursor->next=0;
  }
}


token::~token()
{
 tvalue *prev,*cursor=toke;

 while(cursor != 0)  {
   prev=cursor;                   // walk through the token chain
   cursor=cursor->next;           // delete each node as we go along
   delete prev->value;
```

```
    delete prev;
  }
}


/////////////////////////////////////////////////////////
// define the sole member function
/////////////////////////////////////////////////////////

char* token::nth_token(int num)
{
 tvalue *cursor=toke;  //create a linked list cursor

 for(int i=1 ; i < num ; i++)  // step through num times
    if(cursor->next != 0)      // if not at end of list
      cursor=cursor->next;     // go to next one
    else
      return '\0';             // oops, num too high
  return cursor->value;        // return "numth" token
 }


/////////////////////////////////////////////////////////
// a simple driver function to demonstrate the class
/////////////////////////////////////////////////////////

main()
{
 token x("this is a test");              // create a token object

 for(int i = 4 ; i >= 1 ; i--)           // display the token chain backwards
    cout << x.nth_token(i)  << "\n";
 }
```

It makes sense to define the class *tvalue* as a structure. It really doesn't need to have a private and a public part because it has no function members and is wholly contained within the class *token*. In a simple linked list, this would be the node definition. A character string variable holds the value and a link to the next node on the list. This is the structure that will be used to build the linked list.

The only private member of the class *token* is the pointer to the list of *tvalues*. Most of the work of this class is done by the single constructor, which takes a character string as an initializing variable— *token x("this is only a test")*. If you do not supply this character string in the declaration, an error condition results, and no data object is created. If, however, a correctly formatted character string is sent to *token()*, then the member function creates a linked list, each node of which is a single *word* from the string. The standard library function *strtok()* does the parsing (although you could easily write this *strtok()* in C++).

The initial call to the *strtok()* function is done in the conditional construction that tests for the presence of a string:

```
if((temp=strtok(x,SPA)) == 0)   {
```

Note that the first node on the list is created and filled independently of the loop that strips the other words from the list. This is done primarily because by doing the test, the program has already grabbed the first token. The subsequent *words* are put into nodes by repeated calls to *strtok()*:

```
while((temp=strtok(0,SPA)) != 0)
    cursor->next=new tvalue;
    cursor=cursor->next;
    cursor->value=new char[strlen(temp)+1];
    strcpy(cursor->value,temp);
    cursor->next=0;
}
```

These calls in the loop continue until the function returns a zero to indicate the end of the string. The execution of the constructor leaves the data object of type *token* with a value that consists of the linked list of tokens.

The member function *nth_token()* returns the value of the specified node on the linked list. Thus, a call to *nth_token(3)* returns the value of the third word in the list. A simple *for* loop moves through the linked list until it finds the requested node. If *nth_tok()* is called with too high a number, it returns an *end of string* marker ('\0') to indicate this failure.

The destructor for the token class is straightforward, if a little unwieldy. It steps through the linked list and deallocates each node. If you examine it closely, you will notice that it removes nodes behind itself—a little strange, but reasonably efficient.

In contrast to the earlier example in Listing 4-11, this class consists of two nested classes. One class, *tvalue*, defines a simple linked list. This list is wholly contained in the containing class, *token*. The differences between this class and the earlier one define the notion of a container class. In a traditional linked list, each node is an instance of the class; in a container class, however, the entire list is contained in one class object. Figure 4-4 illustrates this difference.

Linked list:

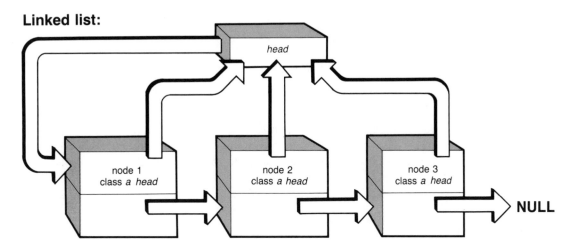

Container class:

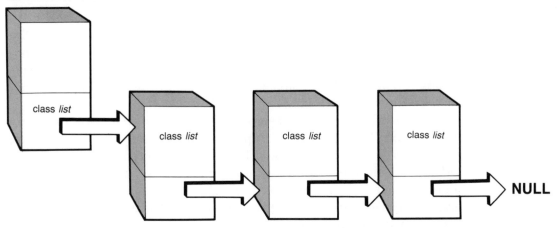

Figure 4-4. Linked lists *vs* container classes

Review questions

1. A _____ variable member is common to the entire class.

2. The _____ pointer contains the address of the current class object.

3. A _____ class holds a collection of data objects.

Programming projects

1. Expand the class in *list.h* to include member functions that add and delete nodes.

2. Use the class defined in *contain.c* to implement a calculator program. This calculator should be able to parse a line such as: 23 + 4 into its constituent tokens and do the appropriate calculations.

Summary

This chapter explored some of the more complicated aspects of the C++ class facility. Added to the basic definition of Chapter 3 were constructors and destructors, the use of *inline* member functions, overloading functions within classes, and the use of the *friend* relationship between functions and class.

Furthermore, you have seen how several important programming problems can be solved in a simpler and more elegant way by using the new *class* data type. Linked lists are easily created by defining a *node* class. The more complex "container" class, which you can use to create tables, lists, and so on, are also much easier to implement. Beyond these examples, the C++ class is the central element that defines this improved programming language.

5

Overloading Operators

5

Overloading Operators

Chapter 3 addressed the problem of modeling complex real-world entities and situations in a computer. The C++ solution revolves around the complex data type called a class. Chapter 4 detailed the way classes interact with the rest of C++ to produce useful and reliable programs. Thus far, however, these discussions have led only to a partial solution to the problem of modeling the real world.

Now, let's address the rest of the issues that have been raised by the definition of classes. For example, one weakness of traditional programming languages occurs when they must handle higher level constructions such as structures. Because these new data types are created by the programmer, they can't be manipulated with the same operators that work with the built-in types. In C, for example, you can't add two structures together, even if the operation is legitimate, as it would be in the case of structures that define complex numbers. You can define an equivalent function that performs addition on particular structures, but you can't magically attach that function to the "+" operator. Thus, to perform the operation, you must use the function call mechanism rather than the simpler syntax of operators. For example, suppose you have defined the following complex number type in C:

```
struct complex  {
    double  real,
            imag;
} x , y, z;
```

In order to give the program the capability of adding two complex numbers, for example, you need to define a function such as *addcplx()*. The actual addition, then, might look like this:

```
z = addcplx( x , y);
```

Most programmers are accustomed to this kind of circumlocution. However, consider how much more clearly the code would evoke its task if it merely read as follows:

```
z = x + y;
```

As you might expect, C++ addresses this shortcoming of C. It gives your programs added flexibility by letting you redefine the existing operators so that they also work with class objects. Not only can you give unique new characteristics to standard symbols such as +, *, and +=, you can even redefine the subscripting symbol and the function call operator (()). Because overloading of the *new* and *delete* operators for memory management is also possible, you gain the ability to create class-specific memory allocation and deallocation routines.

For overloading to be effective, the actions associated with the object must have the same intimate relationship to the value as those of the built-in data types. For example, when you add two integers using the + operator, the code that implements that addition operation knows how an integer is stored and how to manipulate it. You don't have to write code that accomplishes this task bit by bit. C++ gives the same flexibility to programmer-created data types. The aim of the operator overloading mechanism is to short-circuit the external connection between data and action that is found in traditional programming languages, thus forming a more intimate connection between these two aspects of the object.

This chapter explores the operator overloading capability of C++ by offering practical and illustrative examples of useful techniques. For example, the programs in this chapter show you how to use overloaded operators to simplify the manipulation of:

- ▶ complex numbers
- ▶ character strings
- ▶ a circle class
- ▶ a dollars-and-cents data type

Each example demonstrates how to replace function call syntax with a simple and obvious operator.

A Review of Overloading

Chapter 2 discussed the basics of function overloading, and Chapter 4 explained how to use function overloading to provide flexible functions for user-designed classes. For example, one program (Listing 4-6) showed how to use an overloaded constructor function to create class objects with a variety of data formats.

Function Overloading

Before discussing operator overloading, let's briefly review the mechanics of overloading. Several functions with the same name can represent different pieces of code. For example, one *mean()* function might manipulate *double* values, while another—also called *mean()*—might calculate the average of integer values. The program decides which of these functions is specified by a particular function call by matching the actual argument type with the two function definitions. For example, as a very simple solution to a perennial problem, you can specify two *mean()* functions—one for *long* values and one for *double* values:

```
overload mean;
long mean(long);
double mean(double);
```

Each version of *mean()* must have a different definition so that the program can choose the correct code. In this case, the selection is based on the data types of the parameters passed to the function. In the following code fragment:

```
int x, m;
double y, rm;
     .
     .
m = mean(x);
rm = mean(y);
```

the *long* version of the *mean()* function fills the variable *m* because the parameter *x* is *long*. Similarly, *rm* accesses the appropriate function code for a *double* because *y* is a *double*.

You gain important advantages from using overloaded functions. First, you can dispense with the sometimes awkward code that is needed to choose one implementation of a function over another. Second, you no longer need to give functions unnatural names like *fmean()* and *imean()* and place them in some *if* statement that uses a complicated conditional expression to choose one or the other. Third, your program source listings become clean and easy to read because you can replace the circuitous meanderings of complex conditional expressions with more straightforward code.

Extending Overloading to Operators

Operator overloading lets the programmer give new meanings to the operator symbols that already exist in C++. For example, you can construct your own implementation of + or −, the increment and decrement operators (++ and −−), or even the memory allocation operators *new* and *delete*. Remember, too, that when you perform overloading, the existing functionality of the C++ operators is always preserved—for example, ++ still always increments an integer as expected.

Operator overloading—giving multiple meanings to the same symbol—is not as unusual as it first seems. Every programming language uses the procedure to some extent, but, because the overloading is built-in, you might not even realize it has been done. For example, the + that adds two integer values is not really the same as the + that adds two *double* values. In both C and C++, many basic operators are also redefined to perform completely different functions than arithmetic calculations. For example, the * operator, depending on the context, can either be a multiplication operator or it can represent the dereferencing of a pointer variable, letting you obtain the data from the address pointed to. What is new in C++ is that this overloading capability extends to user-defined data types—*class* types.

There are some restrictions to operator overloading, however. Redefinition is confined to existing operator symbols—you can't make up a totally new operator syntax. Operators can be overloaded only in the context of class definitions—you cannot, for example, redefine + for integers or any other built-in data type. You also cannot change the place that the operator holds in the table of precedence. Finally, the capability for defining new operators for pointers is limited. However, even with these restrictions, operator overloading is a powerful tool for program structuring.

Advantages of Operator Overloading

The principal advantage of being able to define new operators to work with classes is that it helps establish *class* types as fully functioning parts of the C++ programming language. Operator overloading permits C++ to become an extensible language in an even more profound sense: The program designer can add to the language specialized data types that promote better data representation, afford modularity, and yet are as easy to use as the basic built-in operators.

By removing the distinction between user-defined types and the traditional types, C++ also opens the door to more efficient code. Now you can extend natural operations to handle similar, but not identical, situations. For example, you can redefine the + operator—used traditionally to indicate the addition of numbers—to concatenate character strings. In C, you can carry out this concatenation only by using a function from the standard library:

```
char s1[10] = "ABC",
     s2[] = "DEF",
     s3[20];
s3 = strcat(s1,s2);
```

Here the concatenation is performed by the function call, so you must be careful that the receiving string variable has sufficient space to store both string values. In C++, by contrast, you can redefine the + operator to represent this same operation:

```
char s1[10] = "ABC",
     s2[] = "DEF",
     s3[20];
s3 = s1 + s2;
```

This code can perform the same work, but the operator syntax is clearer and unambiguous. More importantly, the function of the code is more obvious—concatenation, in a broad sense, is similar to the arithmetic concept of addition. Most programmers who would see the operator used in this context would almost instinctively understand the meaning of the operation.

Operator overloading thus lets you create programming "metaphors" such as the concatenation operator. Figure 5-1 illustrates this concept. A metaphor is simply an extension of the operational concept of one data type to a different, but analogous, type. In the case of

Additions: "adding two numbers"

Concatenation: "adding two strings"

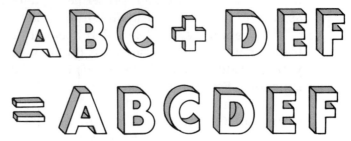

Figure 5-1.   Programming metaphors

concatenation, the notion of numeric addition is given a similar meaning in the context of character strings. Note that this extension of the meaning of addition is not merely a mechanical procedure—the operation of adding two numbers is distinct from the merging of two strings. Therefore, a programming metaphor lets the programmer shift perspectives and see data types, particularly complex ones, in a new light.

Many C++ designers are disillusioned with operator overloading. They feel very strongly that it is a technique that can easily be abused. Some even feel that the specification and implementation of this part of the language needs to be improved. Without taking sides in the issue, it is certainly true that the beginning C++ programmer must approach operator overloading very carefully. It is as powerful as it looks but not as well-behaved or controllable as it seems—that is a dangerous combination. Even more than with function overloading, the beginner can very quickly produce code that is obscure to the point of being opaque—not only to the outside reader but even to the author.

Even the experienced programmer is at risk. The uses and meaning of these operators can become so ingrained that if the meaning of one is switched in one part of a program, it can lead to a confusion of meaning in another. This is especially a problem when you often use the original meaning of an operator inside the function that redefines it.

The safest use of operator overloading is with numeric objects. Defining complex numbers as a class and overloading the usual arithmetic operators is a common, well-behaved example of a clear and balanced use of this facility. However, not every possible overloading situation will be as useful. Keep this in mind as you design your C++ programs.

The Mechanics of Operator Overloading

Before delving into the applications of operator overloading, let's examine the mechanism in C++ that permits you to use this procedure. The key to operator overloading is a special built-in C++ function that lets the programmer substitute a user-defined function for one of the existing operators. The general form of this function is as follows:

```
<type> operator<op>(<parameter list>);
```

First, *<type>* identifies the class type with which the new operator will work; *<op>* represents the operator you want to overload (do not use an intervening space when you supply the operator symbol); and *<parameter list>* is a—possibly empty—list of arguments to be passed to the new operator-function. For example, the declaration of an addition operator for complex numbers might look like the following:

```
complex operator+(complex);
```

Although this example takes only one argument, the parameter list is not restricted to a single variable. Remember, the declaration of a new operator must be followed by its definition. The definition syntax of an *operator* function is the same as it is for any other class member function: A header identifies the class and the particular member, for example:

```
complex::complex operator+(complex x)
```

and is followed by the appropriate code.

After this definition is compiled, whenever the program references the specified operator, a call to this operator function executes these statements. For example, the following code:

```
main()
{
complex x(2,3),
y(4,6);
x+y;
}
```

leaves the variable *x* with a real value of 6 and an imaginary value of 9.

The *cmplx.h* example (Listing 5-1) illustrates how to redefine an operator. This definition of a complex number type includes a constructor, an addition operator, and a display function. (Because the focus here is on the operator definition, the example omits the destructor and other potentially useful member functions.) Recall that each complex number consists of two parts—a real part and an imaginary part. Each of these parts is represented by a *double* value stored in the private section of the *complex* class. The addition of complex numbers involves adding the real parts and the imaginary parts independently to produce a new two-part value. In the example, you must initialize a data object of type *complex* with a value in the form *mm + nni* (you can substitute any numbers in this expression). Figure 5-2 illustrates the form of a complex number.

Note that for convenience, the initializing expression is a character string that the program converts to the appropriate numeric values using character string functions from the standard library. Specifically, *strtok()* divides the string expression into two parts at the + character.

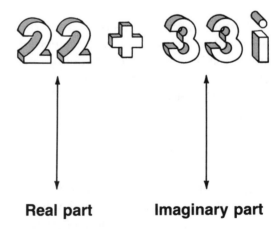

Real part   **Imaginary part**

Figure 5-2.   A complex number

The program assumes that the real part is to the left of this operator and that the imaginary part is to the right. As a further check, the program calls *strtok()* again to search for the *i* character, which traditionally indicates the imaginary part of a complex number. The program then uses the library function *atof()* to convert both strings into numbers.

Listing 5-1.   A complex number class that uses an overloaded "+" operator: *cmplx.h*

```
#include <string.h>

class complex  {
   double real,     // store the real part of the complex quantity
          imaginary;  // ... and the imaginary part
public:
   complex(char*)    // declare a constructor
   complex operator+(complex&) // declare a "+" operator for complex numbers
   char* display() // it's no fun if you can't see the value
};

complex::complex(char* cnum)
{
 real=atof(strtok(cnum,"+"));    // pull off and convert the real part
 imaginary=atof(strtok(0,"i"));  // convert the imaginary part
}

complex complex::operator+(complex cnum)
{
 complex temp;
 temp.real = real + cnum.real;  // add in the new real component
 temp.imaginary = imaginary + cnum.imaginary; //...and the imaginary
 return temp;
}

char* complex::display()
{
 char* temp;                      // create some temporary buffer space
 temp = new char[10];
 sprintf(temp,"%f + %fi",real,imaginary); // fill and format it
 return temp;                     // return the value
}
```

This example focuses on the operator function, which is declared to redefine the + symbol to handle the addition of two complex quantities. This redefinition is quite simple. The complex number that is passed as a parameter is added, component by component, to the *complex* class that calls it.

The action of this operator function is implemented by the following statements in its definition:

```
temp.real = real + cnum.real;
temp.imaginary = imaginary + cnum.imaginary;
```

One of the complex numbers is passed to the function as the parameter *cnum*. The private part of the first class supplies the other value. This class is the calling class, although its position is obscured by the syntax. The program adds together the two real sections, and then it adds the two imaginary ones. In both cases, the result is stored in the variable *temp*. At the end of the operation, this temporary value is returned to the caller.

Note that the redefined symbol—+—is appended to the keyword *operator* and is outside of the parentheses that enclose the list of arguments to the function; this is because the symbol is part of the name of the function and not a function parameter. In the example, the parameter is another complex number to be added to the value of the current *complex* object, the object that contains *operator+()* as a member. Because the operator function returns the result, the function must be declared as type *complex*.

Let's clear up one potentially confusing issue: Remember that the redefinition of the operator—in this case +—takes place only in the context of the class in which the overloading occurs; that is why you can use the standard meaning of the + symbol inside the function definition itself. The values being added here are ordinary *double* values. You cannot overload operators as they apply to built-in data types because new operator meanings can be created only for user-defined types (classes). The *cmplx.c* program (Listing 5-2) is a simple driver that illustrates how you could use this class. This program uses the member function *display()* to produce readable and formatted output.

Listing 5-2.   A drive program that tests the *complex* class type: *cmplx.c*

```
#include <stream.h>

main()
```

```
{
  complex x("22 + 2i"),  // initialize two complex numbers
          y("11 + 3i"),
          z;


  z=x+y;                          // add the numbers together
  cout << form("z=%s\n",z.display());   // display the result
}
```

Review questions

1. The redefinition of built-in operators in C++ is called _____.

2. A programming metaphor occurs when an operation usually performed on one data type is _____ so that it will work on another.

3. Only _____ operators can be overloaded.

Programming project

1. Expand the complex number class by adding definitions for the other arithmetic operators: -, *, and /.

Overloading Binary Operators

In addition to the general restrictions mentioned earlier, there are also restrictions on the way a particular overloaded operator can work. Some of these restrictions arise from the original definition of the operator symbol. First, you must respect the original functional "template" of the operator. For example, you cannot change a binary operator—one that works on two objects, such as the division operator /—to create a unary operator, which works on a single object. In the same way, you can't convert a unary operator to perform binary operations. Also, you must maintain the general form of the operator's syntax even though you might change what the operator does and the objects on which it works. Of course, when you overload operators that can perform either binary or unary functions (such as + and –) you can use them in either context, and C++ will recognize the difference.

Another restriction related to the operator's "template" concerns precedence. Recall that precedence controls the order in which operations are performed when two or more operators are embedded in an expression. For example, in the integer expression $x + y / 2$, the division is performed before the addition because it has a higher precedence. C++ has an explicit and complex set of precedence rules (see the following box). You can change an operator's definition, but you cannot change its precedence; an overloaded operator always retains its place in this list.

Precedence of operators

```
++  -- sizeof (<type>) new delete    evaluates right to left

* (indirection)  & (address of)  + (unary)  - (unary)
* / %

+ -

<< >>

< <= > >=

++ !=

& (bitwise and)    evaluation order not guaranteed

^ (bitwise exclusive or)    evaluation order not guaranteed

| (bitwise or)    evaluation order not guaranteed

&&

||

? (conditional operator)    evaluates right to left

=  +=  -=  *=  /=  %=  >>=  <<=  &=  ^=  |=

, (comma)
```

The constructor in the *string.c* example (Listing 5-3) initializes the string value. The + operator has been redefined as a string concatenation operator that adds characters to the end of an existing string object.

Listing 5-3.   A class with a concatenation operator: *string.c*

```
#include <stream.h>
#include <string.h>


// create a truly dynamic string class


#define MINLINE 55

class string  {
  char *v;                   // create a pointer to the characters
  int len;                   // hold the current number of characters
public:
  string(const char* =0);    // declare an initializing constructor
 ~string() { delete v; }     // define a destructor
  void operator+(char*);     // declare a concatenation operator
  char* dump() { return v;}  // define a simple i/o function
  };

string::string(const char* s)
{
 if(s != 0)  {                      // the constructor has an initializing value
   v = new char[(len = strlen(s))];  // allocate enough memory--set the len
   strcpy(v,s);                     // copy parameter the string
  }
 else  {             // the constructor is called without initializing
   v = new char[MINLINE];    // allocate a minimal amount of memory
   len = 0;   // set the length
  }
}


void string::operator+(char* p)
{
 char *buf;                        // allocate enough memory  for a buffer

 buf = new char[len = strlen(p) + len];     // set the len member
 strcpy(buf,v);                   // copy the original value into the buffer
```
continued

```
        strcat(buf,p);              // concatenate the new value
        delete v;                   // remove old memory allocation
        v=buf;                      // set the string value to the new buffer
    }


main()
{
 string s("this is only a test");     // declare a string type

 cout << form("%s\n",s.dump());  // display the current value
 s + " nothing can go wrong";    // "add" the new characters
 cout << form("%s\n",s.dump());  // display the new values
}
```

The overloading of the + operator in this example demonstrates some of the principles and techniques that increase the effectiveness of a user-defined data type. The meaning of this addition symbol has been extended to encompass the significantly different operation of adding new characters to a string class object. This string class contains a simple concatenation operation that assigns standard C++ strings, which are arrays of characters terminated by a '\0' (the *end-of-string* character), to a *string* class variable. For example, the following code:

```
string p("this is a test");
p + " nothing can go wrong.";
```

appends a literal character string to the variable *p*. (Note that the + operator always adds the string represented by its second operand to the string represented by its first operand.) The *p* variable now contains the original string plus the additional characters and is displayed on the screen by the following code:

```
cout << form ("%s\n", s.dump ())
```

The *form()* function formats the output as a traditional character string.

The definition of this new operator follows the syntax rules that you used to create the complex number class. You declare the *operator+()* function with a type and with a list of parameters. In this case, the only argument to the function is a character string (an array of characters terminated by the null symbol '\0'). After the variable member *v* is appropriately extended, both old and new values are combined in the buffer pointed to by *v*. The new operator is type *void* because it does not return a value; instead it merely alters the left operand. (This procedure might seem odd considering the normal function of the + operator; however, the implementation of the operation is appropriate because the left operand is the only string class object in the program.)

The *string.c* example also contains a short *main()* function that serves as a driver to demonstrate the operation of the class. After it uses an initializing value to declare the string object *s*, the program "adds" a literal character string. Both forms of the string object are then displayed on the screen.

Although it might not be apparent from the code, the *operator+()* function is implemented as a binary operator. The value that is passed as a parameter is the second, or right-hand, operand; the first operand is an object of the *string* class of which this function is a member. This allows the operator function special access to the object. Although the class isn't explicitly in the parameter list, C++ nonetheless implicitly treats it as part of the function; this makes the function a binary operator by default.

The membership of *operator+()* in the class *string* also satisfies another important requirement for operator redefinition—one of the objects involved must be a class object. This example contains one class object and one very basic data type—the traditional character string.

Operators with Two Class Objects

The *string2.c* example (Listing 5-4) illustrates a slightly different con-catenation operator. In this example, the class definition utilizes the < operator to represent the concatenation of one string type onto another. Also, the previous example (Listing 5-3) used an array of characters (a built-in data type) to extend the string object; here, the concatenation involves two class objects, a more complicated situation.

Listing 5-4.   An operator that concatenates two objects of
**   *string* type: *string2.c***

```
#include <stream.h>
#include <string.h>


// create a truly dynamic string class
```

continued

```
#define MINLINE 55

class string {
  char *v;                      // pointer to the string values
  int len;                      // current string length
public:
  string(const char* =0);       //constructor
 ~string() { delete v; }        // destructor
  void operator<(string&);      // concatenates two objects of class string
  char* dump() { return v };    // define a simple display member
 };

string::string(const char* s)
{
 if(s != 0)  {                          // initial value supplied
   v = new char[(len = strlen(s))+1];   // allocate storage
   strcpy(v,s);                         // copy value to string
  }
 else {                                 // using default value
   v = new char[MINLINE];               // allocate minimum storage
   len = 0;                             // show zero length
 }
}

void string::operator<(string& s)
{
 char *buf;                             // create a buffer equal in size to
 buf = new char[len = len + s.len+1];   // both strings
 strcpy(buf,v);                         // copy the original string to the buffer
 strcat(buf,s.v);             //add the contents of the second string
 delete v;                    // replace the old with the new
 v=buf;
}


main()
{
 string s("this is only a test"),           // declare and initialize two
       t(" nothing can go wrong");           // string objects
```

```
    cout << form("%s\n%s\n",s.dump(),t.dump());    // display the current . . .
                                                   // . . . values

    s < &t;                                        // "add" a string object
    cout << form("%s\n",s.dump());                 // display the new value
}
```

The *operator<()* function in this example adds the contents of one string object (sent to it as a parameter) to another. Because this is a binary operator, it requires a left and a right operand. However, only the left operand changes. The right operand—in this case, the parameter value—maintains its value. The *operator<()* function takes advantage of the fact that a member function has privileged access to the private part of the class. Because this privilege derives from the class and not the object, it extends equally to both the implicit and explicit argument value. Thus, the function taps the private part of the parameter class without violating the data-hiding capacity of either of the classes.

The definition of the string concatenation operator in this example is significantly different from the definition of the previous example (Listing 5-3). The primary difference is that this operator concatenates two *string* class objects. The previous operator merely executed a *string fill* operation that altered the value that the *string* class carried, not with a class object, but with an ordinary C character string. Both of these situations frequently arise during program development: The previous case is a kind of *string conversion* because one of the parameters is a non-class type; the current example is a more straightforward concatenation.

Using *friend* Operator Functions for Flexibility

The last two examples show the function that redefines the operator as a member of the same class as the new operator. In this case, the left argument is always implicit, and the class "owns" the function. However, this is not the only way to produce a new operator. You can also redefine an operator by using *friend* functions. The *string3.c* program (Listing 5-5) is the equivalent of the previous example, except that it uses a *friend* function.

Listing 5-5. **An operator defined as a *friend* to a class that concatenates two string objects: *string3.c***

```
#include <stream.h>
#include <string.h>


// create a truly dynamic string class


#define MINLINE 55


class string  {
  char *v;                  // pointer to the actual characters
  int len;                  // current length of the string
public:
  string(const char* =0);             // declare the constructor
 ~string() { delete v; }             // ...and destructor
  friend void operator<(string&,string&); //
  char* dump() { return v;}      // display all
 };


string::string(const char* s)
{
 if(s != 0)  {                 // initial value supplied
  v = new char[(len = strlen(s))]; // allocate storage
  strcpy(v,s);                 // set string value
  }
 else  {                       // no initial value supplied
  v = new char[MINLINE];       // minimal storage allocation
  len = 0;                     // set zero length
  }
}


void operator<(string& a,string& b)  // define the operator using string
{                                    // class references
 char *buf;                          // create a large enough buffer
 buf = new char[a.len = a.len + b.len];  // to store the new value
 strcpy(buf,a.v);                    // copy the old
 strcat(buf,b.v);                    // ...then the new ones
 delete a.v;                         // replace the value
 a.v=buf;
}
```

```
main()
{
  string s("this is only a test"),      // initialize one string object
         t(" nothing can go wrong.");    // ...an another
  cout << form("%s\n",s.dump());         // show the first
  s < t;                                 // concatenate them
  cout << form("%s\n",s.dump());         // show the new value
}
```

Here, the function *operator<()* resembles the one defined in *string2.c* (Listing 5-4). However, rather than using an implied string object as the "right-hand" operand, it uses two explicit objects as arguments. The first string object is altered; the second is not. You must declare the first parameter as a reference because the operator changes it. Although you are not required to declare the second parameter as a reference, doing so saves a little memory space at runtime because C++ doesn't need to create a new string object within the *operator<()* function. (Remember, because the reference type replaces a parameter with the address of the actual argument, a local variable does not have to be created or filled with the value of the actual parameter.) The driver function, *main()*, shows how to use the new operator with this class.

Using a *friend* function to redefine an operator is cleaner and more natural than using a member function. The *friend* approach is further illustrated by *string4.c* (Listing 5-6). In this example, the + operator combines two string objects the same way as the program in Listing 5-5 did; however, instead of altering the first string object, it leaves both operands untouched and stores the result in a new variable. This procedure more closely matches the kind of operation usually associated with the + symbol, even though no syntactical requirements dictate this association. You could implement this example using member functions with no loss in functionality, but your code would lose some of its readability.

Listing 5-6. A *friend* operator function that returns a pointer to a string object: *string4.c*

```
#include <stream.h>
#include <string.h>


// create a truly dynamic string class


#define MINLINE 55
```
continued

```
class string  {
  char *v;                      // pointer to the actual characters
  int len;                      // current length of the string
public:
  string(const char* =0);                   // declare the constructor
 ~string() { delete v; }                    // ...and destructor
  friend string* operator+(string&,string&); // declare a new "+" operator
  char* display() { return v;}              // display all
 };

string::string(const char* s)
{
 if(s != 0)  {                  // initial value supplied
   v = new char[(len = strlen(s))]; // allocate storage
   strcpy(v,s);                 // set string value
  }
 else  {                        // no initial value supplied
   v = new char[MINLINE];       // minimal storage allocation
   len = 0;                     // set zero length
 }
}

string* operator+(string& a,string& b)  // define the operator using string
{
 string* temp;
 temp = new string;                        // allocate a new string
 temp->v = new char[temp->len = a.len + b.len];  // create a buffer
 strcpy(temp->v,a.v);                      // copy the first string
 strcat(temp->v,b.v);                      // ...then the other one
 return temp;  // return the new object
}

main()
{
 string s("this is only a test"),      // initialize one string object
        t(" nothing can go wrong."),   // ...an another
        *result;                       // declare a pointer to a string
 result = s + t;                       // concatenate the two strings.
```

```
   cout << result->display();          // display the contents
}
```

One restriction on operator overloading becomes apparent when you use *friend* functions to create new operators—an operator function must have at least one class object as a parameter. Prior to the current example, this requirement was satisfied by the *this* argument that was implicit in the class in which the operator redefinition function was a member. Listing 5-3, which concatenates a character array onto a string object, demonstrated that an operator function can have a non-class argument. However, you cannot use an operator redefinition function that has *only* non-class arguments, even if you declare it as a *friend* to a class so that it has privileges to access the private area of the class. At least one parameter must always be a class object.

There is one programming situation in which you *must* use the *friend* operator function rather than a member function. If the first argument of an operator redefinition is not a class variable, then you must use a *friend* operator function. Consider the *string5.c* example (Listing 5-7), which concatenates an old-fashioned character string—an array of characters terminated by a '\0'—with a new string object to create a new character string object. If you try to do this with a member function, the first argument is the implicit *this*, and the character string must come first. In this case, you must use the following form:

```
<string object> + <character string>
```

However, this is not what you want to do. Only a friend function allows the programmer to control the order of the arguments to an operator, as in the case of the following example:

Listing 5-7.   A *friend* operator function that returns a pointer to a string object: *string5.c*

```
#include <stream.h>
#include <string.h>

// create a truly dynamic string class

#define MINLINE 55

class string {
    char *v;                 // pointer to the actual characters
```
                                                          continued

```
      int len;                     // current length of the string
   public:
      string(const char* =0);                  // declare the constructor
     ~string() { delete v; }                   // ...and destructor
      friend string* operator+(char*,string&); // declare a new "+" operator
      char* display() { return v;}             // display all
    };

string::string(const char* s)
{
 if(s != 0)  {                      // initial value supplied
   v = new char[(len = strlen(s))]; // allocate storage
   strcpy(v,s);                     // set string value
   }
 else  {                            // no initial value supplied
   v = new char[MINLINE];           // minimal storage allocation
   len = 0;                         // set zero length
 }
}


string* operator+(char* a,string& b)  // define the operator using string
{
 string* temp;
 temp = new string;                            // allocate a new string
 temp->v = new char[temp->len = strlen(a) + b.len];  // create a buffer
 strcpy(temp->v,a);                            // copy first character array
 strcat(temp->v,b.v);                          // ...then the string object
 return temp;                                  // return the new object
}


main()
{
 string s(" nothing can go wrong"),    // initialize one string object
        *result;                       // declare a pointer to a string object
 result = "this is only a test" + s;   // combine character array and string
 cout << result->display();            // display the contents
}
```

Operators with Multiple Overloadings

Be careful not to overlook the matter of the order of operands in an operator function. After all, most operations performed on built-in data types are commutative—they work in both directions. With mixed mode operations—those with an integer and a *double*, for example—you can safely ignore the difference because you know that the compiler will convert the integer to a *double* value before it performs any operations. When you create your own classes and their associated operations, you must explicitly choose the order of the operands. If more than one order is permissible, then you must supply more than one operator function. Fortunately, as with overloaded functions, you can use multiple overloaded operators in a class as long as their argument lists are different.

The *string6.c* example (Listing 5-8) illustrates an operator that supports more than one operand order. Again, the + symbol is the redefined concatenation operator. As in the previous example, the operands remain unaffected, and the operator returns a new string object. The operator supports both calling sequences:

```
<character string> + <string>
```

and

```
<string> + <character string>
```

because the program contains two different definitions of the function *operator+()*. Thus, the *operator+()* function itself is overloaded in this example.

Listing 5-8.   An overloaded *friend* operator function that returns a pointer to a string object: *string6.c*

```
#include <stream.h>
#include <string.h>

// create a truly dynamic string class

#define MINLINE 55

class string  {
```

continued

```
      char *v;                    // pointer to the actual characters
      int len;                    // current length of the string
   public:
      string(const char* =0);                    // declare the constructor
      ~string() { delete v; }                    // ...and destructor
      friend string* operator+(char*,string&);   // declare a new "+" operator
      friend string* operator+(string&,char*);   // ...and an alternative "+"
      char* display() { return v;}               // display all
     };

   string::string(const char* s)
   {
    if(s != 0)  {                     // initial value supplied
      v = new char[(len = strlen(s))]; // allocate storage
      strcpy(v,s);                    // set string value
     }
    else {                            // no initial value supplied
      v = new char[MINLINE];          // minimal storage allocation
      len = 0;                        // set zero length
     }
   }

   string* operator+(char* a,string& b)  // define the operator using string
   {
    string* temp;
    temp = new string;                         // allocate a new string object
    temp->v = new char[temp->len = strlen(a) + b.len];  // create a buffer
    strcpy(temp->v,a);                         // copy the first array
    strcat(temp->v,b.v);                       // ...then the string object
    return temp;                               // return the new object
   }

   string* operator+(string& a,char* b)  // define an alternative
   {                                     // operator function.
    string* temp;
    temp = new string;
    temp->v = new char[temp->len = a.len + strlen(b)];
    strcpy(temp->v,a.v);
    strcat(temp->v,b);
    return temp;
   }
   main()
```

```
{
    string s(" nothing can go wrong"),  // initialize one string object
            *result;                     // declare a pointer to a string object
    result = "this is only a test" + s; // combine character array and string
    cout << result->display() << "\n";   // display the contents
    string x("hello ");                  // initialize a new string object
    result = x + "world";                // add a character array
    cout << result->display();           // show the result

}
```

Creating Unary Operators

Because you must respect the basic "calling template" of an operator symbol, you can use some symbols only for creating unary operators, which have only one operand. A few operators support both single- and dual-operand calling sequences. The following box lists all of the C++ operators that are available for overloading.

Unary, binary, and binary-unary operators				
Unary:	++	--	!	~
Binary:	/	%	()	[]
	new	delete	+=	-=
	*=	/=	|	^
	||	&&	<	<=
	>	>=	<<	>>
	!=	^=	&=	<<=
	>>=	==	!=	
Unary or Binary:	+	-	*	&

Redefining a unary operator is similar to redefining a binary one. You use a symbol with the operator function to create an operator that is unique to a particular class. Either a member or a *friend* function will serve. However, because a unary operator takes only one parameter, the argument you use must be a class argument.

The *circinc1.c* example (Listing 5-9) illustrates a unary operator defined as a member function. This program defines a *circle* class that includes both the current value for the radius of a circle and an increment that increases its size. Member functions for both area and circumference are also defined. The focus of the example, however, is on the *++* operator. This operator has been redefined to work with this new figure, while retaining the essence of the increment operator as it applies to built-in data types. Because the member function *operator++()* is a unary operator, it can take no arguments other than the implied *this* parameter. The private value *incr* increases the size of the radius.

Listing 5-9.   A unary operator redefinition: *circinc1.c*

```
#include <stream.h>


const double pi = 3.1415;


class circle  {
   double radius;      // the key size value
   int incr;           // how much to increment it each time
public:
   circle(double r =0,int i =1)  { radius = r; incr = i;} // create a circle
   double area() { return pi * radius * radius; } // return the area
   double cir() { return pi * 2 * radius; }        //...and the circumference
   void operator++();                              // declare an increment operator
};


void circle::operator++()
{
 radius += incr;
}


main()
{
 circle x(35);

  for(int i = 0 ; i < 10 ; i++ )  {
```

```
cout << form("area=%10.3f\ncircumference=%10.3f\n" , x.area() , x.cir() );
   x++;
  }
}
```

The driver function *main()* illustrates how the new *++* operator works. Note that in the context of an overloaded operator, *++x* and *x++* perform identical operations. The differences between these two forms that occur when the object is an integer type do not translate to its new definition.

The *circinc2.c* example (Listing 5-10) uses the same code as the previous listing, except that it defines *operator++()* as a *friend* to the *circle* class. In this case, you must explicitly pass the class argument as a parameter to the new function. Aside from this difference, the two programs perform identically; they even share the same driver function.

Listing 5-10. A unary operator redefinition as a *friend* function: *circinc2.c*

```
#include <stream.h>

const double pi = 3.1415;

class circle {
   double radius;     // hold the defining value
   int incr;          // this tells us how much to increase the radius
public:
   circle(double r =0,int i =1)  { radius = r; incr = i;} // create a circle
   double area() { return pi * radius * radius; } // return the area
   double cir() { return pi * 2 * radius; }       //...and the circumference
   friend void operator++(circle&);       // declare an increment operator
};


void operator++(circle& c)     // c is a reference to a class object
{
  c.radius += c.incr;     // increase the radius according to current values
}


main()
```

continued

```
{
  circle x(35);

  for(int i = 0 ; i < 10 ; i++ )  {
    cout << form("area=%10.3f\ncircumference=%10.3f\n" , x.area() , x.cir() );
    x++;
  }
}
```

Combination Operators

An earlier example (Listing 5-8) showed that you could create more than one definition and thus overload the operator function. This technique is as useful with operators as it is with ordinary overloaded functions. The same advantages apply—it eliminates redundant selection code and permits a simpler, easy-to-follow programming style. However, with operators, you can take overloading a step further. It's possible to define a function as both a unary operator and a binary one—providing that the "template" of the symbol permits both kinds of operator call. (See the previous box for the appropriate operators.)

A few operator symbols naturally fall into this dual-use category. The most commonly used is the − symbol, which represents either subtraction or a negative number. Both of these uses occur among the numeric data types in C++. Similarly, the + symbol represents either addition or a positive number. The symbols & and ∗ can also be overloaded in this way. These two symbols, however, are even more important in the current context because they are the only operators that can be defined as both unary and binary *simultaneously*.

The *dollars.c* program (Listing 5-11) contains the definition of a class that uses both a + and a − operator. These operators, in turn, each have a binary definition and a unary one. The class itself accepts an initializing value in the traditional dollars-and-cents format and performs addition and subtraction on it. These operations manipulate numbers with a fixed decimal point, numbers such as 11.47 and 12.00. Addition and subtraction on numbers like these are not readily supported by the built-in data types in C++. You can't directly use the integer types—*short*, *int*, and *long*—because they represent whole numbers, and therefore any implied decimal point must be supplied by the user. Real numbers—*float* and *double*—are equally useless because they introduce a round-off error into the calculation. The *dollar* class, however, is constructed to manipulate expressions in the following form:

1.23 + 12.00

and to receive the appropriate result without any round-off error. The display format is the same as the input format. The design of the class uses the basic strategy of storing the current value as a *long* integer—the number of pennies.

Listing 5-11.   An overloaded operator defined as both unary and binary: *dollars.c*

```
#include <stream.h>
#include <string.h>

const char decpt = '.',  // a nom-de-plume for the decimal point
          eos='\0';      //...and one for the end of string



class dollar  {
  long pennies;    // total number of them

public:
  dollar(char *);      // initializing constructor
  friend dollar* operator+(dollar&,dollar&);      // a new "+" operator
  friend dollar* operator-(dollar&,dollar&);      //...and a "-" one
  void operator+()                        // define a unary "+"
          { pennies = (pennies < 0) ? -pennies :  pennies;}
  void operator-()                        //...and a unary "-" one
          { pennies = (pennies < 0) ? pennies : -pennies; }
  char* display();                        // dump the contents
};

dollar::dollar(char* bucks)
{
  char* temp;
  temp = strtok(bucks,".");   // remove the decimal point
  strcat(temp,strtok(0,0));
  pennies = atol(temp);       // convert it to a long
}                                                        continued
```

```
dollar* operator+(dollar& a,dollar& b)
{
 dollar* temp;
 temp->pennies = a.pennies + b.pennies;  // add the appropriate values
 return temp;
}

dollar* operator-(dollar& a,dollar& b)
{
 dollar* temp;
 temp->pennies = a.pennies - b.pennies;  // subtract the appropriate values
 return temp;
}

char* dollar::display()
{
 char* temp;                     // declare a pointer to a buffer
 temp = new char[20];            // allocate a buffer--probably too big!
 sprintf(temp,"%ld",pennies);    // convert to a number
 int p = strlen(temp);           // where's the end of string mark?
 temp[p+2] = eos;                // add a decimal place at the right spot
 temp[p+1] = temp[p];
 temp[p] = temp[p-1];
 temp[p-1] = temp[p-2];
 temp[p-2]=decpt;
 return temp;         // return new value
}

main()
{
 dollar x("12.50"),    // declare and initialize one dollar object
        y("4.25"),     // ...and another
        *result;       // declare a pointer to a dollar object

 result = x + y;                   // simple addition
 cout << result->display() << "\n"; // ...and display

 result = x - y;                   // simple subtraction
 cout << result->display() << "\n"; // ...and display

 -x;                               // create a negative value
```

```
cout << form("%s\n",x.display());    // display it

result = x + y;                      // add the now negative number
cout << form("%s\n",result->display()); //show it
}
```

The key point to notice in this example is the handling of the overloading of the operators. For each binary redefinition, a *friend* function is declared; this returns a pointer to a new object of the class whose value is derived by performing the appropriate operation on the two operands that are imported as arguments. The + symbol adds the current values of the arguments, while the – symbol subtracts the second operand from the first.

The unary version of + is a member function whose only argument is the implied *this* pointer. Whatever the current value of the dollar object, this function converts it to a positive quantity by using a simple invocation of the efficient conditional operator. Note that the function is defined as *inline*. The – symbol converts the value to a negative and acts as an exact complement to the + definition.

Be careful when you overload operators. In this example, you have very little trouble distinguishing the two uses of the operators because their functions—and usually their physical positions in the program— indicate their usage. However, the compiler will not recognize an ambiguous situation, and sometimes this leads to a loss of expressive power in the overloaded syntax. For example, in the current listing, the following combination:

```
result = -x + y;
```

does not work, even though this is a perfectly legitimate expression if you are using integers or *double* values. The ability to create your own operators carries with it the responsibility of considering *all* of the situations in which it might be used.

Review questions

1. What function is used to overload operators within the context of a class?

2. An operator function can be either a _____ of the class or a _____ function.

3. A binary operator has _____ operands. A unary operator is restricted to _____.

4. The basic _____ of an operator must be adhered to.

5. The following symbols can only be tied to unary operations _____.

6. In contrast, these operators _____ can be either unary or binary.

Programming projects

1. Using the class *circle* in *circinc2.c* as a model, define a class for the cylinder.

2. Create a *string* class that has a complete set of operators and functions.

Overloading the () Symbol

In most cases of operator overloading, you will use a common action operator symbol. Symbols such as +, −, and * often suggest analog operations for a class object that mirror the operations of built-in data types. Defining the addition of complex numbers was one example, as was the use of the increment operator ++ for the *circle* class. Even for more tenuous matches—the concatenation of character strings and addition, for example—there is usually a symmetry that suggests a commonsense relationship. Using << and >> with the stream library, for example, obviously symbolizes redirection to many individuals. However, no syntactical rule restricts you to these common operators.

You can use the full range of C++ operators for redefinition. This range includes some unusual choices that can lead either to unreasonable expressions or to unexpectedly powerful expressions. For example, the function call syntax is embedded in the *()* operator. This operator includes two things that the novice programmer often overlooks—first, that it is an operator at all, and, second, that it can be used apart from the function name. This latter point is illustrated by the form of a pointer to a function. Recall that such a declaration takes the following form:

```
int (*f)();
```

The parentheses clearly are more than a grouping operation. In this context, the parentheses separate the variable **f* from the function call created by *()*. Without this form, C++ would interpret the statement as a function named *f* that returns a pointer to an integer value rather than the correct usage of *f* as a function pointer.

With a C++ class, you can take the independence of the *()* operator a step further and actually redefine it as you earlier redefined the *+* operator. The redefinition mechanism lets you capture a function call and interpret it in a way special to an application. This is a very powerful extension of the tools usually available to the programmer. In fact, one possible use of this syntax is the creation of custom type conversion operators.

First, a word of caution. The number of cases in which a redefinition of the function call sequence makes sense is even more restricted than for the more common operators. The purpose of operator redefinition is to simplify the structure of a program. However, the same mechanisms that permit this, if taken to extremes, can cause the opposite to occur, thus obscuring your code and making it impossible to follow.

One interesting and useful redefinition of the *()* operator lets you create a type conversion operator for a user-defined class. You can then use this type cast to convert the class object—or, more usually, part of it—to some other data type. The ability to do an explicit conversion from a *class* data type is even more important in C++, where you often perform type conversions and can easily move values between two related storage strategies.

The *strcast.h* example (Listing 5-12) includes the definition of an enhanced *string* class. The *string* object includes not only the character values that make up the current string, but also the number of characters that are currently contained in the object. (Here, you don't need to use the usual *end-of-string* sentinel—the '\0' character—that characterizes an orthodox C++ character string.) For this object to be of maximum value, you might need to convert it to the traditional built-in string format. You could accomplish this task with a conversion function defined as a member of the *string* class or even as a *friend* to this class. However, because you are converting two similar data types, a type conversion operator is a more appropriate vehicle. Instead of a form such as:

```
string x("this is only a test");
char* y;
y = x.convert();
```

you can use the more telling expression:

```
string x("this is only a test");
char* y;
y = (char*) x;
```

For the first-time reader of the program, the latter form is clearer. It's always valuable to use operators that are familiar to the programmer with new, user-defined variables. In this case, you can use the same type conversion operation for any class variable that you define.

Listing 5-12. An explicit conversion operator defined for a
**   *string* class: *strcast.h***

```
#include <stream.h>
#include <string.h>

// create a truly dynamic string class

#define MINLINE 55

class string  {
    char *v;          // access to the string values
    int len;          // the current string length
public:
    string(const char* =0);   //constructor
    ~string() { delete v; }    // destructor
    void operator<(string*);   // concatenation operator
    operator char*();                  // new type cast operator
};

string::string(const char* s)
```

```
{
  if(s != 0)  {                            // initial value supplied
    v = new char[(len = strlen(s))];       // allocate storage
    strcpy(v,s);                           // copy values
  }
  else  {
    v = new char[MINLINE];    // default  allocate minimum storage
    len = 0;                  // indicate 0 current length
  }
}


void string::operator<(string* s)
{
  char *buf;                               // create a new larger buffer
  buf = new char[len = len + s->len];
  strcpy(buf,v);                           // copy both strings to it
  strcat(buf,s->v);
  delete v;                                // replace original string contents
  v=buf;
}


string::operator char*()
{
  *(v + len + 1) = '\0';   // put an end of string mark at the current end
  return v;
}
```

The conversion syntax is simple. The program checks the last position in the variable member *v* that currently has a value; this is, of course, indicated by the *len* member. It adds one to this value and puts an *end-of-string* mark at the position indicated by this number. This converts *v* into a standard character string so that its value can be returned in the function to be used as a character string. (If you object to using a type cast to change the value of the object, simply copy the value to a *temp* variable of type *char* and perform the same operations.)

There is nothing magical about this usage of the type conversion. The operator syntax supplies the calling sequence: It promises to take the supplied operands and convert them into arguments to the operator function specified—in this case, the arguments are implicit, but many of the examples in this chapter have used explicit ones. After you supply the arguments, the function is no different from any other function.

Statements and definitions hold as true here as in ordinary subprograms. The only difference is in the interface.

The *strcast.c* program (Listing 5-13) contains a driver that lets you test this new class. It creates a class object *temp* and initializes it to a value. The formatted output function *form()* prints the value. (Note, however, that the format it specifies is a traditional character string—a null-terminated array of characters.) The program casts the class object to this built-in type and *cout* displays it on the screen. Without the new operator, only a defined member function could show this value.

Listing 5-13.   A driver program to test the previous example (Listing 5-12): *strcast.c*

```
main()
{
 string temp("Hello World");   // create and initialize a class object

 cout << form("%s\n",(char *)temp); // cast it to an ordinary string
}
```

Let's look at one more example in this section. The class defined in *strops1.h* (Listing 5-14) builds on the functionality of the *string* data type by redefining the *[]* operator, which is used to index into an array. The following example adds this indexing capability to the *string* class.

Listing 5-14.   A redefinition of the [] operator: *strops1.h*

```
#include <stream.h>
#include <string.h>


// create a truly dynamic string class


#define MINLINE 55


class string {
   char *v;    // pointer to internal storage of the characters
   int len;    // the current number of "active" characters
public:
   string(const char* =0);   // declare a constructor with a default value
   ~string() { delete v; }    //...and a destructor
   void operator<(string*);  // concatenating two strings
```

```
  operator char*();                    // converting to orthodox string
  char* operator[](int);               // declare a substring operator
};


string::string(const char* s)        // constructor definition
{
 if(s != 0)  {                        // if initializer specified then...
   v = new char[(len = strlen(s))+1]; // allocate memory AND set len
   strcpy(v,s);                       //...and copy
  }
 else  {
   v = new char[MINLINE];    // otherwise, allocate the standard amount
   len = 0;                  // indicates no active characters yet
  }
}


void string::operator<(string* s)  // define concatenation
{
 char *buf;        // declare a temporary buffer
 buf = new char[len = len + s->len+1];  // allocate a big enough buffer
 strcpy(buf,v);                     // copy the first value to it
 strcat(buf,s->v);                  //...then stick the rest onto the end
 delete v;                          // remove old value
 v=buf;                             // assign new one
}


string::operator char*()  // define type cast
{
 *(v + len + 1) = '\0';   // stick an "end of string" on the end
 return v;                // return the now "altered" current value
}


char* string::operator[](int pos)  // redefine the "[]" operator
{
 return v+pos-1;   // calculate the position specified in v
}
```

It's an easy task to design an indexing operation for the string object defined in this class. Indexing in a regular array of characters merely returns the character at the location requested. For example, the following statement:

```
cout << form("ch=%c\n",ch[5]);
```

returns whatever value is stored at the fifth location in *ch*. The program does not stray too far from this notion, but, because it deals with character strings, it sets up the operator redefinition to return a character string rather than a single character. When you execute the following code fragment:

```
string x("ABCDEF");
cout << form("%s\n",x[3]);
```

you can expect the following output:

```
CDEF
```

The current contents of *x* is displayed starting at the third character and continuing until the end of the string.

The member function *operator[]()* takes as its parameter the position within the string to begin. It uses this number to calculate an offset from the address of the first character in the member variable *v*. Then, it returns this address.

The *strops1.c* program (Listing 5-15) is a driver meant to be used with the *string* class defined in *strops1.h*. It declares and initializes two string objects. After they are concatenated, the program displays the longer one in two ways—as a character string and as a substring starting from the fifth character. This latter operation is possible only because of the redefined *[]* operator.

Listing 5-15.   A driver program for the class defined in the previous example (Listing 5-14): *strops1.c*

```
main()
{
 string s("this is only a test"),    // initialize two strings
        t(" nothing can go wrong");

 s < &t;                             // concatenate them together

 cout << form("->%s\n",(char*)s);  // print out the new, larger string

 for(int i = 0 ; i <= s.len ; i++)  // print it a character at a time.
```

```
     cout << form("*%c",s[i]);


}
```

A Two-Dimensional String Class

The ability to redefine everyday operators underscores the power of operator overloading, but it also sometimes involves some tricky combinations of old procedures and new. Often in the process of redefining an operator, you need to use its original meaning within the *operator()* function. You have seen this in most of the examples in this chapter— for example, to define an = operator for a class, you need to use the built-in power of the symbol in internal operations on the class member. This mixing of levels of meaning can be confusing, but usually it is easy to sort out. What is more difficult is combining old and new operator meanings—not internally in a member function—but in the program itself.

The *strops2.h* example (Listing 5-16) defines a simple class. This class stores and manipulates a character string class, and, as did the previous example, *strops1.h* (Listing 5-14), it also redefines the array-addressing operator to allow access to individual elements in the string. This example, however, creates a two-dimensional string array.

**Listing 5-16.   A class that illustrates the redefinition of the []
operator and creates a two-dimensional array:
*strops2.h***

```
#include <stream.h>
#include <string.h>

class string  {
  char* v;
public:
  string() { v=0; }            // define a simple constructor
  void operator=(char*);   // declare an assignment operator
  char* out() { return v; } //define an output member
  char* operator[](int);     // declare a new [] operator
};

void string::operator=(char* s)  // redefine the assignment
```

continued

```
{
  char* buf;              // declare a temporary buffer
  buf=new char[strlen(s)+1]; // make it big enough

  strcpy(buf,s);  // copy the initializing value
  delete v;       // remove any old value in the type
  v=buf;          // assign the new value
}

char* string::operator[](int pos)  // define the new [] operator
{
  if(pos > strlen(v))  // if the index is too big, return a null
    return 0;
  return v+pos-1;  // otherwise return the specified character
}
```

Unlike the previous example classes, the string defined in this example is much closer to the built-in meaning of a character string in C++. Both this class and the more traditional notion use an array of characters that are terminated by a special flag value, zero. The constructor for this class, *string()*, doesn't let you initialize a class object. It doesn't even allocate memory; it merely assures you that the character member *v* is initially set with a zero value. The program does not define a destructor, although one could naturally extend this class.

In addition to the constructor, the new *string* class contains a simple output member function, *out()*, which returns the value of the storage member *v* in the form of a character pointer. Because *out()* is used by the functions in *stream.h*, in which character strings are appropriate, no explicit type casting is necessary here. Also, this function is small enough for you to declare it *inline*.

One improvement of this character string over the built-in one is the definition of an assignment operator (=). This member lets you use the familiar assignment syntax of other data types in C++ with a character string. The code for *operator=()* is simple. It declares a temporary buffer that is big enough to hold the value on the right-hand side of the = sign. Then, it copies that value into this temporary buffer. (Any previous value stored in the object is removed by the *delete v;* statement.) Finally, the program copies the address of the buffer into *v*. This assignment operator works in a way that is consistent with a programmer's everyday experience of how an assignment works.

The *operator[]()* function is similar to the definition in *strops1.h* (Listing 5-14). It receives the index value as a parameter and adds the value to the address stored in *v* to calculate the position of the desired character. This class offers improved error-checking. If the index is larger than the size of the character string pointed to by *v*, a value of zero is returned to indicate an error condition.

The *strops2.c* program (Listing 5-17) is a simple driver that illustrates the operation of the class. It declares the single string object *s* and assigns a literal string value to it. The resulting value is printed to the screen.

Listing 5-17.   A driver program that illustrates the class in Listing 5-16: *strops2.c*

```
main()
{
 string s;        // declare a string object

 s = "this is only a test";  // assign a value to it

 cout << form("%s\n",s[6]);  // print an arbitrary element of that value
}
```

The *strops3.c* program (Listing 5-18) contains a more interesting *main()* function. This program defines a two-dimensional string array by mixing two levels of abstraction:

▶ an array of objects of class *string* and

▶ an array redefined for string objects.

The code to accomplish this is not restricted solely to the class; it also relates to the way the string object is addressed in the *main()* function.

Listing 5-18.   A driver that illustrates the class in Listing 5-16 and uses both redefined and built-in operators to create a two-dimensional array: *strops3.c*

```
main()
{
 string s[3];    // declare an array of string objects

 s[0]="this is only a test";   // assign a value to each one in turn
```

continued

```
      s[1]="nothing can go wrong";
      s[2]="...go wrong...";
      for(int i = 0 ; i < 3 ; i++)      // print only the second character in
        cout << form("%s\n",s[i][2]);  // each array cell.
    }
```

The first statement in the *main()* function uses the built-in syntax of array creation to declare an array of string variables. Each member of this array represents a string variable and can be assigned a value. For example,

```
s[0] = "this is only a test";
```

puts the value of this literal string into the first location of the array. The *main()* function performs a similar assignment to each cell.

After the variables are filled with values, a *for* loop displays them on the screen. However, in this case, the program displays from the second character in each string value, as follows:

```
his is only a test
othing can go wrong
..go wrong...
```

The following statement in the program performs the above operation:

```
cout << form("%s\n",s[i][2];
```

You can use this form for a variable of this type because the redefined *[]* operator allows the indexing of class objects. The first set of brackets extracts an object of the *class* type from the array. The final set of brackets operates internally on this object. Thus, the final construction is a two-dimensional *string* data type.

Summary

This chapter introduced overloading as applied to the common operators in C++. It showed you how to redefine symbols such as + and − to work with user-defined class types in the same convenient way that they work with built-in types such as *int, double,* and *char.* Within the C++ universe, it makes as much sense to "add" two character strings together as it does to perform this operation on double precision numbers.

The key to overloading lies in the

operator *ops* ();

function. In this function, *ops* can be any defined operator symbol, including compound ones like *++* and *−−*. Furthermore, this function can be a member of any class. This function creates a special calling sequence that mirrors the usual operator usage. For *operator++()*, the code to call it might merely be *x++;* rather than a function call. This kind of usage creates more readable programs that are easier to understand.

This chapter also pointed out the power beyond the formatting inherent in this formalism. By extending common operators to *class* data types, you can create powerful programming *metaphors* that can help you to write even more powerful and complex programs. The streamlining that overloaded operators introduce helps you manage this complexity.

The use of operator overloading was explored through a series of ever more complicated class definitions. Each new definition contained a more complete definition. Even with this detail, many evocative patterns of overloading have been left unstated.

Deriving Classes

6

Deriving Classes

Before examining advanced class relationships, let's briefly review the *class* data type. This structure contains all the elements that make up a programming object—the members that store data items and the member functions that manipulate the data and communicate with the rest of the program. The most important of the class functions are the constructors, which are called when a class object is created. These member functions can perform complex and extensive initializations and other startup actions that complicated classes sometimes require.

Classes are especially important because they help implement models that enable computer programs to simulate complex real-world situations. Classes efficiently manage the complexity of large programs through modularization. Each class contains a *public* part and a *private* part. Members—both variables and functions—declared in the private part of a class are hidden from the rest of the program. The public section is the interface that connects the objects to the rest of the software environment. This lets you solve the details of a program's implementation piece by piece; as you successfully complete each section, you can hide all of the details of the implementation from the rest of the program, so that only the small public interface can affect—or be affected by—other modules.

However, the class alone is not enough to fully support object-oriented programming and design. You also need a way to relate disparate classes to one another. Earlier examples used nested classes, but these are only a partial solution because nested class definitions are not hidden—even if they are defined in the private part of an enclosing class. In any case, a nested class doesn't have the required characteristics to fully relate one class to another. What's needed is a mechanism for creating hierarchies of classes in which class A is a *cognate* of class B, but with added features. C++ has a mechanism for creating such a hierarchy—the *derived* class. The process of deriving classes is called *inheritance*, and it is one of the characteristics that distinguish object-oriented languages.

Derived Classes as a Development Tool

One of the most remarkable features of C++ is the way it lets you build classes on one another. After you define a class, you can use it as the base of an entire family of related, or *derived*, classes. For example, in a graphics library, you might define a *rectangle* class. When you need to define a new kind of rectangle, such as one with rounded corners, you can use the basic features of the *rectangle* class and then add some unique properties to derive a new class of rectangles (see Figure 6-1).

Derived Classes for Better Data Representation

As a more practical example, consider a financial program in which an accounts class contains the identification of a customer as its basic class and adds as derived classes information specific to various kinds

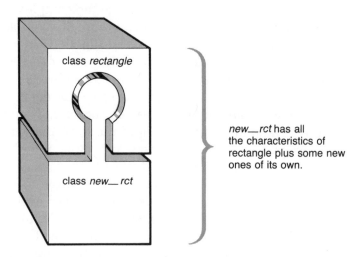

Figure 6-1.   Deriving a new *rectangle* class

of accounts. The original object is preserved; it is merely replicated so that all of its information is available to each derived class that follows. This mechanism helps you produce more efficient and elegant programs (see Figure 6-2). These examples suggest how inheritance lets

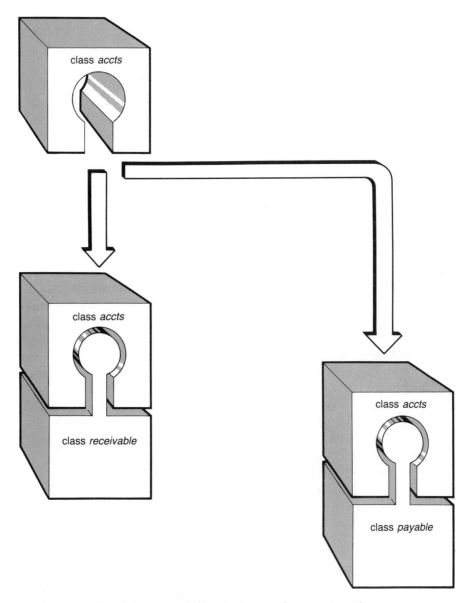

Figure 6-2.   Deriving specialized classes for accounting

you more easily model real-world objects and their interleaving relationships without having to use the obscuring conditional statements and branches found in the traditional C approach.

Derived Classes Promote Modularity

In addition to its usage as a means of representing both the common features and specialized aspects of different data structures, class derivation is also a tool for modularization. For example, a programmer can define a derived class based on an existing class that was produced and compiled outside the current program. Also, a designer can create a library of useful classes by putting the compiled code in a library file and the interface requirements in one or more header files (files that use the extension ".h"). This "library" of classes then could form the nucleus of many programs, yet the details of implementation need not be published. The integrity of the base class is preserved, yet you can customize C++ for a given project to more closely match the application area (see Figure 6-3).

The user of a precompiled class can use the contents of a class library to create derived classes. It is always possible to add members to a derived class, and, although you don't have a comparable "delete" facility, you can merely ignore base class members that you don't need. One great advantage to this procedure is that the derived classes don't alter the base class in any way, and therefore you do not need to recompile it. The base class represents a layer of usable code that no longer needs to be modified. Metaphorically, it underlies and supports the new layer of software. Thus, a derived class is truly a medium of modularization.

In fact, "base class" and "derived class" are relative terms. A class that is derived from one base class can, in turn, be the base of a second class. A hierarchical structure of classes can be produced this way, so that not only the predefined "base" classes, but also the derived classes, can define a layer of finished design. The more refined and specific program code that is produced by this method would also be a substratum of design that can support even more application-specific data structures in the form of derived classes (see Figure 6-4).

Derived Classes Enhance Efficiency

Using derived classes also enhances efficiency. You no longer need to create repetitive code; at each level, the details of the lower levels can

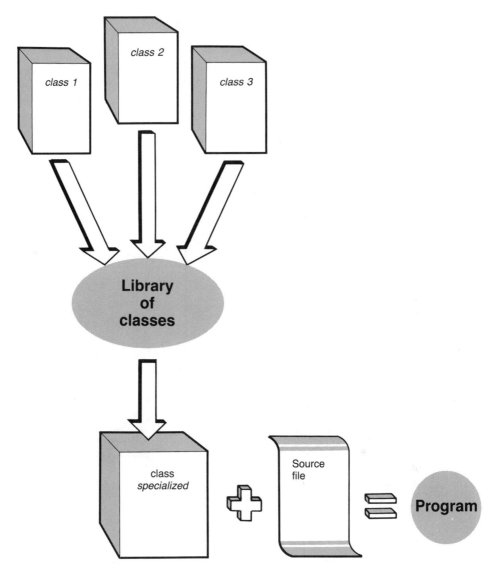

Figure 6-3. Using a library of classes

be grouped with any necessary processing. Indeed, you no longer need to create a series of independent and redundant data structures to handle every possible variation of data organization used in a program. For example, if an accounting program must keep track of individuals with multiple accounts, you no longer have to add code to link the common identification information with a series of unique data structures, one for each kind of account. In C++, you can create the same

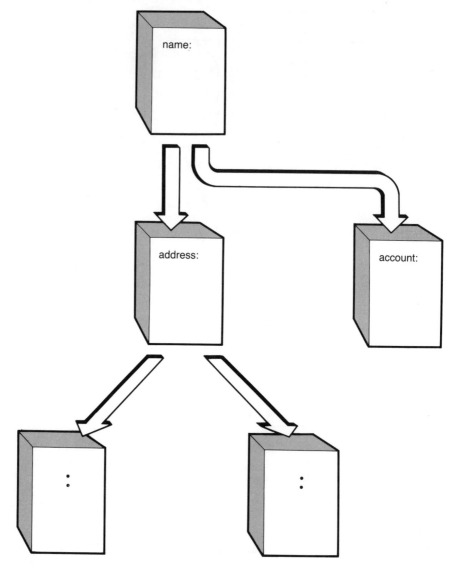

Figure 6-4.   A hierarchical class structure

structure by using a series of derived classes—you maintain the identification information in the base class and put the details of the kind
of account in the appropriate derived class. The customer's name and
other identification data are still available, but now they are retained
within the *account* data type itself. This gives you two immediate advantages—you don't need to create a complex structure of conditionals

to link one set of values to another, nor do you need to include the customer's name whenever you think the program might need it.

Derived classes enable a programmer to save a great deal of effort because blocks of redundant information don't need to be maintained. Using traditional data structures, each time a field or member is repeated, the memory allocation grows, and access time correspondingly slows. Programs also require more time to evaluate Boolean expressions and to work through complex sets of conditionals in order to access the desired set of data. In C++, the derivation of classes arranges the hierarchy of data in a highly optimized and transparent manner.

Class Derivation: A Case Study

Let's examine a situation that often arises in programming—managing a set of information. In this example, imagine that you must handle student records, each of which consists of the following information:

name

year in school (freshman, sophomore, etc.)

dormitory

room number.

You need to manipulate these values to generate bills for room and board or to create a mailing list of all seniors. At first consideration, you might decide to make the record items members of a single class; you might even use a structure to make it more "C-like." However, before you commit to this formulation, examine the data items more carefully. They break down into at least two natural divisions. "Dormitory" and "room number" define the address of the student. "Name" and "year in school" identify the individual. (In reality, the situation is more complex because additional information must be added—grades and classes taken, for example.) However, the point is that information tends to divide itself into related groups. These groups, in turn, are related only by the fact that they belong to the record of one individual.

Similar situations are usually handled by creating individual data types that embrace each group of related information. Typically, these data types themselves are connected in one of two ways—by nesting individual objects in a kind of "super object" or by creating a common value in each otherwise independent data type (see Figure 6-5).

The former case can be represented by the use of class members within a class—a nested declaration. In the latter case, you might, for example, define each group as a class and include a name member in each class. This name member would tie together the otherwise disparate data objects. Of course, you must implement this connection explicitly—and very visibly—in the program code.

The major disadvantage with these typical solutions is that the data abstraction is imperfectly implemented. Even if you define a class within the private part of another class, the scope of the "inner" class is not actually hidden from the rest of the program. In many cases, this might not be an important consideration. However, the scope of the definition is different from the scope of the other items in the class, and this disparity can be confusing in a complicated program.

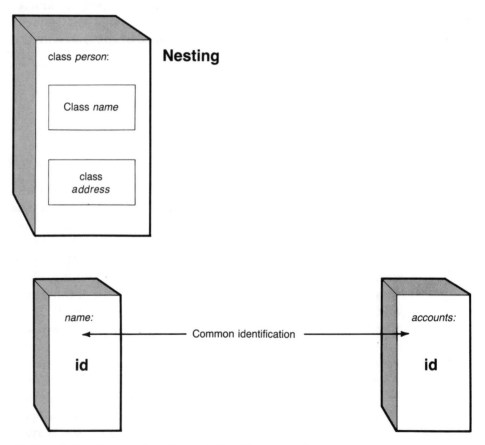

Figure 6-5.   Strategies for relating information

Figure 6-6 illustrates another approach to the problem of combining related data. Here, the earlier student information is divided into two related parts—one contains identification information and the other holds the address. This is precisely what C++ creates when it derives one class from another. The box labeled "on_campus" is derived from the box labeled "student"; it has all the information of the latter object plus the address information that is local to it.

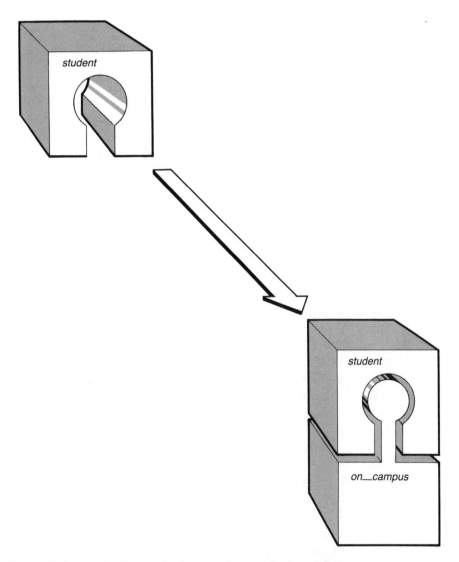

Figure 6-6.   A better solution to data relationships

Derivation, as shown in Figure 6-6, is very different from the simple nesting procedure mentioned earlier. The derived object is, in a sense, still the same type as the base; they can even share pointers! In contrast, the relationship between two nested classes is one of juxtaposition; they are near one another in the program code, but they have no organic connection. In a restricted sense, the derived class has the same capabilities as its base, plus some additional ones. You do not need to redeclare the base members because they are available in the derived class. More importantly, if the base class and all of its member functions are defined, compiled, and stored in an object file, you can use a derived class to change the definition of the data relationships without disturbing any aspect of the base class. Any change to a nested class—no matter how small—requires the recompilation of all of its associated programs and definitions.

One advantage of this enhanced redefinability is that it lets a programmer easily define variations on a similar data object. In a realistic extension of the previous example, you must make allowances for the fact that some students do not live in dormitories, and therefore the program will require more orthodox fields for their addresses. To accommodate this situation, you derive a class that uses the base class but has a different set of address members—street, city, state, and ZIP code (rather than dormitory and room). Now, you have a relationship between a base class and two derived classes. Their relationship is diagrammed in Figure 6-7.

Without the ability to derive classes, you might have had to create two separate and incompatible entities, one for storing address information concerning those students who live on campus and another for those who live off campus. Connections between the two would have to involve some redundant information—a name or, more likely, a unique identification string. Then, you would need to explicitly code all connections into whatever functions will manipulate them, thus creating problems with class definitions. You could use *friend* function definitions, but the coding would be extensive, more complicated, and less clear.

On the other hand, by storing the common information safely in the base class and by deriving extensions as they are needed, you don't need to write explicit code for switching between classes, nor do you need to consult separate entities. Furthermore, as a kind of bonus, if you ever need to create a different kind of address—one that was neither on campus nor off campus—the mechanism is always there. You wouldn't need to rewrite the member functions that accessed the non-address information, you would merely derive a new class.

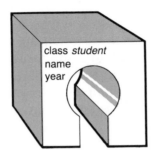

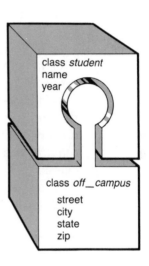

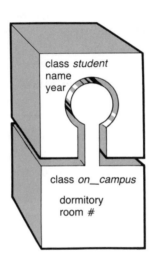

Figure 6-7.   A base class and two derived classes

Creating a Derived Class

Now that you understand the advantages of using class derivation in C++, let's examine the actual mechanics of declaring and using derived classes.

Each derived class must refer to a previously declared base class. This base can be precompiled, or it can be defined in the same program in which the derived class is created. If you do not define the base class before the derived class, you must at least declare the name of the base class first. However, there is nothing syntactically special about the base class, nothing, in fact, to distinguish it from any other class definition. Any class can serve as a base.

The *student.c* example (Listing 6-1) illustrates a simple family that consists of a base class and a class derived from it. This example implements the situation described in the previous section and diagrammed in Figure 6-7; it also demonstrates the basic syntax of the procedure. The definition of *student*, the base class, contains two members in its private section—*name* is a pointer to the student's name, and *year* is an integer variable that indicates the student's class standing. This latter variable contains a number to indicate freshman (0), sophomore (1), junior (2), or senior (3) status. (The choice of values is arbitrary and is based on C and C++ programming tradition.) No constructor is defined here, although the class includes both a simple print function, *display()*, and a creation function for new entries, *create_rec()*. The *main()* function is a simple driver that illustrates how you use these classes.

**Listing 6-1.   A definition of a base and a derived class:
student.c**

```
#include <stream.h>
#include <string.h>



/////////////////////////////////////////////////
// Define a base class                          /
/////////////////////////////////////////////////

class  student  {
   char* name;              // student name
   int year;                // current class standing 1=freshman, etc.
public:
   void display();          // show the name and year
   void create_rec(char*, int);  // put values into a record.
};

void student::display()
{
 cout << form("\nname: %s\nyear: %d\n",name,year);  // show it on the screen
 }
```

```
void student::create_rec(char* n,int y)
{
 name = new char[strlen(n)+1];     // allocate enough memory
 strcpy(name,n);                   // copy the name over to the class
 year = y;                         //...and the year
}


/////////////////////////////////////////////////////
// Define a derived class from student              /
/////////////////////////////////////////////////////

class on_campus : student  {
   char  *dorm,                          // information in addition to
         *room;                          // the student stuff
public:
   void a_disp();                        // declare a simple display member
   void new_student(char*,int,char*,char*);   //...and an input one
};

void on_campus::a_disp()
{
 display();                             // show the base class values

  cout << form("dorm: %s\nroom: %s\n",dorm,room); //...then the new ones
}

void on_campus::new_student(char* n,int y,char* d,char* r)
{
 create_rec(n,y);                        // enter the base values
 dorm = new char[strlen(d)+1];           // allocate memory
 strcpy(dorm,d); //copy
 room = new char[strlen(r)+1];           //...and for this field
 strcpy(room,r);
}

// a simple driver function to test the new classes

main()
{
 cout << "\n=========================================\n";

  student x;                     // start with the base class
```
continued

```
x.create_rec("Joe Smith",1);  // fill it
x.display();                   //...and print it

cout << "\n=========================================\n";

on_campus y;                                     // a derived class
y.new_student("Hank Jones",1,"Foll Hall","L304"); // put the values in
y.a_disp();                                      // get them out
}
```

The most interesting section of this example is the derived class, *on_campus*. The first line:

```
class on_campus : student {
```

both declares this to be a derived class and indicates that the base class is *student*. The rest of the definition of this new class is almost as straightforward as that of the base. Although it also uses no constructor member, the membership of the class includes both a display function, *a_disp()*, and a function that adds objects of this class, *new_student()*. This latter function obtains the values contained in the new *on_campus* class object.

Access to the Base Class

Now, let's examine the relationship between the base class and a derived class. The class *on_campus* includes all of the information that is contained in its base, *student*, but—and this is an important consideration—it has no special access to the private part of the base class. Without the member function *display()* of the *student* class, the *a_disp()* member of *on_campus* could only show the dormitory name and room number. There is a way around this problem—the *protected* section (discussed later in this chapter)—but right now this represents a notable limitation on the relationship. Note, however, that the public member functions of the base class are available to the derived class, as they would be with any other class. Thus, for example, the *a_disp()* member of *on_campus* can freely call *display()* without any further reference to an object of type *student*, because any public member function of the base class is automatically a member function of the derived class. Similarly, *new_student()* depends on the *student* member function *crea-*

te_rec() to initialize the basic data in the class—name and year in school. As with a_disp(), this member is also a part of the on_campus class.

Multiple Derived Classes

The *student2.c* example (Listing 6-2) contains a new derived class, *off_campus*, that uses the *student* class as a base. It also contains a new *main()* that demonstrates the interaction of the now three-part class hierarchy. The new *off_campus* class contains an alternative address format—the traditional number, street, city, state, and ZIP code. It also uses an *a_disp()* member function to display the current values and a *new_student()* member to initialize them.

Listing 6-2. Adding another derived class to the base defined in Listing 6-1: *student2.c*

```
//////////////////////////////////////////////////////
// Derive another class from student                  /
//////////////////////////////////////////////////////


class off_campus : student  {
    char  *street,     // new information to add to
          *city,       // the basic student values
          *state,
          *zip;
public:
  void a_disp();                          // declare a simple display member
  void new_student(char*,int,char*,char*,char*,char*); //...and an input one
};


void off_campus::a_disp()
{
 display();    // put the basic values on the screen
               //...then, the new information
 cout << form("address: %s\n%s, %s %s\n",street,city,state,zip);
}


void off_campus::new_student(char* n,int y,char* s,char* cty,char* st,char* z)
{
 create_rec(n,y);                  // collect the common values    continued
```

```
        street = new char[strlen(s)+1];    // allocate and copy the
        strcpy(street,s);                  // new information
        city = new char[strlen(cty)+1];
        strcpy(city,cty);
        state = new char[strlen(st)+1];
        strcpy(state,st);
        zip = new char[strlen(z)+1];
        strcpy(zip,z);
    }


    ///////////////////////////////////////////////////////////////////
    // A simple driver function to illustrate the family of classes    /
    //    based on student                                             /
    ///////////////////////////////////////////////////////////////////

    main()
    {
    cout << "\n========================================\n";

    student x;                    // start with the base class
    x.create_rec("Joe Smith",1);  // fill it
    x.display();                   //...and print it

    cout << "\n========================================\n";

    on_campus y;                                        // a derived class
    y.new_student("Hank Jones",1,"Foll Hall","L304"); // put the values in
    y.a_disp();                                         // get them out

    cout << "\n========================================\n";

    off_campus z;     // create and show an object of another derived class
    z.new_student("Sally Green",2,"22 Main Str","San Francisco","CA","94113");
    z.a_disp();
    }
```

When you compare the two derived classes, *on_campus* and *off-
_campus*, notice that their member functions have the same names. It
is also apparent that these functions have different names than their
counterparts in the base class. The *display()* function shows the values
that are part of *student*, but *a_disp()* shows the address information
from both *on_campus* and *off_campus*. Because all public members of

the base class are available to the derived class, when you use the same member function name in the base as you do in a derived class, the base's member function becomes unavailable to the derived class. In some circumstances, this can be desirable. If, for example, you use the name "display" in one of the derived classes, it would mask the *display()* member function in the student base class. You also can use the same member names in the two derived classes, however, of course, they are mutually exclusive.

In a derived class, only the member functions can call the base class members. The two example derived classes are symmetrical in design, so what is true for one is also true for the other. In *a_disp()*, the base class member *display()* is called to display the information in the base class—specifically, the name and the year in school. The rest of this function uses *cout* to print the specific information in the derived class—dormitory room and number in the case of *on_campus* and an ordinary address for *off_campus*. Another base class member function is used in *new_student()*; this calls the base's *create_rec()* member function in the first statement.

Explicit References to Members

An alternative construction that allows access to any member function regardless of name uses the C++ reference operator (::) to create an explicit reference to a particular member. The class definition found in *student3.c* (Listing 6-3) uses this procedure. Here, the base name *student* is followed by :: and the member name, *display()*. When using predefined—and often precompiled—class definitions, you aren't always completely free to choose names for variables, so it is useful to have a mechanism that allows you to select a name outside of the present scope.

Listing 6-3. A student class hierarchy redefined using explicit reference operators: *student3.c*

```
#include <stream.h>
#include <string.h>


/////////////////////////////////////////////////////
// Define a base class                              /
/////////////////////////////////////////////////////
```

continued

```
class  student  {
  char* name;                    // student name
  int year;                      // current class standing 1=freshman, etc.
public:
  void display();                // show the name and year
  void create_rec(char*, int);   // put values into a record.
};

void student::display()
{
 cout << form("\nname: %s\nyear: %d\n",name,year);  // show it on the screen
 }

void student::create_rec(char* n,int y)
{
 name = new char[strlen(n)+1];    // allocate enough memory
 strcpy(name,n);                  // copy the name over to the class
 year = y;                        //...and the year
 }


/////////////////////////////////////////////////////
// Define a derived class from student              /
/////////////////////////////////////////////////////

class on_campus : student  {
  char  *dorm,                            // information in addition to
        *room;                            // the student stuff
public:
  void display();                         // declare a simple display...
                                          //...member
  void create_rec(char*,int,char*,char*); //...and an input one
};

void on_campus::display()
{
 student::display();           // explicitly call the student member

 cout << form("dorm: %s\nroom: %s\n",dorm,room); //...then the new ones
 }

void on_campus::create_rec(char* n,int y,char* d,char* r)
{
```

```
    student::create_rec(n,y);              // the base member
    dorm = new char[strlen(d)+1];          // allocate memory
    strcpy(dorm,d); //copy
    room = new char[strlen(r)+1];          //...and for this field
    strcpy(room,r);
}


//////////////////////////////////////////////////////////
// Derive another class from student                     /
//////////////////////////////////////////////////////////

class off_campus : student  {
    char  *street,       // new information to add to
          *city,         // the basic student values
          *state,
          *zip;
public:
    void display();                         // declare a simple display
member
    void create_rec(char*,int,char*,char*,char*,char*); //...and an input one
};


void off_campus::display()
{
 student::display();     // the base one, not the current member
             //...then, the new information
 cout << form("address: %s\n%s, %s %s\n",street,city,state,zip);
}


void off_campus::create_rec(char* n,int y,char* s,char* cty,char* st,char* z)
{
 student::create_rec(n,y);          // another explicit call

 street = new char[strlen(s)+1];    // allocate and copy the
 strcpy(street,s);                  // new information
 city = new char[strlen(cty)+1];
 strcpy(city,cty);
 state = new char[strlen(st)+1];
 strcpy(state,st);
 zip = new char[strlen(z)+1];
 strcpy(zip,z);                                         continued
```

continued

211

```
    }

/////////////////////////////////////////////////////////////////////

    main()
    {
     cout << "\n=========================================\n";

     student x;                    // start with the base class
     x.create_rec("Joe Smith",1);  // fill it
     x.display();                   //...and print it

     cout << "\n=========================================\n";

     on_campus y;                                  // a derived class
     y.create_rec("Hank Jones",1,"Foll Hall","L304"); // put the values in
     y.display();                                  // get them out

     cout << "\n=========================================\n";

     off_campus z;      // create and show an object of another derived class
     z.create_rec("Sally Green",2,"22 Main Str","San Francisco","CA","94113");
     z.display();
    }
```

This example contains the complete hierarchy derived from the *student* class. The difference here is that each class has a *display()* member and a *create_rec()* member. Inside the display member of each derived class is an explicit reference to the base *display()* function. There also is a similar explicit reference to the *student* version of *create_rec()* in the definition of this member. The *main()* function illustrates the use of these objects.

Derived Classes with Constructors and Destructors

Specifying a constructor for a class is often appropriate—and sometimes necessary. Class objects usually are too large and complicated for a simple initialization, and the constructor member function lets you execute as much startup code as you need when you create an object. For example, if a class opens a file and prepares it for writing, a constructor might include compaction code to do *garbage collection* (the freeing of memory used by objects that are no longer needed) every time a new object is created. This is only one of many other possibilities. (Chapter 4 discussed the use of constructors in the context of a single class definition.)

Similarly, the destructor member, if properly designed, can efficiently deallocate a class object (it is good programming practice to return resources that are no longer needed). You also can extend the tasks of the destructor beyond simple deallocation to the performance of a variety of shutdown activities, some only indirectly related to the class of which it is a part. Such uses might include: closing files, flushing buffers, or even reinitializing blocks of memory.

Coordination Between Base
and Derived Classes

Both constructors and destructors also can be a part of a derived class. However, a few minor differences in syntax reflect the more complicated situation of one class being dependent upon another. For example, a constructor or destructor defined for the base class must be coordinated with those found in a derived class. Equally important is the movement of values from the members in the derived class to those members in the base. In particular, you must consider how the base class constructor receives values from the derived class in order to create the complete object.

The first issue—coordination—is resolved by a policy decision of the C++ language definition. If a constructor is defined for both the base class and the derived class, C++ calls the base constructor first; after it finishes its tasks, C++ executes the derived constructor. The commonsense nature of this policy makes it easy to remember—you create the base class first, therefore C++ calls its constructor first. The order of execution of the destructor is equally straightforward. The derived class destructor executes first; after it performs its deallocation and cleanup duties, C++ calls the base class destructor to finish the job. In other words—the last class created is the first destroyed.

Using the Base Class Constructor

One question remains—how do the values that are created in the derived class get to the base class constructor? The answer is not as obvious as the coordination between constructors was. The derived class must explicitly supply the initial values for the base class. This is accomplished by appending the values to the definition of the constructor function of the derived class. The syntax is simple. For example, if the *ex_class* is derived from a base, the header line from the definition of the constructor for this derived class might look as follows:

```
ex_class(int x, int y, int z) : (x,y);
```

The variables in the parentheses that follow the colon are the values that the base class constructor needs to create the base class; they serve the same purpose as calling the base class constructor and passing it these values. Note that if the base class constructor does not require initializing parameters, you do not need to explicitly call it from the derived class constructor, because the compiler invokes the base class constructor automatically.

By definition, a class destructor takes no parameters; therefore, coordinating destructors for base and derived classes is less of a problem. No explicit call from derived class to base class is required. C++ is responsible for coordinating these member functions. Merely remember that the derived class destructor is always executed before the base class destructor.

The *student4.c* example (Listing 6-4) contains a revised version of the *student* class hierarchy. In this version, the base class, *student*, and the two derived classes, *on_campus* and *off_campus*, have constructors. Similarly, it uses destructors to deallocate any resources tied up in these classes.

Listing 6-4.   An example of derived classes that use constructors and destructors: *student4.c*

```
#include <stream.h>
#include <string.h>


const fval = 20;  //specify a format length for display strings



/////////////////////////////////////////////////
// Define a base class                          /
/////////////////////////////////////////////////


class student  {
  char* name;                 // student name
  int year;                   // current class standing 1=freshman, etc.
public:
  student(char*, int);        // put values into a record.
  ~student()  { delete name; }  // define a destructor
  char* display();            // show the name and year
};


student::student(char* n,int y)
{
  name = new char[strlen(n)+1];  // allocate enough memory
  strcpy(name,n);                // copy the name over to the class
  year = y;                      //...and the year
```

continued

```
    }

    char* student::display()
    {
     char* buffer;                          // create a buffer for the display string
     buffer = new char[strlen(name) + fval];
     sprintf(buffer,"\nname: %s\nyear: %d\n",name,year); //prepare it
     return buffer;
    }


    ///////////////////////////////////////////////////////
    // Define a derived class from student              /
    ///////////////////////////////////////////////////////

    class on_campus : student  {
      char  *dorm,                           // information in addition to
            *room;                           // the student stuff
    public:
      on_campus(char*,int,char*,char*);   //...and an input one
     ~on_campus() { delete dorm; delete room; } // define a destructor
      char* display();                      // declare a simple display member
    };

    on_campus::on_campus(char* n,int y,char* d,char* r) : (n,y)
    {
     dorm = new char[strlen(d)+1];                // allocate memory
     strcpy(dorm,d); //copy
     room = new char[strlen(r)+1];                //...and for this field
     strcpy(room,r);
    }


    char* on_campus::display()
    {
     char *buffer;
     int flength = strlen(student::display()) + strlen(dorm) + strlen(room) + fval;
     buffer = new char[flength];
     sprintf(buffer,"%s\ndorm: %s\nroom: %s\n",display(),dorm,room);
     return buffer;
    }


    ///////////////////////////////////////////////////////
```

```
// Derive another class from student              /
//////////////////////////////////////////////////////


class off_campus : student  {
    char *street,       // new information to add to
         *city,         // the basic student values
         *state,
         *zip;
public:
  off_campus(char*,int,char*,char*,char*,char*); //...and an input one
 ~off_campus();  // declare a destructor
  char* display();                        // declare a simple display member


};


off_campus::off_campus(char* n,int y,char* s,char* cty,char* st,char* z):(n,y)
{
 street = new char[strlen(s)+1];    // allocate and copy the
 strcpy(street,s);                  // new information
 city = new char[strlen(cty)+1];
 strcpy(city,cty);
 state = new char[strlen(st)+1];
 strcpy(state,st);
 zip = new char[strlen(z)+1];
 strcpy(zip,z);
}


inline off_campus::~off_campus()
{
 delete street;
 delete city;
 delete state;
 delete zip;
}


char* off_campus::display()
{
 char* buffer;
 int flength = strlen(student::display()) + strlen(street) + strlen(city) +
                           strlen(state) + strlen(zip) + fval;
```

continued

```
   buffer = new char[flength];
   sprintf(buffer,"%s\n%s\n%s, %s %s\n",display(),street,city,state,zip);
   return buffer;
}
```

```
/////////////////////////////////////////////////////////////////////////

main()
{
 cout << "\n=========================================\n";

 student x("Joe Smith",1);
 cout << x.display();                    //...and print it

 cout << "\n=========================================\n";

 on_campus y("Hank Jones",1,"Foll Hall","L304"); // put the values in
 cout << y.a_disp();                             // get them out

 cout << "\n=========================================\n";

 off_campus z("Sally Green",2,"22 Main Str","San Francisco","CA","94113");
 cout << z.a_disp();
}
```

The constructor for the base class *student* first allocates space for the *name* member (the size is determined by the value string entered as a parameter). Because this constructor does not specify default values, it must initialize both this field and the *year* member with the supplied parameters.

The two derived classes also contain constructor members. *on_campus()* allocates space for its variable members, *dorm* and *room*, and initializes them. Note how this constructor supplies the arguments for the base (*student*) constructor:

```
on_campus(char* n,int y,char* d,char* r) : (n,y);
```

The values *n* (name) and *y* (year in school) are collected as parameters when the *on_campus* object is initialized; however, their real purpose is to supply the values to the variable members of the *student* base class, thus their appearance in the second set of parentheses. The *off_campus* class constructor also receives the name and year values during its initialization and passes them to the *student* class.

The destructors for the three related classes deallocate the character strings that store all this information. You need to perform this operation because this memory was allocated using the *new* operator and will continue to exist until the program ends or until the *delete* operator removes it.

Private and Public Base Classes

The default relationship between a derived class and its base might be a little surprising. The base is private to the derived class. Thus, the public members of the base class are treated as if they were private members of the derived class: They are available to the derived class and its members but not to outside classes. For example, consider the following class definition:

```
class base {
    int x;
public:
    base(int);
    int display();
};
```

and the following derived class:

```
class derived : base {
    int y;
public:
    derived(int,int);
    do_it();
};
```

Any member of the class *derived* can access the member function *display()* in the public part of class *base*. However, the same *display()* function is not available to other classes through the derived class—it's not a public member of *derived*—even though the two classes have a tight, dependent relationship. In this respect, the member function *display()* is no different from the variable member *y*—both are hidden in the private part of the class. Of course, you can access *display()* if you create an object of type *base*. Such an object, however, would have no connection to any object of the class *derived*.

Public Base Classes

You can alter the previous default situation, however, by declaring the base class to be public. Then, the public part of the base becomes a public part of the derived class as well.

You accomplish this declaration by preceding the name of the base class with the reserved word *public*. Let's alter the simple example of the last section to reflect this new situation:

```
class derived : public base  {
    int y;
public:
    derived(int,int);
    do_it();
};
```

Note, the list of member functions for the class *derived* includes not only *do_it()* but also *display()*. In fact, an object of the derived class can access *display()*, even though *display()* is not defined as a member of the derived class.

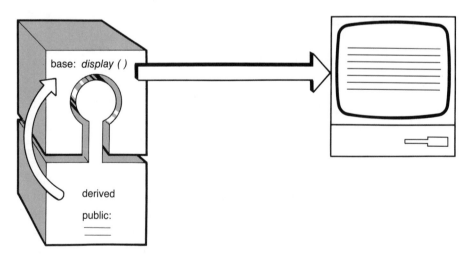

Figure 6-8.   The relationship between *display()* in the *base* class and the *derived* class.

The *address.c* program (Listing 6-5) contains a practical example of a public base class. The class *basic_rec* contains a three-part name—first, middle, and last. A constructor without any default values initializes an object of this class, and a simple destructor deallocates its resources. The member function *show_name()* returns a character string that contains the full name—*first middle last*—in the expected order. A simplified member, *show_last()*, returns only the last name.

Listing 6-5. A derived class with a public base class:
**   *address.c***

```
#include <stream.h>
#include <string.h>


/////////////////////////////////////////////////////////////////////
// define a base class to carry a three part name                   //
/////////////////////////////////////////////////////////////////////


class basic_rec  {
  char *first,              // store typical name information
       *middle,
       *last;
public:
  basic_rec(char*, char*, char*);   // declare a constructor
 ~basic_rec();                      //...and a destructor
  char* show_name();                // a function to display the full name.
  char* show_last() { return last;}  //...and one to give only the last name
};



basic_rec::basic_rec(char* f, char* m, char* l)
{
 first = new char[strlen(f) + 1];    // allocate memory for the members
 middle = new char[strlen(m) + 1];
 last = new char[strlen(l) + 1];

 strcpy(first,f);                     // copy the initial values
 strcpy(middle,m);
 strcpy(last,l);
}                                                      continued
```

```
basic_rec::~basic_rec()
{
 delete first;                       // deallocate the variable members
 delete middle;
 delete last;
}



char* basic_rec::show_name()
{
 char* buffer;                       // create and allocate a buffer;
 buffer = new char[strlen(first) + strlen(middle) + strlen(last) + 1];

 sprintf(buffer,"%s %s %s", first,middle,last);    // format for output
 return buffer;                      // return the formatted output
}
```

```
///////////////////////////////////////////////////////////////////////
// define a derived class based on basic_rec.                          /
///////////////////////////////////////////////////////////////////////



class addr : public basic_rec  {
  char *street,    // set up the address information members
       *city,
       *state,
       *zip;
public:
  addr(char*,char*,char*,char*,char*,char*,char*); // declare a constructor
  ~addr();                                    // declare a destructor
  char* show_addr();                          // declare a display member
};



addr::addr(char* n, char* m, char* l, char* s, char* c,
                                    char* st, char* z) : (n,m,l)
```

```
{
 street = new char[strlen(s) + 1];  // allocate the members
 city = new char[strlen(c) + 1];
 state = new char[strlen(st) + 1];
 zip = new char[strlen(z) + 1];

 strcpy(street,s);  // initialize the variable members
 strcpy(city,c);
 strcpy(state,st);
 strcpy(zip,z);
}


addr::~addr()
{
 delete street;  // deallocate the private members
 delete city;
 delete state;
 delete zip;
}



char* addr::show_addr()
{
 char* buffer;             // allocate and initialize a buffer
 buffer = new char[strlen(street) + strlen(city) +
                              strlen(state) + strlen(zip) + 5];
 sprintf(buffer,"%s\n%s , %s %s",street,city,state,zip); //format output
 return buffer;       // return formatted buffer
}



main()
{
 addr x("Sally","Joan","Brown","123 Main","San Francisco","CA","94113");

 cout << x.show_name() << "\n" << x.show_addr() << "\n";

 cout << "\nLast name= " << x.show_last() << "\n";
}
```

This example also includes the derived class *addr*, which holds the following address information: number and street, city, state, and ZIP code. This class uses straightforward constructor and destructor members. (Note that the constructor explicitly calls the base class constructor and passes it the necessary initial values.) The program includes an additional member function—*show_addr()*—which returns a formatted version of the information contained in the variable members.

The short *main()* driver function demonstrates how the two classes work together. The program creates and initializes an object of type *addr*. It then uses both display member functions to display this information. Note that all of the members of *basic_rec* are accessed through the derived class *addr*.

Creating a Base Class with a Protected Section

Although the relationship between a derived class and its base is a special one, you can access any public part of the base class with a member function of the derived class. The private section of the base class, however, remains locked to the members of the derived class. In this regard, the derived class members are no different than the rest of the program and no direct access is permitted.

This "lockout" of the base class's private section can lead to awkwardly constructed code and, in a few cases, can even work against the kind of data abstraction that C++ was designed to provide. This latter issue is an obvious problem—to access any part of the base class's private section, you must include some public member in the definition of the base class. However, the same public member that allows the derived class access also grants it to the rest of the program; there is no facility for restricting it. In a sense, the more you need data abstraction—for performing delicate operations "inside" a data type—the less protection is afforded. If you need to directly manipulate the internal structure of a class type, the only mechanism available seems to open that internal structure to the entire program.

However, there is a solution to the problem of private versus public access to the base class. C++ has a mechanism that lets you define a third level of security for base and derived classes. A base class can have a "protected" section. This part of the code is treated exactly like the private section of the class as far as access from the rest of the program is concerned; however, it is available to any classes derived from this base. You define a protected section by placing the keyword *protected:* on a line by itself. The scope of this section continues until another label—*public:*, for example—is specified or you insert the brace that ends the class definition. For example, consider the following definition of a simple *base* class:

```
class base  {
     int x;
protected:
     int y;
public:
     base(int);
     show_x_y();
};
```

and the following class derived from it:

```
class derived : base  {
     int z;
public:
     derived(int,int,int);
     show_it();
};
```

Here, any member function of *derived* can directly access its own private variable *z* and the protected variable member of *base*, *y*. However, the (by default private) *x* member is still unavailable.

You now can define three levels of abstraction in a set of classes. Access to the private section of a class is restricted to the immediate members of that class. The protected section is available only to the members of a class and to member functions in its derived classes. Finally, the public section, as always, is available to the rest of the program and defines an interface between it and the class.

The *address2.c* (Listing 6-6) is a modified version of the previous listing. The base class now contains a protected section, which consists of the information found in the private section of the class formatted into a single character string. The constructor member function initializes the protected member, *full_name*, with the rest of the class. The base class also contains a display member, *show_name()*, and a destructor.

Listing 6-6.   A base class with a protected section:
            address2.c

```
#include <stream.h>
#include <string.h>

/////////////////////////////////////////////////////////////////
// define a base class to carry a three part name            //
/////////////////////////////////////////////////////////////////

class basic_rec  {
  char *first,              // store typical name information
       *middle,
       *last;

protected:
    char *full_name;        // the information in formatted form.

public:
  basic_rec(char*, char*, char*);     // declare a constructor
 ~basic_rec();                        //...and a destructor
  char* show_name() { return full_name; } // full name display.
};

basic_rec::basic_rec(char* f, char* m, char* l)
{
 first = new char[strlen(f) + 1];    // allocate memory for the members
 middle = new char[strlen(m) + 1];
 last = new char[strlen(l) + 1];

 strcpy(first,f);                     // copy the initial values
 strcpy(middle,m);
 strcpy(last,l);

 full_name = new char[strlen(first) + strlen(middle) + strlen(last) + 5];
 sprintf(full_name,"%s %s %s",first,middle,last);
}

basic_rec::~basic_rec()
{
 delete first;                        // deallocate the variable members
 delete middle;
```

```
 delete last;
 delete full_name;
}


////////////////////////////////////////////////////////////////////////
// define a derived class based on basic_rec.                          /
////////////////////////////////////////////////////////////////////////

class addr  : public basic_rec  {
  char *street,    // set up the address information members
       *city,
       *state,
       *zip;
public:
  addr(char*,char*,char*,char*,char*,char*,char*); // declare a constructor
 ~addr();                                   // declare a destructor
  char* show_name() { return full_name; }    //access the protected member
  char* show_addr();                         // declare a display member
};


addr::addr(char* n, char* m, char* l, char* s, char* c,
                                    char* st, char* z) : (n,m,l)


{
 street = new char[strlen(s) + 1];   // allocate the members
 city = new char[strlen(c) + 1];
 state = new char[strlen(st) + 1];
 zip = new char[strlen(z) + 1];

 strcpy(street,s);   // initialize the variable members
 strcpy(city,c);
 strcpy(state,st);
 strcpy(zip,z);
}


addr::~addr()
{
 delete street;   // deallocate the private members
 delete city;
 delete state;
```

continued

```
  delete zip;
}


char* addr::show_addr()
{
 char* buffer;              // allocate and initialize a buffer
 buffer = new char[strlen(street) + strlen(city) +
                               strlen(state) + strlen(zip) + 5];
 sprintf(buffer,"%s\n%s , %s %s",street,city,state,zip); //format output
 return buffer;        // return formatted buffer
}



main()
{
 addr x("Sally","Joan","Brown","123 Main","San Francisco","CA","94113");

 cout << x.show_name() << "\n" << x.show_addr() << "\n";
}
```

The derived class *addr* adds basic address information to the name already held in the base. The difference here is that rather than access the public base member function *show_name()*, the derived class directly reads the protected member, *full_name*. The *main()* function illustrates the use of this class.

Review questions

1. The constructor for a derived class must _____ call the constructor for its base class and supply its _____.

2. A program first calls the destructor of the _____ class, then it calls the destructor of the _____ class.

3. If a class is derived from a _____ base class, the public members of the base class are also public members of the derived class.

4. If a base class has a _____ section, the members of this section are public to the derived class, but private to the rest of the program.

Programming projects

1. Using the classes in *address.c* as a model, design a telephone directory system.

2. Create a set of classes to implement a small order-entry system.

---

virtual Functions

Another important feature of derived classes is the "virtual member" function. Sometimes when you derive a group of classes from a base class, certain member functions need to be different in each class. For example, the *display()* function that shows the values of the base class might need to display very different values if it were called from a derived class. Perhaps some of the derived classes could use the *display()* function as defined in the base, while others might require additional items or even completely new formatting. The *virtual function* mechanism lets you effectively accommodate these kinds of changes.

You *could* give different names to each display member function in each different class—the base class member might be *display()*, while the derived class has a corresponding member called *show()*. Although this solution is workable, it is far from ideal. The need to create many unique names for member functions disrupts a unified design and makes the resulting code more difficult to read. Also, this technique of uniquely naming members is opposed to C++'s philosophy of overloading names that perform similar functions.

A better solution—one that was used in Listing 6-3—is to overload the function member name. You could, for example, create the member function *display()* in both the base and the derived class. Then, you could use the scope dereferencing operator (::) to refer to the base class member. This construction uses overloading the way it was intended—the same name represents two different, but similar, operations. This solution is adequate for a simple set of classes, but in a system with many interlocking classes, the details of reference easily become buried in a "spaghetti code" tangle of references.

The best solution is to identify those member functions in the base class that you might need to customize for use in derived classes and then declare them as *virtual* functions. This declaration gives you a simple mechanism for redefining the members in any derived class and has an important advantage over the simple overloading procedure discussed above. When you use a *virtual* function, if a particular member function is not defined in a derived class, but is called through a derived object, then the earlier (base) definition is used. Therefore, the base class definition of the function forms a default definition that the program uses whenever a customized member is not needed.

To declare a *virtual* function, merely precede a member function declaration with the keyword *virtual*. However, you must do this in the declaration line for the function in the base class, even before you mention the data type. For example, the following line:

```
virtual char* display()
```

defines a virtual display function in the context of a base class definition. Note that you do not use the keyword *virtual* in the derived class definition; you merely declare the member as you would any other member function.

You must define a *virtual* function in the base class because the program must have a default function to fall back on. You may or may not define new versions of the *virtual* function in subsequent derived classes, although you can declare them in any class. Because it must be defined in the base class, a program can always access the *virtual* member function through a base class object—assuming that it is a public member of the class. Any redefinition of the *virtual* function in a particular derived class causes the compiler to replace the original definition with the new one whenever the function is used in that class. Thus, the definition in the object accessing the function is the one that is used. Only if no new definition exists does the system resort to the original definition.

The *student5.c* program (Listing 6-7) contains a base class and two derived classes. The virtual member function *display()* is defined in both the base and derived classes. The short *main()* driver function demonstrates the operation of this system.

Listing 6-7.   Derived classes that use *virtual* functions:
**   *student5.c***

```
#include <stream.h>
#include <string.h>


const fval = 20;  //specify a format length for display strings



///////////////////////////////////////////////////////
// Define a base class                                 /
///////////////////////////////////////////////////////

class  student  {
    char* name;                  // student name
    int year;                    // current class standing 1=freshman, etc.
public:
    student(char*, int);         // put values into a record.
    ~student()  { delete name; } // define a destructor
    virtual char* display();     // show the name and year
};

student::student(char* n,int y)
{
  name = new char[strlen(n)+1]; // allocate enough memory
  strcpy(name,n);               // copy the name over to the class
  year = y;                     //...and the year
}

char* student::display()
{
  char* buffer;                       // create a buffer for the display string
  buffer = new char[strlen(name) + fval];
  sprintf(buffer,"\nname: %s\nyear: %d\n",name,year); //prepare it
  return buffer;
```

continued

231

```
}

////////////////////////////////////////////////////////
// Define a derived class from student              /
////////////////////////////////////////////////////////

class on_campus : student  {
  char  *dorm,                           // information in addition to
         *room;                          // the student stuff
public:
  on_campus(char*,int,char*,char*);          //...and an input one
 ~on_campus() { delete dorm; delete room; } // define a destructor
  char* display();                       // declare a simple display member
};


on_campus::on_campus(char* n,int y,char* d,char* r) : (n,y)
{
 dorm = new char[strlen(d)+1];          // allocate memory
 strcpy(dorm,d);                        // copy
 room = new char[strlen(r)+1];          //...and for this field
 strcpy(room,r);
}


char* on_campus::display()
{
 char *buffer;
 int flength = strlen(student::display()) + strlen(dorm) + strlen(room) + fval;
 buffer = new char[flength];
 sprintf(buffer,"%s\ndorm: %s\nroom: %s\n",student::display(),dorm,room);
 return buffer;
}


////////////////////////////////////////////////////////
// Derive another class from student                /
////////////////////////////////////////////////////////

class off_campus : student  {
   char  *street,      // new information to add to
          *city,       // the basic student values
          *state,
```

```
        *zip;
public:
  off_campus(char*,int,char*,char*,char*,char*); //...and an input one
 ~off_campus();                        // declare a destructor
  char* display();                     // declare a simple display member

};


off_campus::off_campus(char* n,int y,char* s,char* cty,char* st,char* z):(n,y)
{
 street = new char[strlen(s)+1];    // allocate and copy the
 strcpy(street,s);                  // new information
 city = new char[strlen(cty)+1];
 strcpy(city,cty);
 state = new char[strlen(st)+1];
 strcpy(state,st);
 zip = new char[strlen(z)+1];
 strcpy(zip,z);
}


inline off_campus::~off_campus()
{
 delete street;
 delete city;
 delete state;
 delete zip;
}


char* off_campus::display()
{
 char* buffer;
 int flength = strlen(student::display()) + strlen(street) + strlen(city) +
                            strlen(state) + strlen(zip) + fval;
 buffer = new char[flength];
 sprintf(buffer,"%s\n%s\n%s, %s %s\n",student::display(),street,city,state,zip);
 return buffer;
}
```

///

continued

```
main()
{
cout << "\n=========================================\n";

student x("Joe Smith",1);
cout << x.display();                    //...and print it

cout << "\n=========================================\n";

on_campus y("Hank Jones",1,"Foll Hall","L304"); // put the values in
cout << y.display();                    // get them out

cout << "\n=========================================\n";

off_campus z("Sally Green",2,"22 Main Str","San Francisco","CA","94113");
cout << z.display();
}
```

The base class *student* has an initializing constructor and de-initializing destructor. It contains only one member function, *display()*, which is a *virtual* member. This member formats the information contained in the private section for display on the screen and stores the result in a character string. The function then returns this string.

The two derived classes, *on_campus* and *off_campus*, have unique redefinitions of the base *display()* member. Each displays the address information unique to its particular class. In *on_campus*, it returns the dormitory name and room number; in *off_campus*, it returns a street address. In both cases, the display is formatted and copied to a character string, which is returned through the function name.

Note the interesting use of the scope dereferencing operator (::). In the *display()* member of the *on_campus* class, it enables the program to bypass the redefinition allowed by the declaration of this function as *virtual* and to recapture the original base class definition. (This is used, of course, as only part of the definition of this member.) The off_campus class uses a similar "out of scope" call.

Complicated Systems of Classes

The concept of a derived class is not an absolute one. The definition of a class contains nothing that distinguishes a base class definition from a class that has no derived classes. Indeed, you can create derived classes from existing classes, even those to which you have only minimal access, such as precompiled classes. Any class can serve as the base for a derived class—even another derived class.

Because base and derived relationships are relative, they can be used as design tools for producing highly structured programs. For example, you can create hierarchies of classes in which the derived class of one becomes the base of another. There is no logical limit to the length of such a chain of interrelated classes. You can use this capability to modularize arbitrarily complex class structures.

The *customer.c* example (Listing 6-8) contains a system of three related classes: a class *customer*, which contains an identification string and a name; a class *account* (derived from *customer*), which contains another identification string and a balance; and a class *cdeposit*, which contains a date and an interest rate. The *cdeposit* class is derived from the *account* class, not from the original *customer* class.

Listing 6-8.   A hierarchy of derived classes: *customer.c*

```
#include <stream.h>
#include <string.h>


/////////////////////////////////////////////////////////////////////
// define the base class with a constructor, destructor, and a     //
//         virtual display() function.                              //
/////////////////////////////////////////////////////////////////////

class customer  {
  char *id,                         // customer identification
       *name;                       // owner's name

public:
  customer(char*,char*);            // declare a constructor
  ~customer() { delete id; delete name; }   // define a destructor
  virtual char* display();          // declare a display member
};

customer::customer(char* i, char* n)
{
  id = new char[strlen(i)+1];       // allocate memory for the id
  strcpy(id,i);                     // copy the initial value
  name = new char[strlen(n)  + 1];  //...and for the name
```

continued

```
  strcpy(name,n);                    // copy the name too
}


char* customer::display()
{
 char* buffer;                       // allocate memory for the display string
 buffer = new char[strlen(id) + strlen(name) + 5];
 sprintf(buffer,"%s\n%s\n",id,name);            // copy the current values
 return buffer;                                 // send it back
}


/////////////////////////////////////////////////////////////////////
//   define an account class derived from the customer class        //
/////////////////////////////////////////////////////////////////////

class account : customer  {
  char* acctid;          // identification of the account number
  long balance;          // current balance in pennies

public:
  account(char*,char*,char*,long =0);  // declare a constructor
 ~account() { delete acctid; }         // define a destructor
  char* display();  // we need a new show member
};


account::account(char* cid,char* cname,char* acid,long b) : (cid,cname)
{
 acctid = new char[strlen(acid) + 1];    // allocate and initialize
 strcpy(acctid,acid);                     // the accound id
 balance = b;                             // initialize the balance
}


char* account::display()
{
 char* buffer;
 int len = strlen(customer::display()) + strlen(acctid) + 20;
 buffer = new char[len];
 sprintf(buffer,"%s%s\n%d\n",customer::display(),acctid,balance);
 return buffer;
}
```

```
/////////////////////////////////////////////////////////////////////
// define another derived class whose base class is account--a base  //
//         class that is itself a derived class                      //
/////////////////////////////////////////////////////////////////////

class cdeposit : account  {
  char* date;
  int percent;

public:
  cdeposit(char*,char*,char*,long,char*,int);  // initialize an object
 ~cdeposit()  { delete date; }                 // define a destructor
  char* display();                             // declare a new member
};

cdeposit::cdeposit(char* i,char* n,char* ia,long b,char* d,int r) : (i,n,ia,b)
{
  date = new char[strlen(d) + 1];        // allocate memory for the date
  strcpy(date,d);                        //...and copy it
  percent = r;                           // initialize the rate
}

char* cdeposit::display()
{
 char* buffer;
 int len = strlen(account::display()) + strlen(date) + 20;  // how big?
 buffer = new char[len];               // allocate space for the display string
 sprintf(buffer,"%s%s\n %d\n",account::display(),date,percent);
 return buffer;
}


/////////////////////////////////////////////////////////////////////
// a simple driver function to demonstrate the class definitions    //
/////////////////////////////////////////////////////////////////////

main()
{
 cdeposit x("L1234","Joe Smith","ACC1234",0,"Jan 22, 1988",5);

 cout << x.display();
}
```

The original base class, *customer*, contains information that identifies an individual. (For the sake of simplicity, this class requires minimal information—merely a name and an arbitrary character string that contains an identification value.) The constructor contains no default values, so each object of this type is explicitly initialized. This is commonsense programming because the program handles unique values. Only one member function, *display()*, is defined; note that it is declared as a *virtual* function. The class destructor performs basic deallocation.

The derived class *account* holds the values of a particular bank account. Again, for simplicity, it contains only an arbitrary identification value and the balance of the account. The constructor accepts as parameters all of the values needed to initialize both this and the base class. The constructor definition explicitly calls the base class initializer. A new version of the display function formats and displays the information in this class. A basic destructor deallocates the account identification string. Because the *balance* member is a simple *long* variable, no explicit deallocation is necessary.

Finally, the program defines a third class—*cdeposit*—which is of type *account*. It does not refer to the original base class, but instead, it grows from an intermediate level. This class definition includes the date and a specific interest rate for this type of account. The date is the date of maturity of the deposit. This constructor contains the values necessary not only to initialize this object but also to initialize its base class (*account*)—and, indirectly, the original *customer* class. The *display()* member function is redefined to recognize the peculiarities of this type. Figure 6-9 summarizes these class relationships.

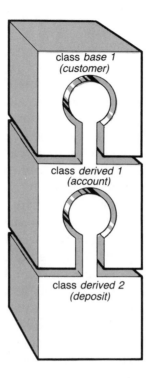

Figure 6-9.   A complex system of classes

Review questions

1. A *virtual* member function must be defined in the _____ class.

2. A _____ member function is defined in the base class and may or may not be redefined in subsequent derived classes.

3. The distinction between a derived class and a base class is _____. You can use a derived class as a base for another class.

Programming projects

1. Flesh out the hierarchy of derived classes in *customer.c* with additional member functions that implement common banking functions. Try to identify those member functions that need to be declared as *virtual*.

2. Use the set of banking classes to create a simple bank management system.

Summary

This chapter explored the capacity of C++ to create systems of related classes. The mechanism for this is the derivation of one class from another. The derived class contains all the information of its base—it both "is" that class, and it is more. The utility of class derivation is unlimited because you can use any preexisting class as a base, even if your access to it is limited to a precompiled version. The derived class lets the designer divide a programming problem into ever more specific modules for an easier and more comprehensible solution.

In addition to the relationship that grows out of the base-derived concept, other aspects of derived classes have been described. Chief among these are *virtual* member functions and protected members. Both of these capabilities generate clear classes and promote modularity. *Virtual* functions are member functions that, once defined in the base class, can be redefined in subsequent derived classes. The members in a protected section of a base class are private to the rest of the program but available to the members of any derived class.

Finally, the notion of systems of classes has been enhanced by illustrating the creation of a hierarchy of related classes. This hierarchy is built on the premise that derived classes and base classes are relative.

7

Using the C++ Input/Output System

- ▶ Basic Input and Output in C++
- ▶ The Stream Class
- ▶ The Input Operator >> and the Standard Input Stream
- ▶ The Output Operator << and the Standard Output Stream
- ▶ Using the Standard Stream Objects
- ▶ Disk File Input and Output
- ▶ A Practical File Program
- ▶ The Standard I/O Functions and the Stream Library
- ▶ Using the Stream Library with User-Defined Data Types
- ▶ Summary

7

Using the C++ Input/Output System

The C standard library has many well-developed input and output routines; to these C++ adds a new and more convenient facility for getting values into and out of a program—the stream library. This set of interlocking data types and functions provides the convenience of built-in I/O statements while maintaining the flexibility of user-defined functions. The C library contains a few massive I/O functions that do all things to all kinds of data; the stream library has a series of smaller functions, each tied to specific data types. Furthermore, the functions in this library are more efficient than those most commonly used in C. This efficiency is also manifested by the greater readability of the C++ output lines.

This chapter introduces the C++ stream library and its most common objects—the standard I/O streams *cin*, *cout*, and *cerr*. It also shows how to extend the stream model to disk files and handle the issues that arise with that transformation. Finally, the chapter offers many concrete examples that show the stream library in action.

Basic Input and Output in C++

To better understand why the stream library in C++ is more convenient than its C counterpart, let's first review how C handles input and output. First, recall that C has no built-in input or output statements; functions such as *printf()* are part of the standard library, but not part of the language itself. Similarly, C++ has no built-in I/O facilities. The absence of built-in I/O gives the programmer greater flexibility to produce the most efficient user interface for the pattern of the application at hand.

The problem with the C solution to input and output lies with its implementation of these I/O functions. There is little consistency among them in terms of return values and parameter sequences. Because of this, programmers tend to rely on the formatted IO functions—*printf()*, *scanf()*, and so on—especially when the objects being manipulated are numbers or other non-character values. These formatted I/O functions are convenient and, for the most part, share a consistent interface, but they are also big and unwieldy because they must manipulate many kinds of values.

The C++ Approach to I/O

C++ uses the mechanism of the class to provide modular solutions to data manipulation needs. Continuing this approach, the standard C++ library provides three I/O classes as an alternative to C's cumbersome general-purpose I/O functions. These classes contain definitions for the same pair of operators—>> for input and << for output—which are optimized for specific kinds of data. These operators are overloaded so that you can add definitions to accommodate new situations without relinquishing their simple, convenient syntax. Thus, you can easily and radically modularize the input output/system with many small I/O functions that have a consistent interface. You don't need to trade convenience for code size.

To the traditional C I/O library, C++ adds the standard stream library, which contains a set of small, specific functions that are more efficient than C's massive general-purpose functions. The standard stream library contains specific functions to perform conversions between the three supported number systems—decimal, hexadecimal, and octal—as well as specialized functions that place strings and individual characters within specified fields. It even contains a *form()* function, which is comparable to the *printf()* family in C.

C++ also supports the input of numbers, characters, and character strings more conveniently and more efficiently than C. Although you cannot explicitly format input as you can with the *scanf()* function, the new library contains much of the functionality of *scanf()*. In order to maintain old programs and to accommodate traditional programmers, the original C library is, of course, available to a C++ program.

The << and >> I/O Operators

From the programmer's point of view, the key to the stream library is the output operator, which replaces the more familiar function call. Instead of writing

```
printf("%d\n",x);
```

to display a message on a screen, in C++, you use the more concise form:

```
int x=123;
cout << x << "\n";
```

This translates as "output the value of x and then output a newline character." Note that you don't need to specify a format for the value in x—the system determines that. This form is more convenient and more obvious than the *printf()* function, but this is not its entire advantage. In addition to its economy of expression, the C++ method introduces more significant improvements as well. For example, in the latter code fragment, the value stored in variable x (123) is easily sent to the display screen. Using the traditional C library, you would first need to convert the numeric value into character string form, because a string is the only data that can be displayed on an output device such as a terminal screen. Usually, you would invoke the convenient, but relatively bloated, *print()* function. As a general-purpose conversion function, *print()* contains all the code needed to handle the many possible combinations of value-to-output transformations. This extra code is linked into each program whether it is needed or not. With the stream library, C++ includes only the code needed for a specific conversion. Generally, this makes the code for I/O operations smaller and faster than the equivalent C code.

The stream library also supplies a similar *input* operator. The following code fragment illustrates its operation:

```
int x;
cin >> x;
```

This places the value typed at the keyboard—or entered by some other method—in the variable x. Because x is declared as an integer variable, it expects an integer value. The input operator automatically performs the conversion. As its corollary did in the output system, this operator replaces the conventional formatted input statement, *scanf()*. This is not a substitution, however, because the input operator does only the data conversions. The *scanf()* function is a complete, formatted input facility that lets you describe the specification of the input line. C++ has no stream input function comparable to the *form()* output function; however, remember that you can always use *scanf()*—or any of the other basic C I/O functions—whenever you need them. The advantages of using the stream input operator are the same as those gained from the output functions—the resulting code is smaller, more specific, and more efficient.

There is an easy way to remember which operator is for input and which is for output: The C++ I/O operators are analogous to the redirection operators in both MS-DOS and UNIX. Thus, just as the < symbol indicates that a command receives its values not from the keyboard but from a file, so the << symbol indicates that the file (usually *cout*) receives its value from a variable or an expression. For example, the following MS-DOS command:

```
dir < file
```

executes the *dir* command with the arguments contained in *file*. Similarly, the following C++ command:

```
cout << x;
```

sends the value stored in *x* to the standard output *cout*. The same relationship exists between > and >>: The following MS-DOS command:

```
dir > file
```

sends the results of the command to a file, and the following C++ statement:

```
cin >> x;
```

puts the value from the standard input into the variable *x* (see Figure 7-1).

As a notational convenience, these operators offer an economy of expression, and their implementation is more efficient than C's general-purpose approach. However, the full impact of this new stream library

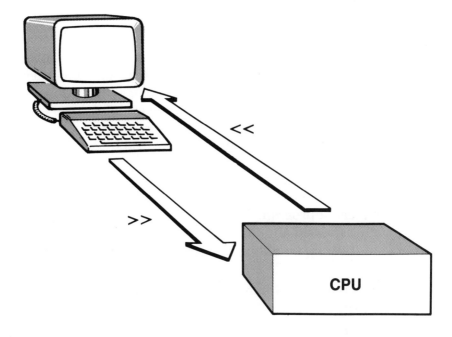

Figure 7-1.   Data flow with ≪ and ≫ operators

goes far beyond these advantages. Let's now unlock the full power of these routines.

The Stream Class

Chapter 3 showed how a C++ class integrates data and related functions into a single structure or object. Therefore, you should not be surprised that the power and simplicity of the stream library derives from its implementation as a series of related classes. These classes include input and output routines defined for each standard data type in C++. In addition to these, by using *virtual* functions and derived classes (see Chapter 5), you can easily add your own I/O routines for user-defined data types. Naturally, these facilities extend to disk I/O as well as to other devices.

The Stream I/O Model

C++ is as consistent with its progenitor language as possible and, there-fore, treats all I/O as a character string operation. This is the origin of the term *stream*—a stream of characters. Both languages also treat disk files as streams—even when they include binary (non-text) values. Re-member this useful metaphor as you examine some of the more subtle and potentially confusing parts of the library.

C++, as with operating systems such as UNIX, uses the file as a basic model for all input and output, even that which goes to the display terminal hardware rather than to the disk. In fact, C++ automatically opens the standard input and output files called *cin* and *cout* whenever you load a program for execution. You can manipulate these files ex-actly as would any user-defined data files.

The stream library is based on the following new classes:

▶ *streambuf*—a buffer type that creates and manages a stream for I/O

▶ *istream* and *ostream*—input and output stream types that define the operations needed to move data between the program and the user

The *streambuf* class contains the basic functions for buffering data, such as allocating a buffer and keeping track of the current position in the buffer. Note that the *streambuf* type merely handles a buffer; it doesn't know where the values come from nor where they are going. Two defined classes, *istream* and *ostream*, are associated with the *streambuf* type and contain the actual operations that implement input and output. Because some input operations differ from those needed for output, C++ uses separate classes. (A single general-purpose type would have been large and unwieldy and would have defeated the purpose of defining special classes.) The principal difference in implementing the two classes occurs in the operator definitions for the >> and the << symbols.

The Standard I/O Streams

When each program begins execution, C++ automatically opens three streams—*cin* (standard input), *cout* (standard output), and *cerr* (standard error). These streams become the interface between the program and the user. Almost every program must use these streams to some extent.

The *cin* stream handles all the input from the terminal keyboard and is of type *istream*. In contrast, *cout* manipulates the terminal display screen and is of type *ostream*. Another standard stream, *cerr*, also of type *ostream*, provides the programmer with a secondary means for reporting error conditions when the mixing of error messages and normal display output might cause problems. These three standard streams correspond to C's *stdin*, *stdout*, and *stderr* files.

You can manipulate the standard streams as you would their C counterparts:

▶ You can redirect them to other devices, even a disk file

▶ You can close and reopen them

▶ You can combine them with each other or with other files

In fact, because both *cerr* and *cout* are connected to the terminal display subsystem, most programs actually display error messages through a different stream than ordinary output. The two streams are logically separate and could be assigned to different devices, or even to a disk file. (Indeed, you can conveniently assign *cerr* to a disk file in programs designed to be run as batch jobs.) In programs that must open several input or output files during the course of processing, you merely declare the additional files as either *istream* or *ostream* classes and then treat them as though they were *cin* and *cout* streams.

The Input Operator >> and the Standard Input Stream

Let's use the standard input stream, *cin*, to examine the operation of the input operator >> in detail. Most of the following discussion also applies to other *istream* objects.

Note that >> is an overloaded operator. C++ supplies a separate function definition for input of each standard data type—integer, real, and character-oriented. You can use the >> operator to direct the input of any value from the keyboard; because this operator is overloaded, the correct function definition for that data type always executes. (Of course, you still have to be sure that the user has entered a valid value, but that is an axiom of real-world programming.) You no longer need to do explicit type conversion or checking, and that is an improvement over the standard C library, in which non-character oriented input must be converted to the required data type.

Flexibility of the >> Operator

The convenience of the input operator is obvious—for the user to enter an integer value, the program requires only the following simple code:

```
int x;
cin >> x;
```

(Remember that the >> symbol was chosen as a mnemonic for the direction of flow—from the input stream (*cin*) to the variable.) However, this operator can do much more. For maximum flexibility, you can cascade operators. For example, the following code fragment:

```
int x,y;
cin >> x >> y;
```

lets the user enter two integer values into a program. One goes into the *x* variable and the other into *y*. This type of cascading has no built-in or practical limit. The following code:

```
cin >> x >> y >> z;
```

introduces three values into the program. The same procedure holds true for real number types—*float* or *double*:

```
double x,y;
cin >> x >> y;
```

(Note that you always use the same operator and the identical syntax, regardless of the type of data involved.) When you use multiple input values, the order of operation is simple and unsurprising: The first variable mentioned is the first filled, and the others are filled in the order of their appearance.

Because the >> operator is overloaded with explicit operational code for each supported data type, there are no restrictions on the kinds of input lines that you can construct inside a *cin* expression. C++

supports any combination of data types in the same line of code. For example, the following lines:

```
char ch;
double x;
cin >> ch >> x;
```

generate the expected values in the correct variables.

The General-Purpose *istream* Input Function

As useful as the input operator is, it does not handle all kinds of input. To create a flexible and useful library, the designer of C++ chose an implementation that reflected the most common usage of such a routine. This is a simple, no-nonsense input routine. The individual programmer must create the flourishes and the code for special cases. The basic nature of the input operator becomes most evident when you use it to handle character string input. Its operation with this data type might surprise an unwary programmer.

Like *scanf()* in the C library, >> reads in a string only to the first occurrence of white space. Consider the following code fragment:

```
char ch[80];
cin >> ch;
```

If the user enters the character string "this is only a test" from the keyboard, only the first word ("this") is placed in the string variable *ch*. The input operator sees the blank space after a word as a signal to end input. The null character that conventionally marks the end of a string in C is then affixed to the end of *ch*. Thus, the >> operator is inadequate for any line-oriented input that might contain embedded spaces or other white space characters.

The *istream* class contains a character string function, *get()*, which serves as a basic input routine that can retrieve a complete string, blank spaces and all. The *get()* function performs no conversions; it merely accepts a character string and places it in the specified variable. Actually, *get()* consists of three overloaded functions that perform basic uninterpreted input. The following box lists the general form of these functions. In addition to its character string function, *get()* supports basic input to a managed buffer and to a single character variable. Note that all versions of *get()* let you specify a character that terminates input.

When you use the default terminator, \n, the function accepts input (including spaces) until the specified length of the variable or buffer is exceeded or until a newline is entered.

The *get()* function in the class *istream*

get(char *string, int *length,* char *terminator*)

where: *string* is a character string variable;
      length is the maximum length of the input string;
      terminator indicates a particular character that will cause termination of input. The default value is '\n'.

      This function will accept characters until either the maximum length is reached or the terminating character is entered.

get(streambuf& *buffer,* char *terminator*)

where: *buffer* is a streambuf object;
      terminator is the character that will stop input.
      Here too, the default is '\n'.

      This function will place input into a managed buffer.

get(char& *c*)

where: *c* is a reference to a character variable.

      This function produces simple character input.

The Output Operator << and the Standard Output Stream

As a complement to the *istream* object that imports values into a program, the stream library also defines an *ostream* type that exports values from the program. The heart of this class is the overloaded output operator <<, which lets you display built-in data types. This operator can perform the basic output function for most programs.

You can also cascade the output operator, and it displays values in the order that they are specified in the line. Thus, the following output expression:

```
int x=123;
cout << "x=" << x;
```

displays:

```
x=123
```

on the screen or on any other output destination that you specify. As with the input operator, there is no built-in limit to the number of elements that you can cascade; however, common sense and good programming practice might dictate a limit of three or four. Of course, you can freely combine different data types on a single line. For example, the following code:

```
int x=123;
double f=1.23;
cout << "x=" << x << "f=" << f;
```

creates a display with the appropriate labels. Note that this code is much simpler than a comparable *print()* statement, which would require format specifiers.

The output operator has a problem that results from the fact that C++ and C have no distinctive character data type. Characters are treated as small integers, and you must explicitly convert them either with the program code itself or by using one of the library functions. Although the << output operator is not defined for single characters, it *can* accept and display a character string. Therefore, you can display a character constant as a character string with only a single character. However, in general, the proper display of character values from variables and expressions must rely on formatted output techniques or on the more basic output functions available in the *ostream* class.

The *ostream* Output Functions

The *ostream* class also contains two primitive output functions. The first of these, *put()*, performs the most basic output operation—it outputs a single character. The *put()* routine accepts an expression that yields a single character and sends the character to the specified display device. This function is the equivalent of the *putchar()* function in the C standard library, and it uses the following syntax:

```
char ch='a';
cout.put(ch);
```

Recall that *cout* is an object of the *ostream* class. The *put()* function is a member of this class, so you must access it either through the *dot* notation (.) or through the *arrow* notation for pointer variables (->).

The second primitive *ostream* output function, *flush()*, clears the output buffer of any characters waiting to be sent to the output destination. Usually, you use this routine with an *ostream* attached to a disk file in order to ensure that all buffered characters have been explicitly written to a file before you close the file or rewrite to it. However, because C++ automatically calls the *flush()* function before it destroys an *ostream* object, you rarely need to explicitly call this function. (This is another example of the useful actions of a class destructor.)

Many programs do not require these *ostream* services. However, remember that they are available and that they are particularly useful for outputting values to disk files and other non-device destinations.

Formatted Output Functions

Included in the stream library—but external to the *ostream* class—are a series of formatted output functions that give the programmer greater control over value conversion and display mechanics. These format functions (described in the following box) were primarily created to be used with the output operator.

The formatted output functions

These functions can be used in conjunction with the output operator to control the position of the values to be displayed. They take the general form:

<type> <name> (<value>,<width>);

`char* oct(long num, int width);`	Displays *num* as an octal number in a field of width characters.
`char* dec(long num, int width);`	Displays *num* as a decimal number in the specified field.
`char* hex(long num, int width);`	Displays *num* as a hexadecimal value in the specified area.
`char* chr(int ch, int width);`	Displays *ch* as a character in the specified position.
`char* str(const char* ch, int width);`	Displays the character string *ch* using a field size of *width*.

The formatted output functions fall into two groups. The first lets the programmer specify only the width of the display field. Each function performs a specific conversion of octal, decimal, or hexadecimal numeric values, as well as single characters or strings. For example, the following code:

```
int x=123;
cout << dec(x,4);
```

displays the value of *x* (123) in a field that is four characters wide (the *dec* signifies decimal, or base 10). If the specified width is too small to hold a value, C++ does not truncate the value—it increases the field width to accommodate it. If you do not specify a field width, C++ uses the default of 0, and the number takes up only enough room to display itself. A negative field width causes the value to be left justified in the field. The default is right justification. Note that C++ provides both single-character and character-string functions.

The second group of output facilities is offered in the *form()* function, which features a complete formatting capability similar to the *printf()* function in the standard C library. The function consists of two main parts—a format string, with which you specify the appearance of the line and the size and formats of the values to be displayed, and a list of expressions that supply the values. For example, the following code:

```
int x=123;
double f=1.23;
char ch='A';
cout << form("x=%d\nf=%f\nch=%c\n",x,f,ch);
```

presents each value and its appropriate title on separate lines, as follows:

```
x=123
f=1.23
ch=A.
```

You create the format string by combining three kinds of elements:

- ▶ regular characters, which are printed as they are written
- ▶ format characters, which specify the output form of a value
- ▶ escape characters, which serve as carriage control specifiers

The most commonly used format characters are the following two-character combinations—%d, %f, %c, and %s, which respectively represent integer, floating point, character, and string values. As format characters are always preceded by a '%', so escape characters are always preceded by a backslash ('\'). The most common escape sequence, '\n', specifies a new line. The *form()* function also lets the programmer specify the field width, and, in the case of real numbers and character strings, the precision. If you are familiar with the operation of *printf()*, you will have no difficulty learning how to use *form()*. The following box presents the definition of this function and a summary of its options.

Formatted output: The *form()* function

The form() function can be used in conjunction with the output operator to specify a range of optional formats and line positions for the output display; it has the general form:

form(char* format_string,<list of expressions>);

The general form of a format specifier is

% <width specifier> <modifier> <format code>

Format codes

Integer values:	u	Unsigned integer
	d	Decimal notation
	o	Octal values
	x	Hexadecimal number
Float or double:	e	Floating point notation
	f	Decimal point display
	g, d, e, or f	Minimizes space while maintaining specified precision
Character-oriented displays:	c	A single character
	s	A null terminated character string

Format modifiers

	–	Left justified display—right justified is the default
	*	Uses the next value in the expression list as the field width specifier

continued

Format modifiers

h	Short integer
l	Long integer
<num>	A display field of *<num>* characters
<num>.<prec> (for float or double)	A display field of *<num>* characters with *<prec>* digits after the decimal point
<num>.<prec> (for character strings)	A field width of *<num>* character but displaying only the first *<prec>* characters from the string

Using the Standard Stream Objects

Now that you know how the stream library relates to the standard input (*cin*) and output (*cout*), let's examine all the details in a complete, concrete example. A simple calculator program, *calcio.c* (Listing 7-1), illustrates the everyday use of these I/O objects. This program accepts an arithmetic expression that uses a single operator—for example, 23 + 45—and returns the result of the specified operation. It continues until the user enters an explicit *stop* command.

Listing 7-1.   A calculator emulation that illustrates stream objects: *calcio.c*

```
#include <stream.h>
#include <string.h>

main()
{
 int x=0,y=0,eval(int*,int*,char*);
 char op;

 while (eval(&x,&y,&op))
```

```
    switch(op)  {
      case '+': cout << "=" << dec(x+y) << "\n";
                break;
      case '-': cout << "=" << dec(x-y) << "\n";
                break;
      case '*': cout << "=" << dec(x*y) << "\n";
                break;
      case '/': if(y != 0)
                    cout << "=" << dec(x/y)  << "\n";
                break;
    }
}

int eval(int *x,int *y, char *op)
{
 char buffer[80],*opr,*find_tok(char*,char*);

 cout << "->";
 cin >> buffer;          // accept an expression from the keyboard

 if(!strcmp(buffer,"stop"))
   return 0;

 if((opr=find_tok(buffer,"+-*/")) == 0)   // find the operator
   return 0;

 *op=*opr;                        // save the operator
 *opr='\0';                       // make two strings out of one
 *x=atoi(buffer);                 // create the first operand
 *y=atoi(opr+1);                  // ...and the second

 return 1;
}



char *find_tok(char* str,char* tstr)
{
 char *prt=str,*tok;

 for(;*prt != '\0';prt++)  {
   tok=tstr;                       // reset the token search string
   for(;*tok != '\0';tok++)
```

continued

```
        if(*prt == *tok)           // if it's a match
           return prt;             // return the location of the operator
    }


    return 0;
}
```

The program consists of three functions: *main()* controls the operation of the program and performs the actual calculation; *eval()* accepts input from the keyboard, evaluates it, and returns useful values to *main()*; and, finally, *find_tok()* extracts the operator from the entered character string.

Note that you must include both the *stream.h* and *string.h* header files to support the functions used in the program. C++ is less forgiving than C when a program tries to use a function that has not been declared. You must even declare those functions that return an integer value before you use them in the program.

The *main()* function consists of a *while* loop that is controlled by the value returned from the *eval()* function. This function passes values through three parameters—*x*, *y*, and *op*. The latter variable controls the *switch* statement in the body of the *while* loop. This *switch* contains a clause for each of the four supported operations (the program omits a default case and error-handling code for the sake of simplicity). The *cout* object provides the output. Note that the program uses the format function *dec()* to permit you greater control over the screen display than would have been possible with the << operator. (You could also replace this function with *oct()* or *hex()*, if you need to work with those number systems.) The division case has an additional conditional because it must check for an attempt of division by zero.

The *eval()* function is the heart of the program. It prompts the user for input and then accepts it as a character string. The advantage of using character-string input is the flexibility that it provides for checking and converting values—the first statement executed after the input, for example, checks for the character string "stop". Note that the simple << and >> operators are all you need to prompt for and to receive values.

If the input value is the stop signal, the function returns zero; if not, it calls *find_tok()*, which returns the operator's position in the input string (the string has the form of "number" "operator" "number"). If *find_tok()* fails to find a legal operator it returns a zero to indicate a problem; thus, the error handling is passed to the calling function, which deals with it further. If *find_tok()* returns a positive value, the program copies that character to the *op* parameter and then alters the input string by changing the character to a null ('\0'). This procedure splits the input into two new strings:

- ▶ one string that begins at the first location of the input string and ends at the position before the operator; and

- ▶ another string that begins in the position immediately following the operator and ends at the last position of the original input string.

Each of these derived strings represents an operand of the expression. The program then uses the library function *atoi()* to convert these substrings into numeric values. If the conversion is successful, a value of one is returned to the calling function.

The *find_tok()* function is similar to the *strtok()* function in the standard library of both C and C++; however, its operation is more specialized. The program passes *find_tok()* two character strings—a string to be searched and a string consisting of important characters, or tokens. The function searches the first string character-by-character and tries to match each of these characters with a character from the second string. If the function finds a match, it returns the address of the current character. A return value of zero indicates a failure to find a match. The variable *prt* serves as a local cursor to allow movement through the string.

The calculator program is a simple example that can be greatly improved. For one thing, its error checking is minimal and needs to be expanded. A fancier user interface would permit expressions with multiple operators. The >> input operator also unduly restricts the format of the input that the program will accept. Specifically, the expression the user inputs can have no spaces because this operator accepts only a character string up to the first blank space character. Nevertheless, the example succeeds in illustrating common uses of the standard I/O objects *cin* and *cout*.

Disk File Input and Output

One important consequence of the two-part design of the stream library—into a *streambuf* object and a stream—is that the same model that performs I/O for keyboard and terminal works just as well when you apply it to a disk file. The same operators and operations perform in precisely the same way. This greatly simplifies a programming task that has always been difficult and confusing.

To facilitate disk file I/O, the stream library defines a *filebuf* object, which is a derivative of the standard *streambuf* type. Like its progenitor type, *filebuf* manages a buffer, but, in this case, the buffer is attached to a disk file. The declaration contains additional items that C++ needs in order to negotiate with a secondary storage device and its operating system interface; the other management functions are inherited from the *streambuf* type. Among the key new functions specific to *filebuf* are *open()* and *close()*; however, also note that new constructors are specifically defined for initializing this derived type.

Opening a File

The first function that you must use with disk files is *open()*. This function makes the connection between the file on the disk and the file being manipulated inside a program. In contrast to C, in which you must send the variable to the function, in C++, the file variable itself contains the open function; its general form is as follows:

```
buffer_name.open(char* file_name,open_mode mode);
```

The *file_name* is a character string that contains the name of a file as it appears to the operating system; this directory name can include a path specification as well as the file name. The only other parameter in the command is a *mode* specifier, which indicates one of the following kinds of access—read, write, or append.

Mode is of type *open_mode*—an enumerated type that has only the following three members:

```
enum open_mode(input=0, output=1, append=2);
```

Each of the above members represents a legal file mode. Input takes values from the file to the program; output sends data to the disk. If you open a file for input, you cannot also use it for output. Using the output mode truncates an existing file, effectively erasing whatever was previously stored there. The append mode lets a program place data at the end of a file without erasing the data in the file. If you attempt to open a nonexistent file for writing—using either the output or the append mode—C++ creates that file. The following is a typical example of an open statement:

```
filebuf file1;
if(file1.open("file.dat",output)==0)
    exit(1);
```

Because the expression *file1.open()* returns a value of zero if the file cannot be opened, a program can easily check the success or failure of the file operation. If the operation is successful, the function returns a pointer to the *filebuf* object itself.

Attaching a File to a Stream

After you open a physical file, you must attach it to a stream—an *ostream* for a file opened for output, or an *istream* for a file opened for input. For example, the following code:

```
ostream file_out(file1);
```

associates the *ostream* object *file_out* with a previously opened file. After a programmer creates this stream object, all operations and functions become available; however, instead of output going to the screen, it goes to a disk file. The same is true for an *istream* object, but, of course, the values enter from the file rather than from the keyboard.

Output and Input with a File

The stream library lets you extend the convenience of the standard I/O to files. You can use the output operator to put values in a file as long as you attach the file to an *ostream* object, as follows:

```
int x=123;
file_out << form("this is a test value=%d\n",x);
```

Similarly, the following shows how you can attach an *istream* object to a disk file and take input from it:

```
filebuf f_in;
if( f_in.open("file.dat",input) == 0)
    exit(1);
istream file_in(&f_in);
```

continued

```
int x;
file_in >> x;
```

This example fills *x* with the next value from *file.dat*. Note the use of an address as a parameter to the *istream* members.

Because *filebuf* and the stream objects are class types, you do not need to explicitly close a file. At the end of the program or when a function terminates, all stream and *streambuf* objects are discarded. The *ostream* class has a destructor that flushes the associated buffer. The *filebuf* destructor closes its file before the function exits. This is sufficient for most cases. However, you can also directly call the *flush()* and *close()* functions. You would need direct access to these functions, for example, if you wanted to change the current assignment to a different disk file.

Testing the State of a Stream

One important attribute of the *istream* or the *ostream* object is its current state. C++ defines four possible conditions:

- ► *_good* indicates that the last access was successful and that the end of the file has not been reached
- ► *_eof* signals that the end of the associated file has been reached
- ► *_fail* is set when the last access was not successful, but it specifies that no data was lost
- ► *_bad* indicates a catastrophic failure of the file

These values are gathered into the following enumerated data type:

enum state_value {_good=0,_eof=1,_fail=2,_bad=4};

and a corresponding state variable in each private section of both the *istream* and *ostream* declarations. You can access the current state of the stream through a series of specific stream functions. For example, if the stream is at the end of the file, *eof()* returns a value of true. Similarly, *fail()*, *bad()*, and *good()* test for their particular conditions. As an example, the following code might read the contents of the file stream *in_file*:

```
for(;;)  {
    if(in_file.eof())
        break;
    in_file >> ch;
    cout << ch;
}
```

This loop continues until the *end-of-file* condition exists, and then the *break* statement exits the loop. You can directly access the state variable through *rdstate()*. This function returns a value that you can compare against the values in the *state_value* data type. (Using the member function maintains the modularity of the class and protects your program against any future changes to its definition.)

In addition to the Boolean functions available within the stream, one function actually lets the programmer access the internal structure of the stream itself. The *clear()* function directly sets the state of the stream. The default value is *_good*, but you can pass any other legal value as a parameter to the function. Use *clear()* sparingly and carefully because it changes the value of a variable that is ordinarily set to reflect the condition of the stream. Circumstances in which you would use the function include devising a recoverable failure:

```
if(in_file.fail())  {
    cout << "recoverable failure\n";
    in_file.clear();
}
```

or forcing a condition that the program requires, such as a premature end of file:

```
while(!in_file.eof())  {
    if(test())  {
        cout << "exiting file early\n";
        in_file.clear(_eof);
    }
    .
    .
    .
```

In both examples, the *clear()* function offers an orderly and efficient way to change the state of the stream.

A Practical File Program

The *comp.c* program (Listing 7-2) illustrates the use of file streams. This program accepts two file names and compares the files character by character. It reports any differences it finds, listing the position and the contents of each file at each point of difference. The program terminates when it reaches the end of the shortest of the two files.

Listing 7-2.   A program that compares two files and reports their differences: *comp.c*

```
#include <stream.h>

main(int argc,char* argv[])
{

  if(argc < 3 )          //check for sufficient input
    cout << "error! you must specify two files to compare\n";

  filebuf f_out1;     // open it or exit
  if(f_out1.open(argv[1],input) == 0)  {
    cout << form("Sorry! I couldn't open %s\n",argv[1]);
    exit(1);
  }

  filebuf f_out2;  //...this one too
  if(f_out2.open(argv[2],input) == 0)  {
    cout << form("Sorry! I couldn't open %s\n",argv[2]);
    exit(1);
  }
  istream file1(&f_out1),file2(&f_out2); //attach the stream

  cout << "comparing files: " << str(argv[1],10) << str(argv[2],8) << "\n";
  char ch1,ch2;
  int n=0;

  for(;;n++)  {
    if(file1.eof() || file2.eof())    //loop until done
      break;
    file1.get(ch1);
    file2.get(ch2);
    if(ch1 != ch2)
```

```
        cout << form("\nposition: %2d\t\t%c\t%c",n,ch1,ch2);
    }
}
```

Note that the program takes input from the command line arguments (this procedure is the same in C++ as it is in C). First, the program checks the count variable *argc* to see if the user supplied sufficient input. If the count does not indicate that two file names were entered, the program exits with an error message. Otherwise, the program attempts to open the first file by creating and opening a *filebuf* variable. If this attempt fails, the program prints an error message and exits. This procedure is repeated with the second file. After both files are successfully opened, the program associates them with two *istream* variables, *file1* and *file2*.

Next, the program prints an information banner on the screen and begins to read the files character by character. Note that the temporary variables, *ch1* and *ch2*, are declared before entering the loop; this is in keeping with good C++ programming practice. The *for* loop increments the line counter *n* and terminates when it reaches the end of either file. The heart of the loop is the conditional that tests each character for equality. If it fails, the program displays the position and the differing characters. No explicit call to the *close()* function is performed because the end of program sequence gracefully closes all files.

This particular program is written as a UNIX "filter." The user enters file names through the standard input device, and the result comes back through standard output. You can use the operating system to redirect both of these—for example, the program could take input from a disk file and return it to another one—without any change to the program code.

The Standard I/O Functions and the Stream Library

This chapter should not give you the impression that the stream library is meant to replace the carefully developed—and debugged!—set of input and output functions in the C library. These functions are not only available in C++, they may be freely mixed with functions from the stream library.

The stream data type was developed to solve a particular problem—basic program I/O. Because the emphasis is on convenience and modularity, complex data input requirements or sophisticated output designs might not be possible using this library alone. However, for that large group of programs that require only simple input and output from keyboard to screen, stream objects offer a safe and convenient tool for rapid software development.

Using the Stream Library with User-Defined Data Types

The programmer can tap the full power of the stream library not only for built-in data types, such as integers and real numbers, but also for classes that are defined within programs. The same convenience and concise notation can be shared by user-defined types. You can use *cout* and *cin* and the operators << and >> with these types as you would use them for more ordinary output.

The advantage of using a consistent I/O scheme is clear—it makes the basic algorithm obvious, particularly to someone reading the program code for the first time. Using input/output functions is often a complicated procedure. Frequently, these operations are unique to a specific implementation or are tied to some hardware peculiarity. Even in the absence of these kinds of problems, programs filled with specialized I/O function calls tend to be both convoluted and confusing. The stream library—true to the philosophy of C++—lets a programmer hide these details within a standard interface.

As the program designer, you face only one issue—examining the new data type to decide what constitutes an appropriate I/O format for it. Once this decision is made, you only need to write the code that implements this format. Because both the output operator (<<) and the input operator (>>) are overloaded functions, your code becomes simply another version of these functions. Thus, you don't need to alter anything in the stream library itself. Your new function merely adds an alternate interface to the stream.

Redefining *ostream*

To create an output function for a new class, you must redefine the following function:

```
ostream& operator<<(ostream&, <class>)
```

to create the desired output for the new class. In this syntax, <class> represents a class declaration. You can accomplish this redefinition in one of two ways.

The simplest situation occurs when a class already has an output function. The *dateout.c* program (Listing 7-3) illustrates this case with the *julian* date class that was presented in Chapter 4. In this example, the new << operator function merely calls the existing output function.

Listing 7-3.   A date class that uses the << output operator: *dateout.c*

```
#include <stream.h>
#include <string.h>

// define some useful constant values

const int months[]={0,31,59,90,120,151,181,212,243,273,304,334,365};
const char* mnames[]={"","January","February","March",
                      "April", "May","June","July",
                      "August","September","October",
                      "November","December"};

class julian  {
    int days;       // number of days since January 1.

public:
    julian(int =0,int =0);  // first constructor: e.g. 12,3

    char *current_date();   // display the current date in month-day format
};



julian::julian(int mon,int day)
{
 days=(mon < 1 || mon > 12) ? 0 : (mon == 1) ? day : months[mon-1]+day;
}


char* julian::current_date()
{
 int mn,dy;

 if(days<=31)  {              // check to see if the month is in January
```
continued

```
      mn=1;
      dy=days;                          // no need to calculate the julian date
    }
  else
    for(int i=2;i<=12;i++)
      if(days<=months[i])  {
          mn=i;                          // set the month number
          dy=days-months[i-1];    // calculate the day
          break;
        }
    char *buffer = new char[20];

    sprintf(buffer,"%s %d",mnames[mn],dy);  // convert to string format
    return buffer;                          //return date string
}

ostream& operator<<(ostream& op,julian x)
{
  return op << x.current_date();
}

main()
{
  julian today(1,31);

  cout << today;
}
```

This example uses a simplified *julian* class. Its constructor initializes a variable declared to be of this type. The date is stored as the number of days since the first of January (for the sake of simplicity, it does not recognize leap years). The output member function *current_date()* returns the current value of an object of the class. This value is put into a character string in the form *month day*.

Although the member function *current_date()* can produce output by itself, you can also call it with an *ostream* operator function. This is what the example does. The following function:

```
ostream& operator(ostream& op,julian x)
```

redefines the output operator so that output is directly available through *cout*. Instead of using the following format:

```
julian x(1,2);
cout << x.current_date();
```

you now can use this version:

```
cout << x;
```

which maintains the consistency of the interface created by the stream library.

The *operator<<()* function calls the *current_date()* member to retrieve a converted form of the value stored in the *days* member of the class. The value is retrieved as a character string, which, in turn, is sent back through the return statement that converts it to an object of type *ostream*. The *main()* function is a simple driver that illustrates the use of these new operators.

Note that because the operator function is not a member of the *julian* class, it cannot access the private part of the class. The only way you can accomplish direct output is by calling a member function such as *current_date()*. This redefined operator cannot be a member of the class (because it already belongs to the *ostream* class), however, it can be a *friend* function. In this case, it has full access to the private data area of the *julian* class. More importantly, this kind of access let's you program the << operator directly, so that you do not need to use an intermediary member function such as *current_date()*. The *dateout2.c* program (Listing 7-4) illustrates this latter case.

Listing 7-4.   A date class that uses the << output operator as a *friend* function: *dateout2.c*

```
#include <stream.h>
#include <string.h>

// define some useful constant values

const int months[]={0,31,59,90,120,151,181,212,243,273,304,334,365};
const char* mnames[]={"","January","February","March",
                      "April", "May","June","July",
                      "August","September","October",
                      "November","December"};

class julian  {
    int days;      // number of days since January 1.
```

continued

```
public:
   julian(int =0,int =0);  // first constructor: e.g. 12,3


   friend ostream& operator<<(ostream&,julian);
};



julian::julian(int mon,int day)
{
 days=(mon < 1 || mon > 12) ? 0 : (mon == 1) ? day : months[mon-1]+day;
}


ostream& operator<<(ostream& op,julian x)
{
 int mn,dy;

 if(x.days<=31)  {                  // check to see if the month is in January
   mn=1;
   dy=x.days;                       // no need to calculate the julian date
  }
 else
   for(int i=2;i<=12;i++)
     if(x.days<=months[i])  {
        mn=i;                       // set the month number
        dy=x.days-months[i-1];    // calculate the day
        break;
      }
   char *buffer = new char[20];

   sprintf(buffer,"%s %d",mnames[mn],dy); // convert to string format
   return op  << buffer;                  // return date string
}



main()
{
 julian today(1,31);

 cout << today;
}
```

The new example is similar to the previous one (Listing 7-3), but instead of using a member function to define the output format, it declares the function *operator<<()* as a *friend* of the *julian* class. This function performs the conversion directly, without the overhead of another function call. It converts the value in days into a character string, *buffer*, which uses the format *month day*. This, then, becomes the object of the return statement. As before, the return statement converts the character string into an object of type *ostream*. As in Listing 7-3, a simple driver function illustrates the new use of the operator.

Both example programs suffer from a lack of adequate error checking. However, they thoroughly illustrate the techniques required for adding any user-defined types to the stream interface.

The Direct Input of User-Defined Types

Just as you can redefine the stream output operators to handle newly created class types, you also can customize input. The techniques are similar. For example, the following function:

```
istream& operator>>(istream&,<class>&)
```

has a reference variable to a user-defined class and the appropriate code to convert normal keyboard input into the values necessary for that class. The reference variable lets a function return a parameter value by setting up a call-by-reference situation. As with the *ostream*, this operator function can either stand alone or be a *friend* of the new class. The *datein.c* program (Listing 7-5) illustrates the latter case.

Listing 7-5. **A date class that uses the >> input operator: datein.c**

```
#include <stream.h>
#include <string.h>

// define some useful constant values

const int months[]={0,31,59,90,120,151,181,212,243,273,304,334,365};
const char* mnames[]={"","January","February","March",
                      "April", "May","June","July",
                      "August","September","October",
                      "November","December"};
```
continued

```
class julian  {
   int days;        // number of days since January 1.

public:
   julian(int =0,int =0); // first constructor: e.g. 12,3

   void new_date(char*);   // declare a member to alter the current date
   char *current_date();   // display the current date in month-day format
};



julian::julian(int mon,int day)
{
 days=(mon < 1 || mon > 12) ? 0 : (mon == 1) ? day : months[mon-1]+day;
}

void julian::new_date(char* rdate)
{
 char *mon, *dy;
 mon=strtok(rdate," ");
 dy=strtok(0," ");

 for(int i=1 ; i <= 12 ; i++)  // find the right month
   if(!strcmp(mnames[i],mon))
     break;

 if(i > 12)       // error condition
   days=0;
 else if(i == 1)   // its January, days and dy are the same
   days=atoi(dy);
 else
   days=months[i-1]+atoi(dy);  //calculate the number of days since Jan 1
}



char* julian::current_date()
{
 int mn,dy;

 if(days<=31)  {            // check to see if the month is in January
   mn=1;
   dy=days;                      // no need to calculate the julian date
```

```
      }
    else
      for(int i=2;i<=12;i++)
        if(days<=months[i])  {
            mn=i;                      // set the month number
            dy=days-months[i-1];   // calculate the day
            break;
        }
    char *buffer = new char[20];

    sprintf(buffer,"%s %d",mnames[mn],dy);   // convert to string format
    return buffer;                           //return date string
}


ostream& operator<<(ostream& op,julian x)
{
 return op << x.current_date();
}


istream& operator>>(istream& ip,julian& x)
{
 char *temp;
 temp = new char[20];

 ip.get(temp,20);

 x.new_date(temp);
 delete temp;
 return ip;
}


main()
{
 julian today(1,31);

 cout << today << "\n";
 cout << "enter new date: ";
 cin >> today;
 cout << today << "\n";
 }
```

This example requires a member function that is capable of changing the value in the data portion of the class because the *operator>>()* function is defined outside of the class. This member function is called *new_date()*. It accepts a character string of the form *month day* and converts it to the Julian date required as the *days* value. The *operator>>()* function receives keyboard input from the stream *ip* through the *get()* function. (Recall that this member of *istream* permits the entry of a character string that includes embedded blank spaces and that the >> operator only accepts input to the first white space character.) The date format includes a space between the name of the month and the day of the month. Keyboard input is stored in the variable *temp*, which the program deletes after the change is made. Note that the stream *ip* must be returned to maintain the consistency of the operator. If you cascade the input operator >> as follows:

```
cin >> x >> y;
```

the *return* statement guarantees that the chain is not broken.

To parse the parameter string, *new_date()* first strips off the month number by using the standard library function *strtok()*. (The month value is the first part of *rdate* and is separated from the rest of the string by a space.) The program then uses *strcmp()* to compare each cell in the constant array *mnames* to the string *mon*. When it finds a match, the number of the index represents the number of the month. This value is then used with the integer array, *months*, to extract the Julian date at the beginning of the previous month. The program then adds this value to the day of the month, and the calculation yields the Julian date.

The *datein2.c* program (Listing 7-6) dispenses with the member function and defines the *operator>>()* function as a *friend* to the class. As was the case with the output operator, this saves the overhead of a function call and lets the function directly access the private area of *julian*. In this example, the necessary values, *mon* (month name) and *dy* (day), are accessed as two elements by using the input operator as it is defined for character strings:

```
ip >> mon >> dy;
```

This takes advantage of the fact that user entry includes a space between the month and the day. The conversion routine is identical to that of the previous example. Again, the *istream* variable, *ip*, must be returned to maintain the "linkage" between the stream operators.

Listing 7-6.   A date class that uses the >> input operator as a
**   *friend* function: *datein2.c***

```
#include <stream.h>
#include <string.h>


// define some useful constant values

const int months[]={0,31,59,90,120,151,181,212,243,273,304,334,365};
const char* mnames[]={"","January","February","March",
                      "April", "May","June","July",
                      "August","September","October",
                      "November","December"};


class julian  {
    int days;       // number of days since January 1.

public:
    julian(int =0,int =0);  // first constructor: e.g. 12,3

    friend ostream& operator<<(ostream&,julian);
    friend istream& operator>>(istream&,julian&);
};


julian::julian(int mon,int day)
{
 days=(mon < 1 || mon > 12) ? 0 : (mon == 1) ? day : months[mon-1]+day;
}


ostream& operator<<(ostream& op,julian x)
{
 int mn,dy;

 if(x.days<=31)  {                  // check to see if the month is in January
   mn=1;
   dy=x.days;                       // no need to calculate the julian date
  }
 else
   for(int i=2;i<=12;i++)
     if(x.days<=months[i])  {
        mn=i;                       // set the month number
        dy=x.days-months[i-1];      // calculate the day
```

continued

```
          break;
      }
    char *buffer = new char[20];


    sprintf(buffer,"%s %d",mnames[mn],dy);  // convert to string format
    return op  << buffer;                    // return date string
}



istream& operator>>(istream& ip,julian& x)
{
 char *mon, *dy;
 mon = new char[20];
 dy = new char[20];


 ip >> mon >> dy;


 for(int i=1 ; i <= 12 ; i++)  // find the right month
   if(!strcmp(mnames[i],mon))
     break;


 if(i > 12)      // error condition
   x.days=0;
 else if(i == 1)   // it's January, x.days and dy are the same
   x.days=atoi(dy);
 else
   x.days=months[i-1]+atoi(dy);  //the number of days since Jan 1
 return ip;
}


main()
{
 julian today(1,31);
 cout << today << "\n";


 cout << "enter today's date: ";
 cin >> today;
 cout << today << "\n";
}
```

Review questions

1. What three major components make up the stream library?

2. What stream objects correspond to C's *stdin*, *stdout*, and *stderr*?

3. Can the >>, input operator be cascaded to allow entry of more than one data item?

4. What two ways can output values be formatted before being sent to the *cout* object?

5. How is a disk file opened and prepared for input or output?

6. What function lets the programmer check for an *end-of-file* condition?

7. What does the *clear()* function do?

Programming projects

1. Expand the calculator program in Listing 7-1 so that it can display output in hexadecimal and octal formats. Add real-number capability. Be sure to add error checking.

2. Modify the calculator program so that it can handle expressions that contain multiple operators.

3. Change the file comparison program in Listing 7-2 so that it can compare two, three, or more files.

4. Using the *julian* class (*datin2.c*) as a model, create a time-of-day class. Be sure to define this class for the << and >> I/O operators.

Summary

This chapter explored the operation of the stream library, a standard C++ library of functions that can be used to generate simple input and output. It was devised as an adjunct to those functions common to C and C++, such as *printf()*, *scanf()*, and, more importantly, file manipulation routines.

In the realm of simple I/O, the stream library offers substantial advantages:

▶ the functions are less general and more specific and thus produce smaller, more efficient program code

► the syntax is more straightforward, particularly with its use of overloaded operators

► a more controlled and consistent interface model unifies both device- and disk-file operations

Nearly every function found in the traditional C library has a counterpart in the stream library, including the following:

► character, integer, and real number input

► formatted output

► character and character string I/O

The benefits of the stream library also can be extended to user-defined classes by redefining the *ostream& operator<<()* and *istream& operator>>()* functions.

8

Using C++ with MS-DOS

8

Using C++ with MS-DOS

This chapter examines the development of C++ programs in the MS-DOS environment. If you are accustomed to software development on "larger" operating systems, such as UNIX, you soon will discover that MS-DOS does not provide standard, integrated tools that support a conscious, structured design methodology. On the other hand, if you work regularly in the MS-DOS environment, you probably are familiar with the many third-party C libraries that attempt to fill this gap. However, these "add-ons" suffer from the drawback that they are merely support programs and therefore do not provide an integral solution. C++ addresses the problem of controllable design in the MS-DOS environment by providing the programmer with an approach that is built into the structure of the language itself.

As you have seen, C++ has all the advantages of C, including efficiency and low-level access, plus high-level structures that directly support structured design. The *class* data type in C++ lets the program designer create objects that can be combined into larger designs and also can be saved and reused in future projects. The hierarchical capabilities inherent in derived classes allow an even greater range for creating coherent designs. At the same time, low-level, operating system, and hardware-specific details can be safely encapsulated in the private parts of objects. None of this power is purchased at the expense of memory or program speed: The size of a C++ program varies only slightly from its C analog, and program speed is similarly controlled.

C++ also offers the MS-DOS programmer the advantage of being a programming language that was designed for an environment only slightly larger than the MS-DOS environment. It is not a massive support subsystem that was pared down to fit on a small machine. In fact, most C++ implementations run well on currently available PC hardware.

The preceding chapters have explored the intricacies of C++ in a general way. So far, all the example programs run on a wide variety of machines—including those that support MS-DOS. This chapter, however, examines in great detail some examples that use features specific to the IBM-PC world. These examples illustrate how C++ can simplify the increasingly complex programming tasks required for this group of machines.

The Project: Creating a Serial Port Object

One of the most arcane, yet useful, parts of a PC is the serial port. America is rapidly becoming a networked nation, and it is increasingly rare to find an owner of a personal computer who does not use a modem to communicate with the outside world. In addition, many projects involve direct communication between computers or between a computer and some peripheral device. Often, these connections must be established through the serial port. As a programmer, you probably will often be called on to implement some form of serial communications, either in a program dedicated to this purpose or in a module for some other program.

However, accessing the serial port is often a complicated and misunderstood process. The need for speed—and thus the necessity for low-level access—militates against the usual techniques of structured programming. Adding serial interface capability to a program often leads to code that is difficult to follow and that tends to obscure overall program structure. The best strategy for the programmer would be to hide the details of serial access from the higher-level parts of the program.

Although there are successful traditional techniques for creating a library of port access functions (some commercial packages even exist), designing a port object as a C++ class gives you all the structure that the other techniques offer, but it also gives you the flexibility of using a serial port in a program as easily as you use a file, an array, or any other common data structure. Now, let's explore this definition in detail.

Basic Elements of the Serial Port

Let's start with the basics—the simple concept of computer-to-computer communication. If you're familiar with the mechanics of serial data transfer, you might want to skip the next two sections.

The general procedure for this type of communication is as follows: a character is encoded as a binary number (its ASCII code), and the number is transmitted one bit at a time (see Figure 8-1). The computer and its operating system handle the translation of the character into a bit pattern. What you need to control is the physical connection between the two systems—a cable (actually a set of wires) and the software connection (the commands and signals that tell the hardware to put a bit pattern on the wire). There are many excellent books that cover these topics in detail, including *Understanding Data Communications* and the *Modern Connections Bible*, both published by Howard

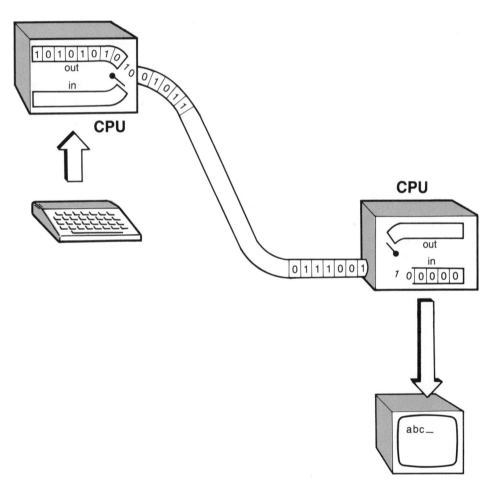

Figure 8-1.   A general outline of bit-by-bit transmission

W. Sams & Company. However, this chapter examines only the minimum number of details that you need to develop a basic working model.

The physical details that you need to know are simple and obvious. In connecting any two systems, the most common plug type is a 25-pin connector known popularly as a DB25 connector. DB9 connectors, which have only nine pins, can also be used. The following discussion assumes that you are using a DB25 connector, but you must adjust the information to fit your local situation.

Each pin on the connector performs a specific service. One pin transmits the bit; one receives it. Another pin indicates that the physical port is ready to receive a new bit (Clear To Send), and one indicates that the port on the sending machine is ready to send (Data Set Ready). Figure 8-2 shows the functions and possible pin allocations for the commonly-used DB25 connector.

In addition to the cable that spans two systems, a "null modem" must be interposed between any direct computer-to-computer connection. This device performs several important crossovers between specific pins on each system. For example, it connects the transmit pin of the sending system to the receive pin of the destination computer. Figure 8-3 shows the other important connections and crossovers.

Except in some specialized applications, the crossover scheme is symmetrical, so that both connected machines can either transmit or receive data.

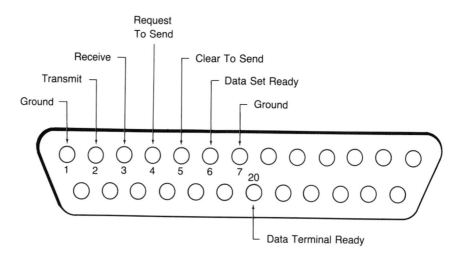

Figure 8-2. Pin assignments for an RS232 port

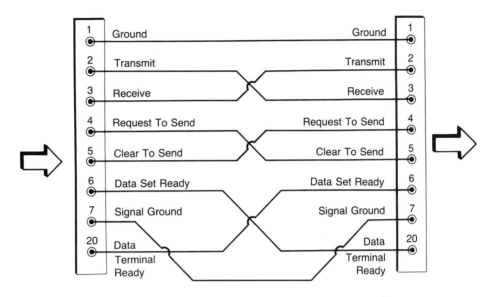

Figure 8-3. Null modem services

The Software Port

The hardware that connects two computer systems is actually only the beginning of data communications. After you set up the cable and physically connect the machines, you must turn your attention to the port as a software entity—a kind of programmable device. The configuration of and access to the port is a collaboration between the underlying hardware and the software of the operating system. This is the realm in which the advantages of C++ become manifest. However, before you examine these advantages, you need to understand the "software port" in greater detail.

An IBM-PC or compatible computer actually creates two ports for the user—*COM1:* and *COM2:* (some newer machines accommodate more). You can access these high-level logical devices in a relatively straightforward manner. The MS-DOS operating system configures and initializes these ports and lets you change many of their parameters. You can use the *mode* command, for example, to change the data transfer speed, or "baud rate," of the port, as well as other key values. Unfortunately, this high-level access is inadequate for all but the most simple of tasks. This convenience of access is purchased at the price of layers of software that reduce the performance of this subsystem. Another important disadvantage is that prior to Version 3.3 of MS-DOS, the operating system recognized only two serial ports.

Actually, the term "port" is ambiguous. Serial and parallel ports are high-level devices. However, the CPU chip itself uses a special address space that is associated with external devices. This port addressing space is, in some important ways, analogous to the direct memory space that contains the system's ROM and RAM storage. Each one of these low level port locations is associated with an address. The CPU provides access to this address with a special machine-code instruction; sending a value to this kind of port is similar to placing a value in main memory. You could create an assembly language module that performs this access and then link it to a C++ program. However, most implementations of C (and, correspondingly, C++) already have a function that lets you access these ports. The examples in this section use the Microsoft C functions *outp()* for writing to and *inp()* for reading from this address space (see Figure 8-4).

At the level below the COM devices, you can readily access the port hardware while still allowing the system to perform the initialization and configuration. The heart of each serial port is a device known as a UART (Universal Asynchronous Receiver Transmitter). From a programmer's perspective this device is a series of seven contiguous one-byte locations that are addressed through the CPU's physical ports, or absolute locations on the processor's bus. The first location contains either the character that has been sent or the character that will be sent. The remaining locations let you access the various control functions and status flags of the UART. By placing special values into these control locations, you can toggle the functions on and off. Analyzing the status of these location values indicates the state of the port.

These port locations are commonly known as *registers*. Figure 8-5 outlines the organization of the serial port. Each serial port has an associated *base* address—*COM1:* is at 0x3F8, and *COM2:* is at 0x2F8—which is the location of the register that contains the data itself. The control and status registers are addressed as offset values from this location. The following example uses only two of these—the data register at *base address* and the status register at *base address* + 5. In fact, only two of the eight bits in this latter byte are important to the serial port program—bit 5 and bit 0 (see Figure 8-6).

Sending a Byte from Port to Port

So far, this brief discussion of the hardware needed to connect two computer systems and the software configuration of the serial port has

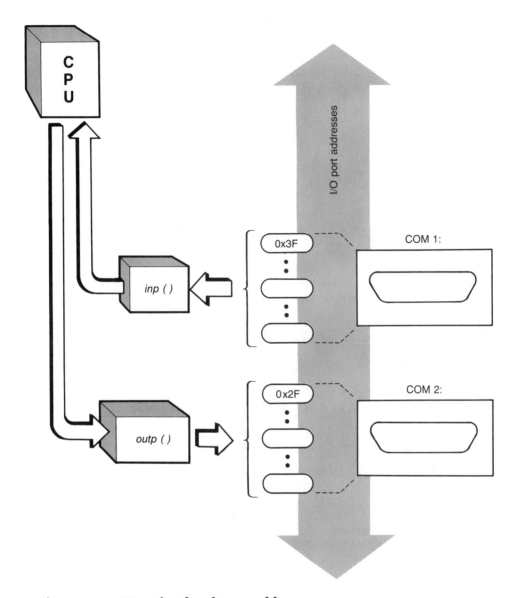

Figure 8-4. **Mapping hardware addresses**

left unstated the basic algorithm for doing any kind of communication. You can use several methods for sending values back and forth between two computer systems. MS-DOS contains two system calls—one designed to send a character to a serial port and another to retrieve a character. The advantage of using these is that all programs that employ these functions are portable. However, the performance level of this

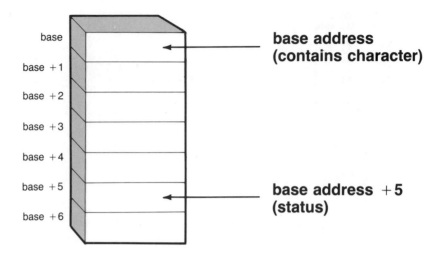

Figure 8-5.   Organization of a serial port

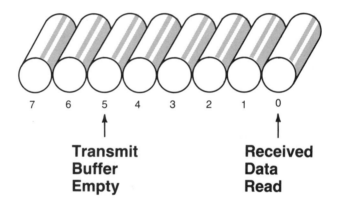

Figure 8-6.   Interesting bits in the port status register (offset 5)

arrangement is unacceptably low. For example, these functions recognize only the first port, *COM1:*, and offer no method for controlling its parameters. A better solution involves going directly to the hardware ports and creating a function that is tied into the interrupt system of the CPU. The advantage of this method is that the code produced will be efficient and will work at any data transmission rate. The disadvantage is that it produces complicated functions that depend on the low-level input/output routines of the *BIOS*. This can lead to problems because there are often small but significant differences between the BIOS of the IBM-PC and the "compatible BIOS" used in some PC clone systems, especially the older ones.

This chapter demonstrates the advantages that C++ has over traditional programming languages when it comes to taming hardware and making it easier to deal with. These programs steer a middle course between using the basic MS-DOS I/O functions and the correspondingly complex, interrupt driven ones. The programs directly access the hardware ports, but they depend on clean and efficient C++ code to effect the transfers rather than on the more effective interrupt driven functions. You can consult many good sources about how to create these more sophisticated systems. The modular nature of C++ will let you easily convert these examples for use with interrupt driven systems.

Transmitting a Character

To send a character to another port, you must perform the following three distinct actions:

- ► initialize the receiving port so that it agrees in all respects with the transmitting port
- ► wait until the receiving port is ready to accept a new character
- ► send the character through the transmitting port

This simple three-step process hides a great deal of low-level detail; fortunately, the programmer can safely ignore most of it.

Initializing the ports is a one-time operation. Once you set a port to a specified configuration, it stays in that configuration until you reset it. In a typical situation, a single port configuration is used for many character transmissions. This initialization requires several accesses to the low-level hardware ports that make up the high-level serial port.

The second step in the transmission process is to test the status of the port. The receiving port signals that it is ready for another character by setting bit 5 in the status register at location *base address* + 5. The transmitting program must continually monitor this hardware location, so that it knows when to send another character.

The final step is to send the character itself. This is an easy process—you simply perform an output operation to the port's base address. The underlying hardware subsystem sends the character, bit by bit, through the line to the receiving port. The operating system automatically coordinates bit transmission; the serial port program needs only to coordinate at the character level.

Let's translate these three steps into some C++ code:

```
for(;;)  {
   status=inp(com+5);
   if((status & 0x20) != 0)  {
     outp(com,ch);
     break;
    }
 }
```

Recall that the *inp()* function accepts a hardware port address as a parameter and returns the value that is currently stored in that port. Here, the status register is stored in a variable called *status*. (This function is part of the Microsoft C library; other compilers might provide this function under a different name.) To extract the appropriate bit value, the program performs a logical *and* operation on the status byte and a mask variable that contains a template of all zeroes except for the fifth bit position. (The hexadecimal value 0x20 produces the appropriate bit pattern—0010.) If bit 5 is not set, the resulting value is 0. However, if the receiving port is ready for a new character, the status bit is set, and the value that results from the *and* operation is greater than zero.

Note that these examples perform no explicit initialization. Because the programs use the standard serial ports, they depend on the operating system to perform this necessary step in the process. Remember that you do not open and close ports as you do files; ports remain open and available as long as the computer is running.

When *status* becomes greater than zero, the program can send another character out the port. This is accomplished by using the hardware port output function *outp()*, which takes two parameters—the base address of the port and the character to be sent. As it did with *inp()*, the UART subsystem performs the bit-by-bit transmission. A *break* statement exits from the wait loop. If the result of the masking operation is zero, control passes to the *for* statement and the process begins again.

Receiving a Character

Receiving a character at the serial port—the complementary operation to sending—requires a similar three-step process:

- ► initialize the port
- ► wait until the transmitting port is ready to send a new character
- ► perform an input operation on the port

The initialization step is the same for the receiving port as it was for the transmitting port. Even the wait loop is similar. Of course, the goal in this case is to perform input, and the code to accomplish this task is as follows:

```
for(;;)  {
  status = inp(com+5);
  if((status & 0x01) != 0)  {
    ch = inp(com);
    return ch;
  }
}
```

As with the transmit code, a wait loop is established to read the status of the port. This time the important part of the status register is bit 0, which contains the "data ready" status. As soon as this is set, the port can read a new character. This is accomplished by invoking the *inp()* function to read the base address. The resulting value is returned, thus accomplishing a graceful exit from the wait loop.

A Serial Port Class

Now that you understand the basic algorithm, let's integrate this low-level software access with the high-level features of C++. One problem with a serial port in any ordinary C program is that it always appears as a special entity, as something that must be treated differently from variables, memory locations, or even disk files. Also, too many of its details are visible; it carries a lot of baggage for such a simple operation as sending a character from one system to another. The best way to handle the port is to devise a way to "package" it so that most of its details can be ignored and access can be reduced to the same simple operation that manipulates any other value-handling object.

The solution is a *port* class, with which you can define variables of type *port* and use them anywhere in a program where you need this kind of access. What's even better, you don't need to explicitly open the port, send the values, and then close the port. You can hide all of these details inside the port definition.

What elements do you include in the *port* class? You have a wide latitude here, and you should choose with an eye to its eventual use and expansion. Let's take a first pass at a *port* class definition:

```
class port  {
   unsigned com;
   char* name;
public:
   port(int,char*);
   ~port();
   void pchar(int);
   int gchar();
};
```

You need to include the base address of the port, or at least some way of identifying it to the system; this goes into *com*. Because it is useful to have a user-defined name as well, the example adds a simple character string member called *name*. You should put both these members in the private part of the class for a number of reasons, not the least of which is to protect the rest of the program from knowing too much about the actual configuration of a serial port.

As the class is configured, the member functions available for access are general-purpose functions consistent with a wide range of serial port configurations. After all, at this basic level you merely want to send a character out to a port (*pchar()*) or to read the next character at the port (*gchar()*). It's hard to imagine a general-purpose serial port that wouldn't allow these two operations. The code is, of course, hidden in the implementation of the class. If you obtain new serial hardware or, more likely, you decide to use a more sophisticated access routine, the rest of the program need not be changed. The *port.h* example (Listing 8-1) shows one implementation of this class.

Listing 8-1.   A simple *port* class: *port.h*

```
// NO_EXT_KEYS is a necessary flag value for Microsoft C
// version 5


#define NO_EXT_KEYS


// include the necessary header files
```

```
#include "\c5\include\conio.h"
#include <string.h>

const com1 = 0X3F8,        // set the address of the standard ports
      com2 = 0X2F8;

class port  {
  unsigned com;            // base address of the port
  char* name;             // user supplied port name

public:
  port(int,char*);             // initialize the port
 ~port() { delete name; }      // perform cleanup
  char *wport() { return name;} // what's in a name?
  void pchar(int);        // send a single character to the port
  int  gchar();           // get a single character from the port
};


port::port(int pnum,char* n)
{
 name = new char[strlen(n)+1];   // set up the port name member
 strcpy(name,n);                 // initialize it to user value
 com = (pnum != 1) ? com1 : com2; // set the port address
}

void port::pchar(int ch)
{
 unsigned status;
 for(;;)  {                      // wait loop
   status=inp(com+5);           // get status
   if((status & 0x20) != 0)  {  // check it
     outp(com,ch);              // send the character out
     break;                     // exit the wait loop
   }
  }
}

int port::gchar()
{
 int ch;
 unsigned status;
```

continued

```
for(;;)  {                    // initialize wait loop
   status=inp(com+5);         // get status
   if((status & 0x01) !=0)  { // check for character ready
     ch = inp(com);           // get it from the port
     return ch;               // send it to the caller
   }
 }
}
```

This listing shows the complete definition of a simple *port* class. Several lines in this file need to be clarified. The *#define* at the top of the file is a necessary flag value for the Microsoft header files; without it, the C++ preprocessor cannot set up the compile properly. Along the same lines, you should explicitly call the *conio.h* header file. Depending on the way you have set up your directories, C++ might not recognize this file as a standard file. The *string.h* header file is needed because you must use the string manipulation functions in the standard library. (You might have to change these details to conform to the compiler your C++ package uses.)

MS-DOS 3.1 and earlier versions recognize only two serial ports. This port class is set up in a similar way, although you could easily add any number of ports as long as you know the hardware address of the UART. The nice thing about *COM1:* and *COM2:* is that they are always at the same addresses—0X3F and 0X2F, respectively. These values are assigned to a pair of constants that the class uses later. Note that you should always *wire* this type of information into the class rather than requiring that other programs that use this class know about ports and addresses. As you'll see in the definition of the constructor, all the calling function needs to supply is 0 for *COM1:* and 1 for *COM2:*.

The constructor for the class, *port()*, takes two parameters—a number to indicate the port and a name for that port. A small member function, *wport()*, can access this name, but nothing is done with it in the current example. Still, this type of redundancy is useful because it gives the designer another way of referring to this object. A program could easily create more than one port object and have them all refer to the same physical port; this is, in fact, a typical situation. Using only the port address, you might have trouble differentiating these objects. Using names, differentiation would be a straightforward matter.

The *port* class doesn't really *open* the port in the strictest sense of the word. The ports are available as soon as the operating system is loaded, and they remain open until you turn off the computer. This class merely gives you access to these resources. As a result, the initialization step, which is part of the task of the constructor, does little more than set the proper port address in the private member *com*. It accomplishes this by using a condition operator to test the port number (*pnum*) supplied as a parameter. Note that if the user enters an illegal port number, the program uses *COM1:* as the default. The constructor also allocates and copies the supplied value from the parameter *n* into *name*. The destructor similarly has little to do; it merely returns the memory locations used by *name* to the pool of available space.

At the heart of *port* are two I/O functions—*pchar()* sends a single character out the port specified by *com*, and *gchar()* gets the character waiting at this port. The code that implements these member functions uses the algorithms discussed earlier. A wait loop continually tests the status of the port, and the *inp()* and *outp()* functions directly access the hardware ports.

An Enhanced Port Class

Now that you have solved the basic problem of moving a single character between two systems, you can build on this framework to create a data type that transfers an entire line of text. Because text in the real world is often handled line by line rather than character by character, this is an important design consideration. The *port2.h* example (Listing 8-2) shows the declaration of a new *port* class.

Listing 8-2. A declaration of an enhanced *port* class: *port2.h*

```
class port   {
    unsigned com;        // base address of the port
    char* name;          // user supplied port name
    void pchar(int);     // send a single character to the port
    int  gchar();        // get a single character from the port

public:
    port(int,char*);              // initialize the port
    ~port() { delete name; }      // perform cleanup
    char *wport() { return name;} // what's in a name?
    void send(char*);      // send a line out the port
    char* receive();       // get a line from the port
};
```

This new declaration and the original have two differences. The most striking difference is the addition of two new member functions, send() and receive(). However, this isn't the only change. The *pchar()* and *gchar()* functions have been moved from the public part of the class to the private part, so that they are available only to the member functions.

Isolating the two basic character functions makes sense. These members are most sensitive to the underlying hardware—if it changes, they must change as well. The public part of a class should serve only as an interface to the rest of the program. By removing these low-level access routines from it, you can be assured that no other part of the program will come to depend on the idiosyncrasies of this particular implementation.

The code for the new member function *send()* is in Listing 8-3. This simple function is built on repeated calls to the now private *pchar()* member. The character string to be sent to the remote system is passed into *send()* as a parameter. A *for* loop moves through the string character by character, passing each character to the port one at a time. Because it returns no value, the *send()* function is declared *void*.

Listing 8-3.   The new member function *send()*

```
void port::send(char* buffer)
{
 for(int i=0 ; i <= strlen(buffer) ; i++)
   pchar(buffer[i]);
}
```

The complement to *send()* is *receive()*, the code of which is in Listing 8-4. This function does the reverse of *send()*. It constructs a string by adding each character to a buffer as it comes across the communication line.

Listing 8-4.   The member function *receive()*

```
char* port::receive()
{
 char buffer[80];

 for(int i=0 ; i < 80 ; i++)          // loop through the buffer
   if((buffer[i]=gchar()) == '\0')    // fill char by char
     break;
 return buffer;                       // send it back
}
```

The *receive()* function takes no parameters. It declares a temporary buffer that is filled inside a *for* loop by repeated calls to the *gchar()* member function. One problem that you must resolve is how big to make the buffer. Because this port has been created to be a line-oriented object, 80 characters seems to be the most reasonable size for the buffer. In fact, the loop continues until it receives an *end-of-string* mark, '\0'. At that point, the new value of the buffer is returned to the caller. (For the sake of simplicity, these functions omit error-handling.)

In order to use this new class you need some testbed programs. The *sendstr.c* (Listing 8-5) program sends a specific character string out the port. You must specify the string on the command line, and the program tests for this before it continues. If the string contains embedded blanks, you must enclose them in double quotation marks (") or the program interprets them as more than one command line argument. Note that you must adjust the port declaration to your local configuration; this example uses *COM1:*.

Listing 8-5. A send program based on the enhanced *port* class: *sendstr.c*

```
#include <stream.h>


main(int argc,char* argv[])
{
 port x(0,"com1:");      // declare a port variable


 if(argc == 1)  {        // command line message only
    cout << "please include message\n";
    exit(1);
  }
 x.send(argv[1]);        // send it to the port
}
```

The complementary receiving program, *recvstr.c*, is in Listing 8-6. The receiving computer is set up to accept data on *COM2:*. This program first declares a buffer and a port. A quick call to the *receive()* member of the port inside a *strcpy()* transfers the value from the wire to *buffer*. You display the value in this character string variable in the usual way.

Listing 8-6.   A receive program based on the enhanced *port* class: *recvstr.c*

```
#include <stream.h>

main()
{
 char buffer[80];                 // create a message buffer
 port x(1,"com2:");                // declare a port
 strcpy(buffer,x.receive());  // fill buffer
 cout << form("%s\n",buffer);  // display it on screen
}
```

Programming projects

1. Expand the class definition in Listing 8-2 to include explicit initial-ization in the constructor. Modify the destructor to return the port to its normal configuration.

2. Reimplement the port members *send()* and *receive()* as over-loaded operators.

A Hierarchy of Port Classes

The serial port on an IBM-PC is obviously a useful device. You can use it to communicate with a mainframe or another PC—either directly or through a modem—or even to communicate with peripheral devices, such as printers or mice. These applications will have some common elements and some elements that are unique to specific situations. A printer might need special *setup* sequences; a modem might require a special character to communicate with the device itself. The example *port* class has already evolved from performing simple character trans-fers to sending and receiving a character string. How do you accom-modate the need to build new features onto a common base of func-tionality?

Whenever you face a situation in which a core of common functions can be used by several specialized applications, the C++ derived class offers an efficient and structured solution. Rather than create a family of disparate objects, each one unconnected to the others even though they often share the same code, you should isolate the common operations and put them in a base class. After you create this base, you can derive an entire series of specialized classes from it. Each would contain special operations for a particular task without unnecessarily duplicating the basic configuration.

The Base Class

The base class for a serial port is similar to the original *port* class. However, several modifications need to be made to make it more general. For the revised declaration, see *port3.h* (Listing 8-7).

Listing 8-7.   A modified *port* to serve as a base class: *port3.h*

```
class port  {
  unsigned com;          // base address of the port
public:
  port(int)  { com = (pnum != 1) ? com1 : com2; } // set address
  void pchar(int);       // send a single character to the port
  int  gchar();          // get a single character from the port
};
```

The *send()* and *receive()* members have been removed—they should be members of the derived class. Also gone is the *name* member. The new *port* is designed as a more generic serial device, something very basic upon which you can build specialized and unique devices. Because the *name* member is missing, the vestigial access to it, *wport()*, must also be removed. The constructor is modified accordingly, so that its only parameter is the port number. The base class does not have a destructor.

This stripped base class now includes only *com*, the address of the hardware that underlies the port, a constructor that sets this address in *com*, and the basic character functions *pchar()* and *gchar()*. This selection underscores the design goal of finding the minimum functions common to any port.

The *pchar()* and *gchar()* functions have the same implementation as they did in the original definition. The constructor member, however, is simpler because it needs only to set the address of the port. In fact, it is now simple enough to be defined as an *inline* function.

The Derived Class *serial*

The base class is an earlier and more "primitive" definition of *port* that retains only the most elementary ability to send to and receive from the port. Now, let's configure a more realistic port, one that can transmit entire messages between two computer systems.

First, you need to create a new class that treats the serial port as a character string device. The declaration for this new class, *serial*, is found in *serial.h* (Listing 8-8).

Listing 8-8. A declaration of a derived *serial* class: *serial.h*

```
class serial : port  {
  char *dname;
public:
  serial(int,char*);
  ~serial()  { delete dname; }
  char *wport() { return dname;} // show the port name
  void send(char*);      // send a line out to the serial device
  char* receive();       // get a line from the serial device
  };
```

The declaration indicates that the class *serial* is derived from *port* and that this is a private base class. The latter attribute is consistent with the basic design criterion—the base class should contain only the common functions. It is neither desirable nor necessary for any specific *port* type to allow direct character access to the port. For the most part, the specialized classes will define highly restricted kinds of access. You don't want to give another programmer the capability of "breaking" the specification by going beneath the structure to the underlying functionality of the basic hardware itself; this would defeat the purpose of defining a *port* class. By declaring the base as private, you restrict the character access functions to internal use by the derived class. Therefore, these functions won't be directly available through a variable declared as type *serial*.

The only private member of *serial* is the port name, *dname*. None of the code responsible for character transmission uses this value, but you can use it as an identifier for programs that open and close many different ports that share the same physical device. (This might be useful in a multitasking PC operating system such as OS/2.) In any case, the member *wport()* is included to let you access this character string. The destructor is the same as the original *port* class destructor, and it is certainly small enough to be defined as *inline*.

The constructor function *serial()* is similar to the constructor in the earlier *port* class. However, it performs an additional task: It not only accepts the parameter *pnum* for itself, but it also passes the parameter to its base class *port* for initialization. Its only other task is to set *dname* (see Listing 8-9). The *send()* and *receive()* member functions are identical to their counterparts in the original *port* class.

Listing 8-9. The constructor for the class *serial*

```
serial::serial(int pnum,char* device) : (pnum)
{
  dname = new char[strlen(device)+1];  //set up the port name
  strcpy(dname,device);                // initialize it
}
```

Finally, let's test this new class in a program. The *sendstr2.c* program (Listing 8-10) sends a line of text to the serial port. You must include the line of text as a command argument, or the program exits with an error message. The example expects the serial port to be *COM1:*, but you can, of course, rewrite it to accommodate any configuration.

**Listing 8-10. A sample send program to test the *serial* class:
sendstr2.c**

```
#include <stream.h>

main(int argc,char* argv[])
{
  serial x(0,"com1:");  // declare a serial object

  if(argc == 1)  {       // scold them for no message
     cout << "please include message\n";
     exit(1);
   }
  x.send(argv[1]);   // send it
}
```

The complement to the send program, *recvstr2.c*, is in Listing 8-11. This accepts a string of characters from the port and displays them on the screen. This program is set up for *COM2:*, but you can use it with any port that your system supports.

Listing 8-11.   A receive program to complement the send program: *recvstr2.c*

```
#include <stream.h>

main()
{
 char buffer[80];

 serial x(1,"com2:");      // declare a serial type
 strcpy(buffer,x.receive()); // get a string and copy it
 cout << form("%s\n",buffer); // display it
}
```

Programming projects

1. Reimplement the *port* base class (Listing 8-7), so that it uses the MS-DOS interrupt system.
2. Using *port* as a base class, define a class that handles a serial printer. Include alternate character sets and the necessary peripheral initialization.

Packaging a Class

This chapter has focused on one interesting example that uses C++ within the context of MS-DOS. It showed the important interaction of the hardware, the operating system, and C++ and how to design some new data types, the *port* and *serial* classes. You can use these classes as a resource for many different programs that need to access the serial communication port. You only need to solve a problem once; then, you can create an object that you can use over and over again.

Another aspect of this object must be discussed—how to package it for reuse. So far, the main purpose of this chapter was to look at the details of the specifications and definitions. To this end, both the specification of the class—the variable members and member functions— and the code that implements the member functions have been included in the same file. However, this simple approach is neither the only possibility nor even the best one. Let's now investigate a different organization.

Two Tasks in Creating a *class* Data Type

The creation of a *class* data type can be divided into two relatively well-defined tasks:

► the declaration of the class

► the definition of the member functions

The declaration sets the basic structure and the organization of the new type. You identify the types and names of all of the variable members of the class. You also must specify the return type of each member function as well as its parameter list. The blueprint of the operation of the class is complete when you assign each member to either the private, public, or protected sections of the class.

The definition of the member functions, in contrast to the declaration of the class as a whole, involves writing the code that implements each function. This traditional programming task need not be physically juxtaposed to the declaration. After you create the template for a class, the implementing code needs only refer to the template. It makes sense to put the class definition in a header file and the implementation of the class in a separate file. After you compile the latter file, you can use it in its object form by including the header in each file in which a class of this type is defined and linking in the object file. The header file then serves as a kind of bridge between the program that uses the class and the actual instructions that were used to compile it.

However, there are some restrictions to this procedure. The declaration of the class must come before any function definitions. Also, you must specify some *inline* functions within this declaration. Although these restrictions might seem contradictory, they really are concerned with two different things.

Compiling and Forgetting

After you create a new data type—such as the example *port* class—and debug it, you do not need to recompile the code every time you use it. To use this class, all you really need to do is to link the object file that contains its implementing functions with the new program. In other words, you can compile a class definition to an object file—one with the extension *.obj*—and use this while keeping the source file in a safe place. If your business is creating software modules, this procedure makes even more sense—you don't relinquish any secrets because you will not be distributing any source code.

Of course, creating an object form of a class is not as simple as the previous paragraph implies. One important element is missing. You must also create an interface module to serve as a bridge between the object code and the program that will use it. The class declaration is that bridge. In addition to the object code, you must supply the user of the module with a file that contains this declaration. The *port4.h* example (Listing 8-12) shows the contents of an interface file for a simple *port* class. The interface file is typically a header—or *.h*—file, which must be included in each file that contains code that refers to the new class.

Listing 8-12. An interface file for a simple *port* class: *port4.h*

```
const com1 = OX3F8,        // set the address of the standard ports
      com2 = OX2F8;


class port  {
  unsigned com;            // base address of the port
  char* name;             // user supplied port name


public:
  port(int,char*);               // initialize the port
 ~port() { delete name; }        // perform cleanup
  char *wport() { return name;}  // what's in a name?
  void pchar(int);         // send a single character to the port
```

```
   int  gchar();          // get a single character from the port
};
```

This two-step approach of using an object file and a header file let's you add even more structure and modularity to a program.

Programming projects:

1. Repackage the *port* class as a library; that is, an object code file that contains the implementation of the class member functions and a header file that serves as an interface to these functions.

2. Do the same to the class *serial*. Remember to implement this class using the new version of *port*.

The Complete *port* and *serial* Class Listing

For your convenience in using the serial port code in your own projects, *portclas.h* (Listing 8-13) contains the entire declaration and definition of the class *port*. In like manner, *serclas.h* (Listing 8-14) shows the complete *serial* class. In the interest of clarity, the discussion in this chapter omitted some minor parts of these definitions.

Listing 8-13.   The complete *port* class definition: *portclas.h*

```
#define NO_EXT_KEYS

#include "\c5\include\conio.h"
#include <string.h>

const com1 = OX3F8,      // set the address of the standard ports

      com2 = OX2F8;

class port  {
   unsigned com;         // base address of the port
   char* name;           // user supplied port name            continued
```

```
  void pchar(int);        // send a single character to the port
  int  gchar();           // get a single character from the port
public:
  port(int,char*);        // constructor initializes the port
 ~port() { delete name;} // destructor performs cleanup
  char *wport() { return name;} // report ports name
  void send(char*);       // send a line out the port
  char* receive();        // get a line from the port
};

void port::pchar(int ch)
{
 unsigned status;
 for(;;)  {
   status=inp(com+5);      // loop until ready to send
   if((status & 0x20) != 0)  {
     outp(com,ch);         // send a character out
     break;
    }
  }
}

int port::gchar()
{
 int ch;
 unsigned status;
 for(;;)  {
   status = inp(com+5);   // loop until character waits
   if((status & 0x01) != 0)  {
     ch = inp(com);        // get it
     return ch;            // send it back
    }
  }
}

port::port(int pnum,char* n)
{
 name = new char[strlen(n)+1]; //set up the port name member
 strcpy(name,n);               // initialize it

 com = (pnum != 1) ? com1 : com2;
}
```

```
void port::send(char* buffer)
{
 for(int i=0 ; i <= strlen(buffer) ; i++)    // empty the buffer
   pchar(buffer[i]);                          // out the port
}


char* port::receive()
{
 char buffer[80];

 for(int i=0 ; i < 80 ; i++)
   if( (buffer[i] = gchar()) == '\0') // loop until end of string
     break;
 return buffer;               // return buffer full
}
```

Listing 8-14. The complete serial class definition: *serclas.h*

```
#define NO_EXT_KEYS

#include "\c5\include\conio.h"
#include <string.h>

const com1 = 0X3F8,      // set the address of the standard ports

     com2 = 0X2F8;


///////////////////////////////////////////////////////////////
// BASE CLASS:  port
///////////////////////////////////////////////////////////////

class port  {
  unsigned com;          // base address of the port
public:
  port(int p)  { com = (p != 1) ? com1 : com2; } // constructor
  void pchar(int);       // send a single character to the port
  int  gchar();          // get a single character from the port
};

void port::pchar(int ch)
{
```

continued

```
    unsigned status;
    for(;;)   {                        // character output
      status=inp(com+5);
      if((status & 0x20) != 0)   {
        outp(com,ch);
        break;
        }
      }
    }


  int port::gchar()
  {
   int ch;
   unsigned status;                    // character input
   for(;;)   {
     status = inp(com+5);
     if((status & 0x01) != 0)   {
       ch = inp(com);
       return ch;
       }
     }
   }


  //////////////////////////////////////////////////////////////
  // DERIVED CLASS:  serial
  //////////////////////////////////////////////////////////////

  class serial : port   {
    char *dname;
  public:
    serial(int,char*);
   ~serial() { delete dname; }
    void send(char*);        // send a line out to the serial device
    char* receive();         // get a line from the serial device
   };


  serial::serial(int pnum,char* device) : (pnum)
  {
   dname = new char[strlen(device)+1];  //set up the port name
   strcpy(dname,device);                // initialize
  }
```

```
void serial::send(char* buffer)
{
 for(int i=0 ; i <= strlen(buffer) ; i++)  // send it character
   pchar(buffer[i]);                        // by character
}

char* serial::receive()
{
 char buffer[80];

 for(int i=0 ; i < 80 ; i++)
   if( (buffer[i] = gchar()) == '\0')  // build string in buffer
     break;
 return buffer;
}
```

Summary

This chapter illustrated the creation of three simple classes that access the serial port of the IBM-PC. Each version was an enhancement of the previous one. The first example explored basic character transmission. A simple class with a constructor, destructor, and two character-oriented member functions—*pchar()* and *gchar()*—let you send a single character out the port and receive it at the other end. To this character-by-character capability, the next example added special members to the class that allowed a single character string to be sent through the serial port. This created a more useful data type. Finally, the last example used the concept of derived classes to create a hierarchy of *port* data types. Starting with a simple core of input/output capabilities— essentially the same as the original *port* class—as a base, the chapter demonstrated how to define specialized *port* classes to handle specific types of situations.

Also discussed were some important design and style issues. You saw how to use the inherent structure of a class definition—its two-part nature of declaration and definition—to create an even more modular and more structured program.

Using C++ on the UNIX System

Using C++ on the UNIX System

E. William Leggett

In recent years, the UNIX Operating System (OS) has become a popular software development environment. See, for example, Waite, Martin, and Prata's *UNIX System V Primer*, published by Howard W. Sams & Co. The chief reason for this growth is that the system provides many compilers, assemblers, and other software development tools, including a wide variety of file-handling utilities. Now that inexpensive versions of UNIX are available for PCs, you can even develop MS-DOS software in the richer UNIX environment. In fact, many of the programs in MS-DOS are based on similar utilities that have been available for years on the UNIX system.

All of the programs in this book (with the exception of those in Chapter 8) work under UNIX as well as on the PC under MS-DOS. However, more advanced "systems" programs, such as some file-handling utilities or sophisticated screen graphics programs, often use hardware-specific or OS-specific function calls and device-handling characteristics. For example, for a program to do a reasonable job with bit-mapped graphics or window management, it must either use a layer of hardware-specific functions or use a package such as MIT's *X Windows*. This chapter shows you how to develop facilities that help UNIX programs communicate with each other. So that you fully understand what this entails, let's first briefly examine the basic characteristics of the UNIX system.

A Brief Introduction to UNIX

The UNIX system was developed in the early 1970s at AT&T Bell Laboratories specifically as a software development environment. Throughout the years, it has acquired myriad software development tools, such as programming languages, networking facilities, document preparation tools, editors, source code version control, and other utilities too numerous to mention here. Early in its development, it was largely rewritten in the then newly-developed C language. Most of its tools are written in C and can be easily ported from one UNIX system to another. By virtue of its many software development aids and its availability to universities, it has become quite popular.

UNIX is a *multitasking* operating system that permits many programs to be running at the same time. For example, under UNIX, a programmer can read electronic mail while running the *make* program-builder "in the background"; the processor allocates time to both processes, but the program "in the foreground" is the one associated with keyboard input. Of course, a single processor, can run only one task at a time. However, several processes can be partially completed concurrently; for example, one can execute CPU instructions while another waits for disk access.

In fact, many UNIX users can execute several such tasks simultaneously, making UNIX an example of a *multiuser* operating system. Typically, a UNIX system has several users "logged in" and working at once; the programs of one user do computations while other users perform input, read files, or drink a cup of coffee, thus optimizing use of the computing resource. However, even on a single-user PC or workstation, the operating system's ability to run simultaneous background processes can be a tremendous asset.

To prevent all these processes and users from encroaching on each other's data, the UNIX system uses *virtual memory mapping*, so that one user's pointers can only access and change the locations assigned to that user. That is, an extra mapping step ensures that one user's data address AA00 is mapped to a different region of "real" memory than another user's location AA00 (see Figure 9-1).

By contrast, MS-DOS is not multitasking: One program must wait while another executes, even if the other program's output is displayed on the screen in another window. OS/2 is multitasking, but not multiuser: The programs of a single PC user share the CPU, each briefly using the processor in a "time-slicing" manner.

The concept of a *process* or *task*—a program with its own code, data, stack, and thread of execution—is fundamental to UNIX and other

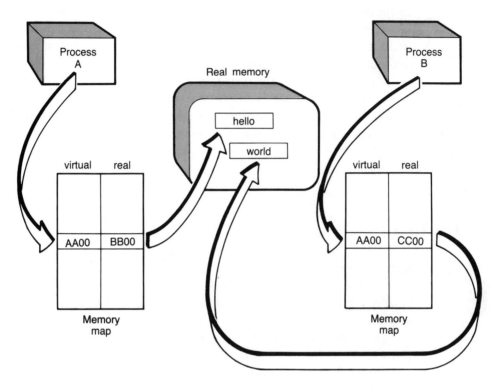

Figure 9-1.   Virtual memory map protection

multitasking operating systems. The primary job of a multitasking operating system is equitably providing the necessary system services to the various processes while protecting the tasks from each other.

UNIX and OS/2 use memory management techniques to protect and serve multiple tasks. Because most programs do not intentionally write in the operating system code space, both UNIX and OS/2 permit processes to share code, thus reducing memory requirements. (MS-DOS typically does not use memory management to protect multiple switched, memory-resident processes.)

Because multiple processes must share resources (usually only one process at a time can use a printer or read the keyboard), a multitasking operating system usually has a separate "kernel," or collection of system routines for accessing the disk, deciding which process accesses the CPU next (scheduling), allocating memory, and so on. These routines are typically accessed by special traps or *system calls*. The operating system handles the hardware "interrupts," which indicate events such as mouse movement or that a disk block was read, and also issues the I/O commands to devices on behalf of all users. This allows multiple processes to use system resources efficiently and, more importantly, protects processes from each other.

However, there are times when you want processes to interact or to cooperate to finish a job. For example, you might need a printer spooler interface to accommodate several client processes, so that they do not have to wait while the printer is in use. The main example in this chapter shows how C++ can neatly encapsulate such interprocess cooperation in the UNIX system.

Why Use C++ Under UNIX?

C++ was developed on the UNIX system at Bell Labs by Bjarne Stroustrup. Thus, it is not surprising that it has a full set of UNIX library routines and that, to date, much C++ code has been written on UNIX systems.

As noted in the previous section, a multitasking operating system naturally partitions itself as a collection of objects (memory segments, hardware devices, files, processes, and so on), each with a set of allowed operations and security fences. UNIX begs to be rewritten in an object-oriented language such as C++, which can safely encapsulate such functionality. AT&T and SUN Microsystems might possibly be using C++ to write the successor to System V Release 4 UNIX (combined System V and Berkeley Software Distribution, BSD, UNIX).

In addition to the design of a system or application (which can be made clearer using object-oriented techniques), the main obstacle to producing quality code is the lack of a formal interface between modules written by different people on a multiple-person project. Even one-person efforts can benefit from a clear separation of functionality and a precise specification of object interfaces, as anyone who has looked at his or her code after a year or so can attest! C++ provides significant built-in facilities for data hiding, which helps to avoid such problems. ANCI C's function prototypes also support strong typing, but ANSI C lacks data-hiding mechanisms.

Using the public/private mechanisms enforced by the C++ translator, a systems programmer can, for example, build a module (class) for handling a process control block and be certain that no one can use that object in any way not explicitly granted. Most people who have worked on a multiple-person application with a tight deadline (aren't they all like that?) agree that guidelines and conventions are rarely enough. C++ is successful because, when used correctly, it guarantees type/class security without resorting to cumbersome "export-to" lists, syntactic straitjackets, or vague English descriptions or documentation standards that are tedious to use and easily circumvented. C++ enables programmers to state relationships and interfaces succinctly, thus avoiding the uncertainty and confusion that arises even in the best "Programming Standards" manuals.

Systems programming, or writing the facilities that allow applications processes to cooperate, is difficult to get exactly right. In it, the messages, processes, and "interesting event" communications and queues are prime candidates for C++ classes and objects. Also, the additional interface structuring of C++ is even more useful in this type of development. Now, let's examine UNIX multitasking and cooperating processes and see how C++ can neatly encapsulate some of the trickiest UNIX System V code.

Using UNIX System Multitasking

The success of the UNIX system is due not only to its many utilities, but also to the philosophy behind much of its development. This "UNIX philosophy" is most eloquently demonstrated in Kernighan and Pike's *The UNIX Programming Environment*. The main idea behind the UNIX philosophy is to build small, efficient tools, while providing the structure for combining them in powerful ways.

The ideal UNIX tool has few options and few dependencies on other utilities with which it might be asked to interact. For example, because UNIX developers noticed that most processes have one primary input file (device) and one primary output file (device), they established that the connecting of these input and output streams to other programs or files should be like a circus parade of elephants, with the trunk of one holding the tail of the other. Thus, an ideal program does not have built-in dependencies on where its data comes from and where its data goes to.

Most people identify the UNIX system with its *shell*, or the command language interpreter that serves as the primary interface for UNIX users. The *shell* provides a succinct notation for connecting the I/O of various tools and utilities to other programs and files. Thus, you can connect a series of programs as a "pipeline" of processes, the output of each becoming the input of the next, as shown in Figure 9-2.

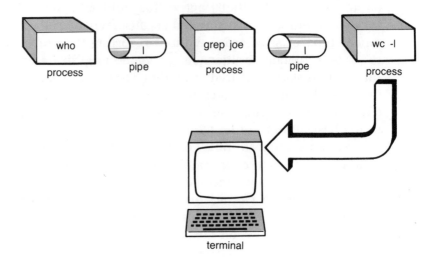

Figure 9-2.   An example of a UNIX pipeline

The *who* command usually lists the people logged onto the system at the terminal. In this example, its output is diverted to the *grep* program (*grep* stands for "generalized regular expression pattern matcher") with the argument "joe", which outputs only the lines that contain the string "joe". Finally, the output of *grep* is "piped" to *wc*, a word-and-line-counting program, which (with the "-l" option) prints the resulting number of lines on the terminal, its output device. Thus, you can easily discover how many terminal lines Joe is logged onto without constructing a special utility for that purpose.

Pipes address a problem that is the reverse of that of memory protection—how to share information in a protected environment. However, pipes are not adequate if UNIX processes do not have a common ancestor or if their communication is not predictable. These cases require another mechanism. Then, if they need to cooperate through a mechanism other than the pipeline, how do they do it?

The kinds of programs that need to communicate by a more general means than pipes are often system programs, such as "demons" that control special devices or multiactive-window display screens. Because the concurrency of programs cannot be known beforehand, it is nearly impossible for the system to provide normal pipes between them. They could communicate through files. But, if multiple processes are protected from altering each other's data, then how does one process know when it is safe to write in a file to be read by another? System

V UNIX file locking can help solve this problem, but in real-time applications, such as for robot control, this method might be too slow. Resource sharing in which time is not critical, such as for a printer spooler, is best implemented with simple lock files.

UNIX System V has several interprocess communication (IPC) facilities that you can use with processes that need to cooperate more efficiently. These facilities are:

▶ "Named" Pipes

▶ IPC Messages

▶ Shared Memory

▶ Semaphores

Named Pipes or FIFOs

Normal UNIX system pipes require the two communicating processes to share a common ancestor. The parent process opens both ends of the pipe and attaches the output of one process to the front end and the input of the next process to the business end. If a demon process, such as one that UNIX executes at startup to manage a print spooler queue, needs to respond to user processes as they request service, it can open a *named pipe*, or *FIFO* (First-In, First-Out queue), for reading and then patiently wait for some writer to open the other end and send a message. Many such writers can use the *FIFO* to send messages to the reader. Writes to named pipes are guaranteed to be *atomic*; that is, part of one message will not be mixed in with part of another. However, when several messages are queued in the pipe, the demon might have difficulty determining where one ends and the next begins.

Continuing with this example of a FIFO object, the UNIX *init* process that started the printer spooler demon does not know in advance when a program will start printing its output; therefore, it cannot reserve a "regular" pipe ahead of time. Thus, when a program sends its output to an *lp* process through a regular pipe, the *lp* process writes to a special file (the System V FIFO of the printer demon).

Using a *fifo* class object, the code for *lp* might look something like the following:

```
#include "fifo.h"

    fifo    print_fifo;
```

continued

```
fifomsg fifo_msg(60, lp_cookie);

print_fifo.attach("/usr/spool/lp/print.fifo");

fifo_msg.addmsg(filename);
fifo_msg.endmsg();
print_fifo.sendmsg(&fifo_msg);
```

This code allocates a FIFO called *print_fifo* and a message, *fifo_message*, which contains a special character (a "magic cookie") to help the spooler demon delimit messages in the queue. The application then attaches to the FIFO, puts in its message the file name to be printed, declares that it has ended the message, and sends it to the demon through the named pipe.

The *fifo* class object might also include a partial interface, as follows:

```
class fifomsg {
    int     size; // max size of message
    char    cookie; // first character is a "magic cookie"
    char *  body; // body of message to send

public:
    fifomsg(int maxsize, char magcookie)
      { size = maxsize; cookie = magcookie;
        body = new char[maxsize];
        body[0] = NULL; }

    void addmsg(char * newstring)
      { strcat(body, newstring); }

    void endmsg() { strncat(body, "\n", 1); }
};

class fifo {
    int     fd; // UNIX file descriptor

public:
    void attach(const char * name)
      { fd = open(name, O_RDONLY); }

    void sendmsg(fifomsg * msg)
```

```
        { write(fd, msg, strlen(msg)); }
};
```

Messages on the FIFO have a maximum length and contain a special marker to simplify finding the beginning of messages (the "magic cookie") in addition to the body of the message. The *attach()* and *sendmsg()* *fifo* member functions then merely call *open()* and *write()*, respectively.

Of course, this implementation lacks necessary error and string bounds checking. However, if you add that error-checking, this FIFO object will be sound enough to use in a number of applications. Thus, object-oriented programming lets you create classes that have well-specified, safe interfaces and that you can easily reuse in other applications.

How did UNIX create the FIFO and get it to the */usr/spool/lp* directory in the first place? The answer is that the UNIX *mknod* command uses the *-p* option to create a named pipe node, or special UNIX FIFO file, in a directory. Of course, the *lp* demon must know the node name of its FIFO and open it for reading.

UNIX IPC Messages

A previous section briefly discussed how messages could be used for interprocess communication. In System V, *IPC messages* are mailboxes kept in the kernel's address space. They offer two advantages over named pipes: They let you allocate a big enough buffer to hold all the expected messages and—the key difference—they maintain each message as a distinct entity. Thus, even if an errant process puts a garbage message on the stack, the reader can ignore it and continue with the next valid message. If a message sender process needs a reply, then that process can open its own message queue and, in the request message it sends, include the key that identifies its reply message queue.

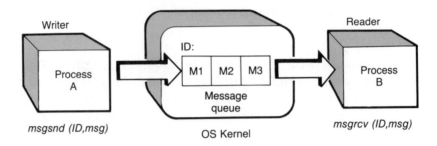

Figure 9-3.   UNIX System V message-passing

If you rewrite the *lp* program of the previous example as an IPC message queue instead of a FIFO, its code might look as follows:

```
#include <sys/types.h>
#include <sys/ipc.h>
#include <sys/msg.h>
#include "msgs.h"

    msgq     print_queue;
    ipc_msg  ipc_msg(60, lp_cookie);

    print_queue.attach(LP_KEY);

    ipc_msg.addmsg(filename);
    ipc_msg.endmsg();
    print_queue.sendmsg(&ipc_msg);
```

Note that only a few changes—the variable and class names—were necessary; the functions and their arguments are almost identical to those of the FIFO example. This suggests that you could have used true object-oriented methods by defining an *ipc* base class and deriving the *fifo* and *msgq* classes from it.

The implementation, however, is not quite as similar. The differences between the examples are important, because they show how you can change an implementation without changing the interface to the user. This is the essence of object-oriented programming.

```
class ipc_msg {
        struct  msgbuf sndbuf; // in sys/msg.h
    int     size; // max size of message
    int     sndsize; // size of message sent
```

```
        char *  body; // body of message to send

public:
    ipc_msg(int maxsize, char magcookie)
      { size = maxsize; sndbuf.mtype = magcookie;
        body = new char[maxsize];
        body[0] = NULL; }

    void addmsg(const char * newstring)
      { strcat(body, newstring); sndbuf.mtext = body;
        sndsize = strlen(body); }

    void endmsg()
      { strncat(body, "\n", 1); sndsize = strlen(body); }

    int len() { return sndsize; }
};


class msgq {
    int     mqid; // UNIX message queue ID

public:
    void attach(const int key)
      { mqid = msgget(key, 0); }

    void sendmsg(const ipc_msg * msg)
      { msgsnd(mqid, msg, msg.len(), 0); }
};
```

The *msgbuf* structure is defined in *sys/msg.h* and includes a *long mtype* and a *char * mtext*. The key point here is that IPC messages provide intrinsic message separation; thus, the "magic cookie"—which cannot be used in the body of the message—is not needed. The System V message buffer also has a separate, built-in message type code that permits a receiver to ask for all messages in its queue of a certain type before reading messages of other types. The *msgget()* routine is a UNIX System V system call that returns the (internal) message queue identifier associated with the specified key (think of it as a special file *open()* for message queues), and the *msgsnd()* system call sends a message (much like a file *write()*) to that queue. The key must be specified to prospective clients (usually in a header file). Thus, the message queue ID is an internal system identifier that resembles a file descriptor for an open file.

Shared Memory

One of the most efficient means of sharing data is to map the same block of "real" addresses in two or more processes' virtual space (at the same or different addresses). Then, any of these processes can read or write in the area. See Figure 9-4.

Note that each process does not need to put the data at the same virtual (private) address; however, if you store pointers in the shared area, you must map them all to the same location, and no pointer should point to a "private" non-shared address of any process. Of course, if both processes try to write to the same location at the same time, chaos can ensue. A later example uses shared memory and demonstrates how to resolve these problems.

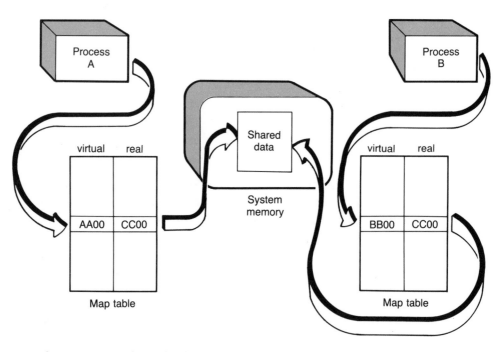

Figure 9-4.   Shared memory mapping

Semaphores

Semaphores are a popular method for controlling access to a resource, such as a shared memory region. A semaphore can be a binary value, which indicates whether or not a resource is available, or a counting value, which indicates how many of the resources are available. If none are available, the semaphore has a non-positive value, and processes must wait for a resource to be "posted," or returned to the pool. If a binary semaphore is zero, it indicates that the resource is unavailable. For counting semaphores, a zero or negative value indicates the number of processes that need the resource (in addition to those resources in the pool already being used).

The name *semaphore* comes from the idea of the train semaphore signaling system developed in the 19th century to avoid collisions. If the semaphore is in use (not positive, or arm out), then the section of track is being used and should not be entered. When the semaphore arm drops down (becomes positive), then a waiting train is free to enter the shared section of track. (The semaphore analogy was developed by E. W. Dijkstra.)

System V semaphores are arcane, to say the least. The main program in this section uses them to efficiently resolve the common access problem of shared memory and to show you how to use System V semaphores. Another way to think of a binary semaphore is as a gate to an enclosure in which a resource can safely be used without interference from other processes. Figure 9-5 shows a binary semaphore as a train signal and as a gate.

The next section explains how to use shared memory and semaphores to provide safe shared access to a common buffer.

Monitors and Critical Regions with System V

The previous section discussed various IPC mechanisms for solving a concurrent reader/writer problem (the reader was the *lp* demon). Suppose you want to implement a temporary buffer in memory that will be shared by many writers and a single reader. This would be useful in a factory automation control system: The writers might return values from sensors on assembly lines, and then the reader could correlate the loads on the lines to display the overall status and perhaps compare the activity on the lines to increase efficiency. The main example in

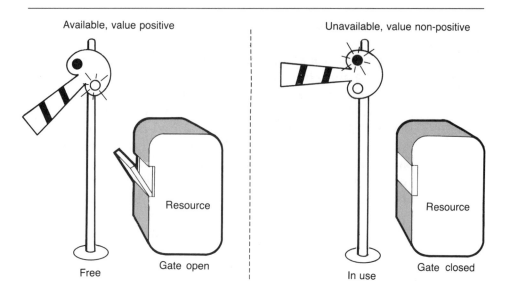

Available, value positive   Unavailable, value non-positive

Resource

Resource

Free   Gate open   In use   Gate closed

Figure 9-5.   A binary semaphore

this chapter is not that specific; it shows how writers can safely write complete messages into a common log buffer from which a single reader can pull the messages. You could use these programs for keeping a log of system activity or for holding messages that are generated by multiple processes for debugging purposes.

The example uses shared memory to hold the log message lines, so it must prevent the processes from writing the same record at the same time and keep the reader from updating the read pointer while a writer is using it. The program must also address how the reader knows when the buffer is empty and when it contains something to read, and how a writer knows when the buffer is full and when it has space for writing a new record.

Sometimes multiple processes must access a resource, but they cannot be allowed to use it at the same time. When this occurs in a program, the code sections that access the resource are called *critical regions*. One way to protect a shared log region is to use a *monitor* structure. (The term *monitor* was devised by C. A. R. Hoare.) Typically, you use a semaphore to stand guard at the gate of the monitor to allow only one process at a time to be active inside it. Then you can use another semaphore/gate to signify that the buffer contains lines of log messages and yet another to signify that it is not currently full, or that the buffer has room for another log message line. The shared memory area and its semaphores implement the monitor for the critical buffer region as shown in Figure 9-6.

In Figure 9-6, Process A is waiting to enter the monitored region. Process B has entered the monitor (it "shut the gate") and is about to update the *"non-full"* semaphore, or open the gate to the waiting Process C. More complete descriptions of these actions follow, and a later section provides an overview of how to implement this monitor and its semaphores.

Problems in Concurrent Processing

When you program for any concurrent processing system, you must adhere to several basic principles:

► Avoid "race" conditions

► Avoid deadlock

► Avoid livelock

► Try to be fair

A "race" condition exists when, for example, two writers try to write the same record at the same time. Unfortunately, the race is not always to the swiftest—usually both lose, resulting in hopelessly scrambled data. Avoiding this condition is one of the main reasons for devising the monitor.

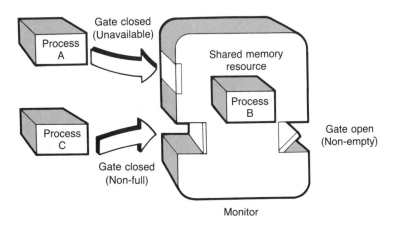

Figure 9-6.   Semaphores and shared memory as a monitor

Deadlocks are more subtle and therefore more difficult to avoid or detect. Much of the discussion in a typical operating systems textbook is concerned with the problems of providing services while avoiding deadlock. The simplest example of a deadlock occurs when two processes each have a resource and want the other's. If neither can be forced to give up its resource, they will forever remain locked in a "deadly embrace."

Using the buffer example, suppose a writer process is inside the monitor and is waiting for the buffer to become non-full. If the reader process acquires the non-full semaphore first, then tries to enter the monitor, the two processes will wait for each other forever. That is, each has a resource the other needs, yet neither will surrender its resource nor stop waiting for the other process to release the resource it has. This deadlock occurs when neither process can proceed; thus the resources are useless. The solution is to not allow a process to acquire another semaphore unless it is inside the monitor first (has acquired the monitor semaphore). Because a process inside the monitor is always alone, it cannot be deadlocked.

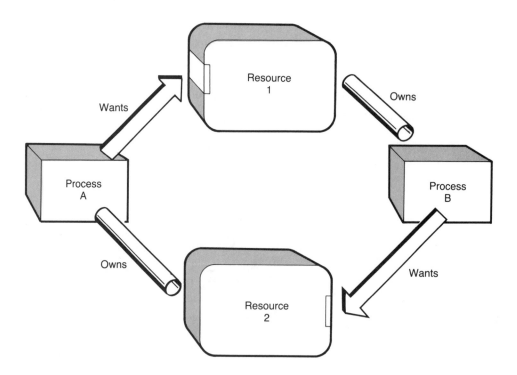

Figure 9-7. Deadlock

Now, consider another problem that might develop if the reader has the monitor semaphore (is inside the monitored region) and is waiting for the non-empty semaphore to become true. Suppose a writer wants to put a record in the buffer and then post the non-empty semaphore. The writer can't get inside the monitor to write its record; it can't get the reader to release the monitor so that it can update the semaphore the reader is waiting for! Thus, the writer is "livelocked"— it knows what to do, but it can't get into the monitor to do it.

Figure 9-8 shows that if Process B retains the monitor semaphore while waiting for the other semaphore, then Process A cannot post that semaphore, as this can only be done from inside the monitored region.

The classical solution to this problem with monitors is to require that whenever a process inside the monitor lacks a resource, it must surrender the monitor until that resource is available. A process should never "sleep" (wait indefinitely) with the monitor semaphore in its possession (that is, inside the monitor), or a deadlock or livelock will surely occur.

In Figure 9-9, Process B had the monitor (semaphore G), but needs the unavailable resource NF, so it has relinquished the monitor (making G available) and waits outside the monitor for NF to be available. Meanwhile, Process A can acquire the monitor (semaphore G), enter the monitor, and post (free) the semaphore NF. Later, when NF is posted and A leaves the monitor, B will be able to enter the monitor and use the resource NF now available.

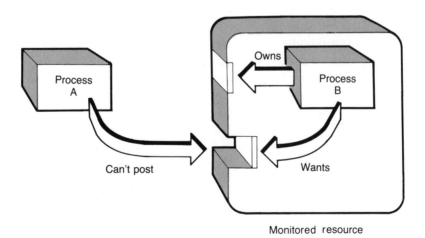

Figure 9-8. Livelock

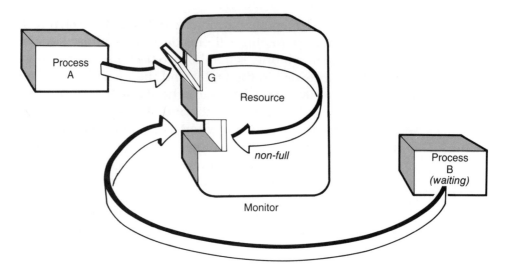

Figure 9-9.   Sleep outside the monitor

Avoiding Concurrent Processing Problems

The buffer example must treat the reader fairly when it is waiting for the non-empty semaphore and treat multiple writers fairly (in the order of their requests) when they are waiting for the non-full semaphore. In order to be fair, the UNIX operating system maintains first-in, first-out queues for processes waiting for the resource protected by the semaphore. Some monitor implementations go even further and, when a process posts a waited-for semaphore, the posting process immediately steps outside the monitor to let the waiting processes acquire the monitor and use the desired (now available) resource.

In Figure 9-10, Process A is in the monitor and thus has the monitor semaphore, G. Processes B and C are queued waiting for the monitor semaphore; when A leaves the monitor and frees G, B will get it and enter the monitor first.

The implementation in this chapter lets the reader in when a writer is done and lets a writer in when the reader is finished. However, for greater system efficiency, when the reader process accesses the buffer, it reads all the records available. Thus, writers defer to the reader.

To review, the example implementation will allocate a shared memory region that multiple writers and one reader can attach to their address space. It will use a monitor semaphore that allows only one process at a time to change shared memory, a semaphore for "buffer

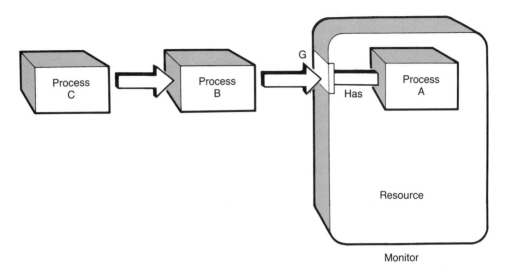

Figure 9-10.   Wait in order for a semaphore

not-empty," and a semaphore for "buffer not-full." The next section shows how to use the low-level system calls of UNIX System V to implement this design.

As you examine this C++ example, keep in mind that the proper use of the *data abstraction* facilities of C++ can guarantee that deadlock and race conditions cannot occur. The data abstraction interface does not permit access to internal data, except as specifically allowed through the public interface. Thus, because C++ lets you confidently reason about the properties of an object—and even formally prove freedom from deadlock—you can safely use the class in other applications. If you coded the same example with traditional C structures, you would find it difficult to enforce the use of the carefully-constructed access methods.

Developing the Shared Memory Error Log

This section contains the C++ code that implements a shared memory error log buffer protected by semaphores. The example allows only one reader, but many writers. The log messages of the writers will never become scrambled even though all the processes, including the reader, run concurrently. This code solves the classical *producer/con-*

sumer problem shown in many operating system textbooks, in which many processes produce data (writers) and one process consumes it (the reader). For example, a disk controller is a consumer of the disk block read/write requests produced by processes using file data. Of the many such examples of producers and consumers of protected data in an operating system, the following is both simple yet instructive.

The shared memory option for interprocess communication is the best solution for many applications. FIFOs have problems with message delimiters, and IPC messages are subject to internal system limits that are typically much smaller than those of shared memory regions. Also, system calls copy message and FIFO data to destination buffers in the kernel, whereas with shared memory properly protected with semaphores, the read and write copying occurs in user (not system) space, because the shared segments are mapped in all processes' virtual data space. In real-time applications, or even in heavily-used multiprocessing applications, the extra copying of large amounts of data can cause a severe loss of performance. Using shared memory often results in less copying in some situations. For example, a FIFO writer creates a message in its virtual address space; then it makes a system call that copies the data to an internal system buffer. When the FIFO reader makes its system call, the data is again copied to the reader's virtual address space. Using shared memory, the two extra copies to and from system space are avoided.

The example program has to address the following issues: First, it must obtain the monitor and the read/write semaphores (permission); then, it must provide the read and write primitives and allow a process to wait (sleep) if a resource is not available; finally, it must make sure processes surrender the monitor when they are waiting for a read (non-empty) or write (non-full) semaphore. The goal of data abstraction is to provide these services in a way that is safe and cannot be easily circumvented.

The solution offered by the sample program demonstrates the separation of concerns, implementation hiding, and the structuring concepts of object-oriented programming in C++. As a result, the final reader and writer test programs are very short and clear. If you change the class implementations without changing the public interface, you would need only to relink with the new implementation routines; the reader and writer code would be exactly the same.

Of course, it is the object-oriented structure of C++ that allows such a concise and elegant solution. You could program a very similar-looking solution using C, but the program would not have the advantage

of the protection and the hiding of private implementation data that
C++ provides.

Starting the Development Process

First, let's make a precise formulation of the problem. Multiple processes must be able to post error log messages to a shared memory
region, from which a dedicated reader process will access them and
either put them in a special file or write them on a terminal. In this
case, the reader merely prints the messages at the terminal.

Note that this simple error log example is an abstraction of a function of a telephone switch maintenance system. The maintenance system gets input—error and warning messages—from several switches. It
then sends these messages to a message logger that looks for correla-
tions in the error messages and has message-per-unit-time thresholds.
According to the severity of the error messages and their rate of receipt,
the logger can trigger an alarm bell or display a warning message on
a special console. Important messages are logged in special files. This
"message browser" is an example of the type of expert system used in
telephone switch maintenance.

The writers in this example also display their messages at the
terminal as well as writing them to shared memory. Not only should
the log messages from different writers not be scrambled in shared
memory, they also should not be scrambled on the terminal. The display of writers' messages to the terminal for debugging purposes is
also protected by the monitor! The screen of the terminal itself seems
to offer natural limits to the size of the shared log buffer: Messages
shouldn't be more than 80 characters long and shared memory should
hold only as many as 24 of them at a time. A more general solution
would treat the shared area as a heap and allow variable-length messages; the details of such an implementation are not included here.

Before you actually start writing code, ask yourself the following
questions: "What should happen if a writer tries to write a message
and shared memory is full?" "What happens if the reader finds the
buffer area empty?" "How does the program respond if two or more
writers simultaneously try to access the log when the reader is trying
to read?"

Other parameters that need to be considered include the number
of messages written or read at once. In this example, the writers will
write only one message at a time; the reader will read as many messages
as exist in the buffer when the reader gains access to the shared mem-

ory monitor. When a message is read, the program displays it on the terminal and then discards it. (In a real use of this technique, you might want to save the messages in various files or keep running totals based on message severity.)

The 24 lines in the shared memory log buffer will be used in a circular fashion, with the read pointer following the write pointer in the buffer area as messages are read and written. The buffer lines are used circularly; when the last is filled, the first line is the next to be written.

An Overview of Program Files

The complete shared log buffer example consists of the following files. The program and header files comprise *shlog.h*, which contains message keys, line and buffer sizes, semaphore control values, and other miscellaneous definitions. The *logmem.h* file contains the *logmem* shared memory log class definition. The *semaset.h* header file contains the *semaset* semaphore set class. The *semaset.cpp* and *logmem.cpp* files contain the implementations of the semaphore set and memory log class member functions; the contents of these files are broken into several separate listings to keep them manageable. The *writer.cpp* and *reader.cpp* files contain the C++ code for the writer and reader processes. Listings also include a simple UNIX *makefile* for managing the building of the modules and processes. Figure 9-11 shows the relationships of these files.

The semaphore set and shared memory log server routines called by the client reader and writer processes could have been placed in a System V shared code library. During the course of your own programming, you will usually store such real object class implementations in a library archive and link them as necessary with client programs.

Constants and Key Values

The *shlog.h* header file (Listing 9-1) contains common constants such as *TRUE* and *FALSE* as well as parameters for System V shared memory and semaphore system calls. (Please refer to the UNIX Programmer's Reference Manual for details about these system calls.) It also includes parameters for the shared log size, *SHBUF_LINES* and *SHLINE_SIZE*, so that you can easily change its size in one place and let *make* remake the implementations and test processes. Note that the listing uses the

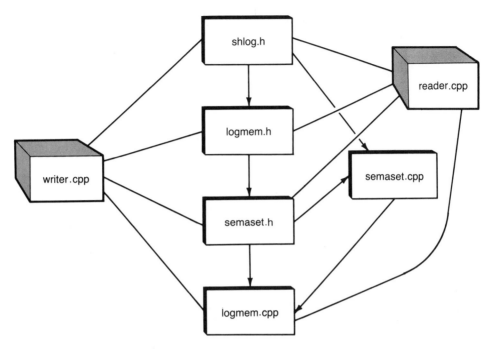

Figure 9-11.   Relationships of files and processes

C++ *const* constant declaration rather than the common C #*define*; you can include *const* names in the symbol table for easier debugging.

Listing 9-1.   Constants and keys: *shlog.h*

```
/* shlog.h common constants, etc. for shared mem logs */

#ifndef SHLOG_H

extern int errno; // UNIX system call error code
extern int getpid(); // UNIX program to return process ID


const int SUCCESS = (0);
const int FAILURE = (-1);
const int TRUE = (1);
const int FALSE = (0);

const int IPC_PERM = 0666; // IPC get permissions
```

continued

```
const int LOG_SEMA_KEY = 'L'; // key used to get sema set
const int SHLOG_KEY = 'S'; // key used to get shared log
const int LOG_READER = 1; // caller is log reader
const int SEMAS_OWNER = 1; // caller is semaset owner
const int LOG_WRITER = 0; // caller is one writer
const int SHBUF_LINES = 24; // number lines in shared mem
const int SHLINE_SIZE = 80; // size of buffer lines
const int SH_SEMAS = 3; // need three semas for log
const int SH_SEMA_OPS = 5; // number sema ops in one call

const int SH_MON_SEMA = 0; // monitor semaphore index
const int SH_NFULL_SEMA = 1; // buffer not full sema index
const int SH_NEMPTY_SEMA = 2; // buffer non-empty sema index
const int SH_SEMA_TRUE = 1; // binary semas init value
const int SH_SEMA_FALSE = 0; // binary semas unavail value

#define SHLOG_H
#endif
```

Defining the Shared Memory Log Class

All of the data for the shared memory log object is private, so no client process can directly access this data. Only the actual implementation routines can access such data and use the internal member functions. Thus, C++ greatly facilitates data abstraction and information hiding, the only overhead being the word *public:*. The declaration of the member functions also includes the argument list prototypes (although most of these routines take no arguments). Listing 9-2 contains the class definition for the shared memory log.

Listing 9-2.   The class definition of the shared memory log file: *logmem.h*

```
/* logmem.h class for shared memory log file */

#ifndef LOGMEM_H

class logmem {
    struct  shmem {
        short readidx; // read buffer line index
        short writeidx; // write buffer line index
```

```
        char  buff[SHBUF_LINES][SHLINE_SIZE]; // buffer of lines for log
    } * shmem; // address memory attached at

    semaset  * semas; // semaphore set for monitor
    int     id; // ID of shared memory area returned
    key_t   key; // key used to get area
    int     owner; // owner/creator PID of shared memory
    int     blines; // total number of buffer lines
    int     bsize; // size in bytes of buffer lines

    int remove(); // remove shared memory region
    int markfull(); // post buffer full (writer)
    int marknempty(); // post buf not-empty (writer)
    int marknfull(); // post buf not full (reader)
    int markempty(); // post buffer empty (reader)
    int empty(); // returns whether buffer empty
public:
    logmem(int flag); // constructor; flag for reader
    ~logmem(); // destructor (memory freed)

    int detach(); // detach from shared region

    int monnfull(); // wait mon, notfull (writer)
    int monnempty(); // wait mon, not empty (reader)
    int postmon(); // post mon (exit monitor)

    int read(char * line); // read record; adv read ptr
    int write(char * line); // write record; adv write ptr

    void dump(); // dump values for debugging
};

#define LOGMEM_H
#endif
```

The *shmem* structure has only a pointer declared for it. Because it is shared data, this area must be allocated only once and shared by all users. Similarly, the program uses a pointer to the semaphore set in the *logmem* data; the set is allocated separately merely to demonstrate variety.

In operating system theory, the problem of keeping one process out of a section of code or a region of data while another process executes a critical update is called the *mutual exclusion problem*; however, although more than one client can't be allowed in at once, all processes desiring entry should eventually be serviced. To solve the mutual exclusion problem, mentally draw a wall around the shared memory area. You must limit access to this special area through a monitor that will guard the entrance by allowing only one process at a time inside to change shared memory. This monitor is represented by a monitor semaphore.

The shared memory area of the example is protected by a "monitor" that strictly controls entry and exit. The monitor gate is a semaphore: When it is down (has a positive value), a process may enter the monitored region to perform a function; when it is up (has a zero or negative value), a single process is using the resource, and other processes must wait in a queue until the resource is available.

What if the reader tries to enter the monitor, but there's no data inside? If it gets inside the monitor to wait, then no writer can enter, thus creating a "livelock." Another semaphore, the *non-empty* semaphore, solves this by allowing the reader to wait outside the monitor.

What if a writer wants access and the buffer is full? Another semaphore, this one specifying *non-full*, allows writers to wait outside the monitored region for available buffer space.

Finally, if a writer writes a line that makes the buffer non-empty, it must activate the reader by posting, or incrementing, the *non-empty* semaphore. Similarly, the reader must post when the *non-full* transition occurs.

Figure 9-12 shows the final picture of the shared memory region with its monitor and semaphores and semaphore waiting lines.

Now, let's use the System V system calls to code the access routines.

Using the Semaphores: the *semaset* Class

The *semaset* class is defined in a general manner, so that it can be used with applications other than the shared memory log. For this reason, the array of operations is allocated in the constructor, and only the pointer *sops* appears in the data. The number of semaphores in the set and the number of operations (essentially the number of "semaphore things" done in one atomic system call, such as "get monitor, free monitor, get not-empty, free not-empty, get monitor") are arguments to the constructor, *semaset()*. Several of the semaphore member functions and operations use default values for trailing arguments, so that the semaphore set can provide counting semaphores. (Note, however,

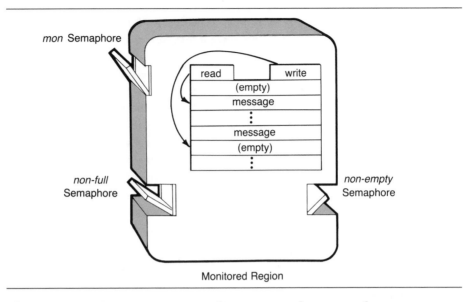

mon Semaphore

non-full
Semaphore

non-empty
Semaphore

read   write

(empty)

message

⋮

message

(empty)

⋮

Monitored Region

Figure 9-12.   Log memory monitors, semaphores, and queues

that this example uses only binary versions of these semaphores.) Listing 9-3 contains the semaphore declarations.

Listing 9-3.   The semaphore set class: *semaset.h*

```
/* semaset.h semaphore set class for shared memory log file */


#ifndef SEMASET_H


class semaset {
    int    id; // ID of semaphore set returned
    key_t key; // key used to get semaphore set
    int    owner; // owner of semaphore set
    int    nsemas; // number of semaphores in the set
    int    nops; // max number of concurrent sema ops
    int    curops; // current number of sema ops built
    struct sembuf * sops; // pointer to array of sema ops


public:
    semaset(int ckey, int numsems, int maxops, int flag);  // constructor
    ~semaset(); // destructor
```

continued

```
int init(int semnum, int resources); // resources is initial value
int remove(); // remove semaphore set system ID

int post(int sema, int val=1);    // indicate resource release
int wait(int sema, int val=1);    // get resource; wait if unavailable
int wait0(int sema); // wait for semaphore to become 0
int doset0(int sema); // clear semaphore (set to zero)
int is0(int sema);   // is the semaphore's value 0?
int isp(int sema);   // is the semaphore's value positive?
int dosema();   // do semaop() on array of ops filled
int clear();   // clear ops array (end or cancel ops)

void dump();   // dump semaphore values for debugging
};

#define SEMASET_H
#endif
```

The Semaphore Operations

Following are declarations of a set of three semaphores and an array of five semaphore operations. The semaphore operations array is the System V method of connecting semaphore operations in an *atomic* fashion, so that no other process can access a resource and invalidate an earlier operation in the set if a later set operation is being waited for. It also prevents deadlock.

Waiting for "non-full" and "non-empty" Conditions

The code that permits a writer to access the buffer can be the most confusing of the example's semaphore operations. To get through the monitor gate and write a log line in the shared memory buffer, the following operations from *logmem.cpp* (Listing 9-4) must be performed:

Listing 9-4.   Enter the monitor when the buffer is not full: *monnfull()*

```
// used by writer to get access to buffer
int logmem :: monnfull()
```

```
{
    if (id == 0)
        return FAILURE;

    // first, get the shared memory monitor
    // wait until it is available, then grab it
    semas->wait(SH_MON_SEMA);

    // then free the monitor, in case you have
    // to sleep if the buffer is full!
    // give up the monitor semaphore
    semas->post(SH_MON_SEMA);

    // next wait until the buffer is not full,
    // so you have room to write.
    // wait until it is not full
    semas->wait(SH_NFULL_SEMA);

    /* then free the not full sema, so don't lock reader out */
    semas->post(SH_NFULL_SEMA); // wait until not full

    /* when you can do work, grab mon again for exclusion */
    semas->wait(SH_MON_SEMA); // wait until available

    // now that array of atomic operations is built,
    // do the sema operations
    int ret;
    if ((ret = semas->dosema()) == FAILURE)
        return FAILURE;

    /* clear out operation array buffer */
    semas->clear();

    return SUCCESS;
}
```

Let's discuss this code in detail. First, a discussion of this type doesn't appear anywhere in the System V manuals, and the section on semaphores in the Programmer's Guide merely presents a program for testing all the possible options of semaphore operations. Although the program is useful, it does not explain why semaphores are manipulated in that particular way. (Note that the Programmer's Reference Manual has an error in the calling sequence that is repeated in the *sys/sem.h* file distributed with the UNIX version of C++!)

The use of the semaphore set is best explained in terms of the concurrency principles of the previous section. First, a reader must wait for the monitor semaphore; waiting for another semaphore first can cause deadlock. This is the first *semas –>wait(SH_MON_SEMA)* operation in the listing. When the reader enters the *monitor*, it frees the monitor guard semaphore, so that if it must wait for the *buffer non-empty* condition, it will wait "outside" the critical region and allow another process to access the monitor. This avoids livelock. When the *non-empty* semaphore is posted, the reader resumes execution and reacquires the monitor semaphore so it can do its work. However, first it re-posts the *non-empty* semaphore, because that semaphore is a binary one—meaning "non-empty is true"—and it needs to be incremented to show its true value (the *semas –>post(SH_NFULL_SEMA)*). Thus, if the process has to wait for *mon* after it has waited for *non-empty*, then the *non-empty* semaphore will be correct while the reader waits.

Actually, the *wait()* and *post()* calls merely record their operations in the semaphore operations array, so that the system call in *semas –>dosema()* performs them as described above. After the system call completes, the *semas –>clear()* function resets the operations array by setting the count of valid operations to zero.

You must use the semaphore array, rather than simply executing single semaphore operation system calls, because the chain of calls must be atomic. For example, if a writer does not claim the monitor semaphore while checking the *non-full* semaphore, then another writer process could acquire the monitor and invalidate the condition (by writing the last buffer slot) before the first writer reclaims the monitor. On the other hand, a writer must surrender the monitor semaphore before checking the *non-full* semaphore, because if it is false, the writer must wait until a reader posts it. The semaphore array and single system call let the writer provisionally relinquish the monitor while checking the *non-full* semaphore—just in case it has to wait. If a writer does not have to wait, then it can regain the monitor knowing that the semaphores it just checked were not invalidated by another writer.

The "monitor and buffer non-empty" access routine (Listing 9-5) is also from *logmem.cpp*.

Listing 9-5. Enter the monitor when the buffer is non-empty: *monnempty()*

```
// used by reader to get access to buffer
int logmem :: monnempty()
{
    if (id == 0)
        return FAILURE;

    // first, get the shared memory monitor
    // wait until it is available, then grab it
    semas->wait(SH_MON_SEMA);

    // then free the monitor,
    // in case you have to sleep if the buffer is empty!
    semas->post(SH_MON_SEMA); // give up monitor semaphore

    // next wait until the buffer is not empty,
    // so you have something to read
    semas->wait(SH_NEMPTY_SEMA); // wait until not empty

    /* free the not-empty sema, so writers are not locked out */
    semas->post(SH_NEMPTY_SEMA); // free non-empty semaphore

    /* when you can do work, grab the mon again for exclusion */
    semas->wait(SH_MON_SEMA); // wait until available

    // now that array of atomic operations is built,
    // do the sema operations
    int ret;
    if ((ret = semas->dosema()) == FAILURE)
        return FAILURE;

    /* clear out operation array buffer */
    semas->clear();

    return SUCCESS;
}
```

Note that the above routine is very similar to the previously described *monnfull()* routine.

Semaphore *wait()* and *post()* Member Functions

Now, let's examine the code for *wait()* and *post()* from the semaphore set implementation module, *semaset.cpp* (see Listing 9-6).

Listing 9-6.   The *wait()* and *post()* semaphore functions

```
/* val is number of posts (freed resources); default is one */
int semaset :: post(int sema, int val = 1)
{
    if (id == 0)
        return FAILURE;

    if (val <= 0) // if zero or negative, disallow
        return FAILURE;

    if (curops >= nops)
        return FAILURE;

    sops[curops].sem_num = sema; // semaphore array index
    sops[curops].sem_op = val;  // post resources
    sops[curops++].sem_flg = 0;  // nothing to undo

    return curops; // return ops in array so far
}


int semaset :: wait(int sema, int val = 1)
{
    if (id == 0)
        return FAILURE;

    if (val <= 0) // if zero or negative, disallow
        return FAILURE;

    if (curops >= nops)
        return FAILURE;

    sops[curops].sem_num = sema; // semaphore's array index
    sops[curops].sem_op = -1;  // get resource; else sleep
    sops[curops++].sem_flg = SEM_UNDO; // if die, post it
```

```
    return curops; // return number ops in array so far
}
```

Note that the *semaset::wait()* and *semaset::post()* routines merely put an element in the array of "atomic" operations that the *semop()* system call performs when called from *semaset::dosema()*. Once again, this guarantees that one semaphore operation cannot be "undone" by another process before the next semaphore operation is done. The semaphore set and array notion works because UNIX is a "single-thread, non-preemptable" kernel. Of course, if a process must wait for a semaphore's resource to become available, the kernel deactivates it until its turn comes up again in the semaphore sleep queue. That is why the program posts *mon* before waiting for *non-empty* or *non-full*.

What to Do About "UNDO"

The use of the *SEM_UNDO* "undo semaphore operation" flag needs some explanation. If a process dies (exits) while waiting for a resource (or, for example, is interrupted by an alarm timer), thus interrupting the *semop* system call, UNIX keeps track of which semaphore the process is waiting for. The operating system then posts the semaphore if the process is taken off the semaphore wait queue. Do *not* "undo" a post operation, although it is legal to do so in the system call, because the buffer does not become *non-empty* if the writer of the last-written record exits all the wait queues, the monitor, and the system kernel.

This might not be obvious. My first implementation of the semaphore members had an "undo" on the post calls, but when the last writer exited, so did the post of the *non-empty* semaphore, and the reader was not able to read the last records written in the buffer! However, if a counting semaphore represents the number of server processes available to perform some service, then you need to "undo" their posts when those processes die or are interrupted and unavailable. "Undo" only when the claim on a resource (wait) or the availability of a resource (post) should no longer be in effect if the waiter or poster dies.

The Semaphore Set System Call

The *dosema()* routine that actually performs the system call and the *clear()* routine are implemented as shown in Listing 9-7 (from *semaset.cpp*).

**Listing 9-7. Atomic semaphore operations: *dosema()* and
*clear()***

```
int semaset :: dosema()
{
    if (id == 0)
        return FAILURE;

    /* operations can block; if successful return, */
    /* then all were done */
    /* all array operations tried in order */
    /* in kernel "atomically" */
    if (semop(id, sops, curops) == FAILURE)
        return(FAILURE);

    return SUCCESS;
}


int semaset :: clear()
{
    if (id == 0)
        return FAILURE;

    int ret = curops;
    curops = 0; // no current operations; wipe them all out

    return ret; // return number operations flushed
}
```

Note that the *dosema()* routine uses the following argument:

```
struct sembuf * sops;
```

This pointer to an array of semaphore operations is the argument as
is it used in the System V Programmer's Guide semaphore tester program. However, the discussion there and the argument declaration in
the System V Programmer's Reference Manual claims it should be as
follows:

```
struct sembuf ** sops;
```

This is clearly wrong. The ** construct represents "a pointer to a pointer to a value," while a single * represents "a pointer to a value," or a single rather than a double indirection. This error extends to the *sys/sem.h* function prototype. Presumably, this will be corrected in a future version of the manuals.

The *clear()* function merely resets to zero the count of operations stored in the semaphore operations array. This function is executed after the semaphore system call returns, and the operations array must be cleared for the next use.

Leaving the Monitor

When a process finishes its task inside the monitored region, it posts the monitor semaphore to free the resource for other processes (see Listing 9-8, from *semaset.cpp*).

Listing 9-8. Exit the monitor: *postmon()*

```
int logmem :: postmon() // free up shared memory monitor
{
    if (id == 0)
        return FAILURE;


    /* assume you have the shared memory monitor */


    /* post monitor sema for other shared memory processes */
    semas->post(SH_MON_SEMA); // post mon not in use


    /* now that the array of atomic operation(s) is built, */
    /* do the sema operations */
    int ret;
    if ((ret = semas->dosema()) == FAILURE)
        return FAILURE;


    /* clear out operation array buffer */
    semas->clear();


    return SUCCESS;
}
```

This simple call places only one operation in the array, the request to post the monitor semaphore, *semas →(SH_MON_SEMA)*. The *dosema()* call then does only one semaphore operation—that post—which cannot wait.

Writing and Reading Messages

Now, let's look at the shared memory log read and write member functions.

Writing Messages

The read pointer always points to the next line in the buffer to be read; the write pointer points to the next available location for a written log line. If the read and write pointers are equal, then either the buffer is full or it is empty. The read and write "pointers" are actually indexes, because different processes can have different virtual addresses for the shared memory buffer. If a writer used an actual pointer in shared memory with its (virtual) address, then a reader, which might attach shared memory at a different location, would not be able to use that pointer correctly. If the buffer is empty, the program sets the read and write pointers (indexes) to zero.

If the writer causes the buffer indexes to be equal, then the buffer is full and is so marked. When the writer finishes, the buffer must be non-empty, so the writer sets that semaphore. Listing 9-9 shows the code for the *write()* function.

Listing 9-9. The shared log buffer writer function: *write()*

```
// write a line to the buffer
int logmem :: write(char * line)
{
    /* line must point to buff big enough to hold a line */
    if ((id == 0) || (line == (char *)NULL))
        return FAILURE;

    /* can't be full, because you write only one at a time */
    /* and you just waited for not-full */

    /* else copy caller's line into shared memory buff line */
```

```
    int to = shmem->writeidx;
    strncpy(shmem->buff[to], line, SHLINE_SIZE);

    if ((shmem->writeidx = ++shmem->writeidx % SHBUF_LINES)
        == shmem->readidx)
    {
        /* then buffer is full */
     markfull();                    // mark it full
    }

    marknempty();                   // buffer now not empty

    return SUCCESS;
}
```

When the writer is executing the *write()* function, the buffer cannot be full because the writer waited for the non-full semaphore, has the monitor semaphore, and thus is the lone process in the monitored region. The semaphore operations for the writer could be included in the *write()* function, but they are not combined so that the writer's program structure more closely resembles the reader's program structure. After a record is written in the log, the buffer is marked full if the read and write indexes are now equal. The buffer is also marked as now being *non-empty* by setting the *non-empty* semaphore's value to 1. This is a "mark" rather than a "post" because the semaphore is a binary semaphore. If every successful writer posted the *non-empty* semaphore, its value would become greater than one, and the semaphore would become a counting semaphore rather than a binary semaphore (which takes only the values zero and one). If you use counting semaphores (as suggested in Exercise 9-3), then you can use "post" to indicate the number of records written. The semaphore's value would then represent the number of resources (log records) available (waiting to be read).

Note that the program uses *strncpy()*, so that the copy is "safe" (a long line sent to the write routine cannot overwrite part of the next line). Always use *strncpy()* rather than *strcpy()* whenever possible. The *strncpy()* function lets you limit the number of characters that can be copied; if no *end-of-string* null character is found before the limit is reached, the copy ends. With *strcpy()*, a bad pointer (for example, using ** instead of *) might copy thousands of characters before encountering a null character to stop it. This error is most often seen with bad string arguments to *printf()* in C.

Reading Messages

The *read()* routine (Listing 9-10) is different from *write()*. Although only one record at a time can be written to shared memory, the reader can read all the messages in the buffer. Thus, it performs an extra check (another system call) to see if there is still another record to read. Note that the reader cannot wait for *non-empty*, because it has the monitor!

Listing 9-10.   The shared log buffer reader function: *read()*

```
/* read a line from the buffer */
int logmem :: read(char * line)
{
    /* only creator can be reader/consumer */
    if (owner != getpid())
        return FAILURE;

    /* line must point to buff big enough to hold line */
    if ((id == 0) || (line == (char *)NULL))
        return FAILURE;

    /* must test, because do multiple reads in monitor */
    if (empty())
        return FAILURE;

    /* else copy a record into the caller's line */
    int from = shmem->readidx;
    strncpy(line, shmem->buff[from], SHLINE_SIZE);

    if ((shmem->readidx = ++shmem->readidx % SHBUF_LINES)
       == shmem->writeidx)
    {
       // then buffer is empty
       shmem->readidx = shmem->writeidx = 0;
       markempty();               // mark it empty
    }

    marknfull();                  // buffer is now not full

    return SUCCESS;
}
```

Notice that there can be only one reader, the shared memory and semaphore set owner/creator. To allow multiple readers, you would have to change the constructors, because the program uses the simplification that the single reader does the actual memory allocation for shared memory and creates the semaphore set.

Some Design Issues

After the last record is read, the program uses the convention of resetting both read and write indexes to zero. This action is not required, and no function depends on it. It merely makes debugging easier.

The read and write routines are the true "monitor" routines, in that they are the critical regions of code that multiple processes should not enter at the same time. The monitor semaphore is the System V device that excludes more than one process from those critical regions. The *non-empty* and *non-full* semaphores and their queues represent the conditions that can be signaled and waited for (outside the monitor) in the classical monitor paradigm. The semaphore operations array used with the semaphore set represents the conditional waiting characteristic of a classical monitor.

The reader and writer routines contain the monitor entry and exit semaphore operations merely for the purposes of exposition. To be truer to the monitor model and to information hiding principles, you might only use *read()* and *write()* operations at the client/user level and completely hide all of the semaphore waiting, posting, and marking inside the *logmem* class.

The semaphore "mark" routines merely set the binary semaphores to zero or one (see Listing 9-11, from *logmem.cpp*).

Listing 9-11. **Semaphore "mark" full or empty routines:**
**   *markfull()*, *markempty()*, *marknfull()*, and**
**   *marknempty***

```
// used by writer to indicate buffer full
int logmem :: markfull()
{
    if (id == 0)
        return FAILURE;


    /* assume have shared memory monitor */
```

continued

```
    /* post that buffer is full */
    /* by setting sema "not full" to false */
    semas->doset0(SH_NFULL_SEMA);

    /* set0() does not use semaop() */

    return SUCCESS;
}



// used by reader to indicate buffer empty
int logmem :: markempty()
{
    if (id == 0)
        return FAILURE;

    /* assume have shared memory monitor */

    /* post that buffer is empty */
    /* by setting sema "not empty" to false */
    semas->doset0(SH_NEMPTY_SEMA);

    /* set0() does not use semaop() */

    return SUCCESS;
}



// used by reader to indicate buffer not full
int logmem :: marknfull()
{
    if (id == 0)
        return FAILURE;

    /* assume you have shared memory monitor */

    /* if semaphore is already 1, then just return */
    if (semas->isp(SH_NFULL_SEMA))
        return SUCCESS;

    /* post that buffer is not full */
    semas->post(SH_NFULL_SEMA); // post that buffer not full
```

```
    /* now that the array of atomic operation(s) built, */
    /* do the sema operations */
    int ret;
    if ((ret = semas->dosema()) == FAILURE)
        return FAILURE;

    /* clear out operation array buffer */
    semas->clear();

    return SUCCESS;
}


// used by writer to indicate buffer not empty
int logmem :: marknempty()
{
    if (id == 0)
        return FAILURE;

    /* assume you have the shared memory monitor */

    /* if the semaphore is already 1, then just return */
    if (semas->isp(SH_NEMPTY_SEMA))
        return SUCCESS;

    /* post that the buffer is not empty */
    semas->post(SH_NEMPTY_SEMA); // post buffer not empty

    /* now that the array of atomic operation(s) is built, */
    /* do the sema operations */
    int ret;
    if ((ret = semas->dosema()) == FAILURE)
        return FAILURE;

    /* clear out operation array buffer */
    semas->clear();

    return SUCCESS;
}
```

The System V semaphore routines provide a function for setting a semaphore to zero. However, the program does not use the normal *wait()* function because it wants to *force* the semaphore to be zero, not *wait* until it is zero!

Setting a semaphore (initializing it) is not done via the system call *semaop()*. Semaphores are initialized using the *semctl()* system call, as shown in the *semaset::doset0()* routine discussed later.

You might want to consider implementing a different version of the *semaset* class in which the *non-empty* semaphore is a counting semaphore that indicates the number of unread log messages in the buffer and the *non-full* semaphore is a count of the number of empty lines. Although this might make the *empty()* check in the reader routine unnecessary, you must be careful that the reader does not wait inside the monitor when the *non-full* semaphore drains to zero, as it might if you simply coded a *wait()* call. If the reader waits while it has the monitor semaphore, you have a "livelock."

If you do change *semaset*, you don't *need to* change *logmem*, although you might want to change it to take advantage of the counting semaphores, perhaps for greater efficiency or more error checking. You also do not need to change the reader and writer processes. This is what data abstraction and object-oriented programming are all about!

Constructors and Destructors

The constructor for the semaphore set is straightforward (see Listing 9-12). After some simple security checks (which could be strengthened), the *semget()* system call gets the ID for a semaphore set (see Listing 9-12). Because all routines use the same key value, they share the semaphore set. Also, each process has its own buffer of semaphore array operations, which the constructor allocates using the C++ *new* operator. (The destructor uses the *delete* operator to delete these buffers.) Again, the program allocates the semaphore set in this manner to more clearly demonstrate the use of constructors and destructors. It could have defined the *semas* member without the pointer ⁕ and let the compiler automatically handle the *new* and *delete* operations.

Listing 9-12. The *semaset* constructor and destructor: *semaset()* and ˜*semaset()*

```
/* semaset.c implement routines for set of semaphores */

#include <stream.h>
#include <sys/types.h>
```

```
#include <sys/ipc.h>
#include <sys/sem.h>
#include "shlog.h"
#include "semaset.h"

semaset :: semaset(int ckey, int numsems, int maxops, int flag)
{
    id = key = owner = nsemas = nops = curops = 0;
    sops = (struct sembuf *)NULL;
    errno = 0;              // clear UNIX system call error code

    if ((numsems <= 0) || (maxops <= 0))
        return;

    /* get the semaphore (1 means one sema at a time) */
    if ((id = semget(ckey, numsems, IPC_CREAT | IPC_PERM))
      == FAILURE)
        return;             // errno is set by system

    key = ckey;  nsemas = numsems;  nops = maxops;
    if (flag & SEMAS_OWNER)
        owner = getpid();

    // get sembuf array from free store
    sops = new sembuf[nops];
}


semaset :: ~semaset()
{
    if (id == 0)
        return;

    delete[nops] sops;      // return sembuf array to free store
}
```

The *semget()* system call returns a kernel semaphore set ID for the given key. If the key is already in use, it returns the existing ID, so that all users of the set use the same semaphores. However, each semaphore set user must have its own semaphore operation array, because several processes can simultaneously be waiting for, posting, or "marking" different semaphores.

Listing 9-13 shows how *init()* (the reader/creater function) initializes the semaphores. When all processes finish using the semaphores,
remove() removes them from the system.

**Listing 9-13. Initializing and removing the semaphore
functions: *init()* and *remove()***

```
int semaset :: init(int sema, int resources)
{
    errno = 0;          // initialize system error code

    if (id == 0)
        return FAILURE;

    if (owner != getpid())
        return FAILURE;

    if ((sema < 0) || (sema > (nsemas - 1)))
        return FAILURE; // make sure sema num is in set

    if (resources < 0)        // if negative, disallow
        return FAILURE;

    union semum arg; // initial val arg to semctl is unusual
    arg.val = resources;

    // initialize semaphore in set to desired initial value
    if (semctl(id, sema, SETVAL, arg) == FAILURE)
        return FAILURE;         // errno is set by system

    return SUCCESS;
}


int semaset :: remove()
{
    errno = 0;          // clear UNIX system call error code

    if (id == 0)
        return FAILURE;

    if (owner != getpid())
```

```
            return SUCCESS;

        union semum arg;     // arg is 0 for sema set removal
        arg.val = 0;

        /* remove the semaphore set from the system */
        if (semctl(id, nsemas, IPC_RMID, arg) == FAILURE)
            return FAILURE;              // errno is set by system

        id = key = owner = 0;

        return SUCCESS;
}
```

The System V *semctl()* system call initializes semaphore values. Another *semctl()* call also removes the semaphore set ID, which effectively removes it from the kernel. Only one process should perform these operations—the reader. (You need to change this to allow multiple readers.)

The *logmem* constructor (Listing 9-14) is more complicated, because it contains the shared memory region pointer and the set of semaphores. Note that *logmem* also contains an instance of the *semaset* class, rather than being derived from that class. Therefore, this example follows the practice of "top-down decomposition" rather than the full object-oriented, inheritance paradigm. However, you could derive special-purpose shared memory regions or semaphore sets from these examples following the inheritance model. These are merely simpler to present.

Listing 9-14.   The *logmem* constructor and destructor:
                  logmem()* and *˜logmem()

```
/* logmem.c implement routines for log file shared memory */

#include <stream.h>
#include <string.h>
#include <sys/types.h>
#include <sys/ipc.h>
#include <sys/shm.h>
#include "shlog.h"
#include "semaset.h"
#include "logmem.h"
```

continued

```
logmem :: logmem(int flag)
{
    id = key = owner = blines = bsize = 0;
    shmem = (struct shmem *)NULL;
    semas = (semaset *)NULL;

    errno = 0;
    int bytes = (SHBUF_LINES * SHLINE_SIZE) + (2*sizeof(int));

    /* get the shared memory region */
    /* only reader can create shared memory */
    if ((flag == LOG_READER)
        && ((id = shmget(SHLOG_KEY, bytes,
        (IPC_CREAT   IPC_PERM))) == FAILURE))
        return;           // errno is set by system
    else if ((id = shmget(SHLOG_KEY, bytes, IPC_PERM))
        == FAILURE)
        return ;          // errno is set by system

    shmem = new shmem;

    if ((shmem = (shmem *)shmat(id, 0, 0)) == (shmem *)(-1))
    {
        shmem = (shmem *)NULL;   id = 0;
        return;
    }

    if (flag == LOG_READER)
        shmem->readidx = shmem->writeidx = 0;

    semas = new semaset(LOG_SEMA_KEY, SH_SEMAS,
        SH_SEMA_OPS, flag);

    if (flag == LOG_READER) // if reader, init semaphores
    {
        semas->init(SH_MON_SEMA, SH_SEMA_TRUE);
        semas->init(SH_NFULL_SEMA, SH_SEMA_TRUE);
        semas->init(SH_NEMPTY_SEMA, SH_SEMA_FALSE);
    }

    key = SHLOG_KEY;
    blines = SHBUF_LINES;  bsize = SHLINE_SIZE;
```

```
    if (flag == LOG_READER)
        owner = getpid();
}


logmem :: ~logmem()
{
    if (id == 0)
        return;

    if (owner == getpid())
        remove();        // delete shared memory region

    delete semas;
}
```

The *semget()* system call allocates the shared memory region and gives it a unique ID based on the given key. Note that the *logmem* constructor attaches shared memory with the *shmat()* system call and also creates and initializes the semaphores, so that all log users share them. The destructor removes the shared memory area from the system; the creator also removes the semaphore set.

The *remove()* operation, called by the reader only, removes the semaphores and then removes the shared memory segment from the kernel. The writers merely call *detach()*, which uses the UNIX *shmdt()* system call to remove the shared space from their address space (see Listing 9-15).

Listing 9-15.   Exiting shared memory: *remove()* and *detach()*

```
int logmem :: remove()
{
    errno = 0; // clear UNIX system call error code

    if ((owner != getpid()) || (shmem == (shmem *)NULL))
        return FAILURE;

    if (id == 0)
        return FAILURE;

    if (owner == getpid())
        if (semas->remove() == FAILURE)
```

continued

```
                    return FAILURE;


        /* if own shared memory, then remove from system */
        if (owner == getpid())
            if (shmctl(id, IPC_RMID, (shmid_ds *)NULL)
              == FAILURE)
                return FAILURE;


        return SUCCESS;
    }




int logmem :: detach()
{
    errno = 0;  // clear UNIX system call error code

    /* detach from shared memory segment */
    /* (does not remove it from system) */
    if ((id == 0) || (shmdt((char *)shmem) == FAILURE))
        return FAILURE;


    return SUCCESS;
}
```

Other Functions

Finally, let's examine the rest of the routines of the program, including the dump routines used in debugging the implementations. The *read()* operation uses the *logmem::empty()* operation to see if continued multiple reads are possible.

Listing 9-16.   Other *logmem* functions: *empty()* and *dump()*

```
int logmem :: empty()
{
    if (semas->isO(SH_NEMPTY_SEMA))
        return TRUE;
    else
        return FALSE;
}
```

```
void logmem :: dump()
{
    if (shmem != (shmem *) NULL)
        cerr << "read idx: " << shmem->readidx
            << " write idx: " << shmem->writeidx << "\n";


    return;
}
```

The semaphores have additional functions, not all of which are used in this application. They are used to discover if a semaphore is zero or is positive (not zero) and set a semaphore to zero (note that the *semctl()* call accomplishes this, not *semop()*).

Listing 9-17. Other *semaset* functions: *wait0(), is0(), isp(), dose0(),* and *dump()*

```
int semaset :: wait0(int sema)
{
    if (id == 0)
        return FAILURE;

    if (curops >= nops)
        return FAILURE;

    sops[curops].sem_num = sema;    // semaphore's array index
    sops[curops].sem_op = 0;        // return if sema 0; else sleep
    sops[curops++].sem_flg = 0;     // if die, nothing to undo

    return curops;                  // return number of ops in array so far
}



int semaset :: is0(int sema)
{
    errno = 0;                      // initialize system error code

    if (id == 0)
        return FAILURE;

    if ((sema < 0) || (sema > (nsemas - 1)))
        return FAILURE;             // make sure sema num is in set
```

continued

```
        union semum arg;              // initial val arg to semctl is unusual
        arg.val = 0;

        int ret;
        // determine semaphore's current value
        ret = semctl(id, sema, GETVAL, arg);

        if (ret == FAILURE)
            return FAILURE;           // errno is set by system

        if (ret == 0)
            return TRUE;
        else
            return FALSE;
    }


int semaset :: isp(int sema)
{
    errno = 0;                    // initialize system error code

    if (id == 0)
        return FAILURE;

    if ((sema < 0) || (sema > (nsemas - 1)))
        return FAILURE;                      // make sure sema num is in set

    union semum arg;                 // initial val arg to semctl is unusual
    arg.val = 0;

    int ret;
    // determine semaphore's current value
    ret = semctl(id, sema, GETVAL, arg);

    if (ret == FAILURE)
        return FAILURE;           // errno is set by system

    if (ret > 0)
        return TRUE;
    else
        return FALSE;
    }
```

```
int semaset :: doset0(int sema)
{
    errno = 0;                      // initialize system error code

    if (id == 0)
        return FAILURE;

    if ((sema < 0) || (sema > (nsemas - 1)))
        return FAILURE;             // make sure sema num is in set

    union semum arg;                // initial val arg to semctl is unusual
    arg.val = 0;                    // clear semaphore (set to 0)

    // initialize semaphore in set to desired initial value
    if (semctl(id, sema, SETVAL, arg) == FAILURE)
            return FAILURE;         // errno is set by system

    return SUCCESS;
}



void semaset :: dump()
{
    cerr << "num ops: " << nops << " cur ops: "
            << curops << "\n";

    for (int i = 0; i < curops; i++)
            cerr << "sembuf[" << i << "]: "
            << form("n: %d op: %d flg: %d",
                sops[i].sem_num, sops[i].sem_op,
                sops[i].sem_flg) << "\n";

    return;
}
```

Reader and Writer Test Processes

Now that the implementations of the semaphores and the shared memory region are complete, users can reap the benefits of these efforts, made surer and easier with C++. The test driver routines are almost embarrassingly simple, spending most of their time using the provided objects, rather than being involved with the details of semaphore and shared log implementations. More importantly, users of the *logmem* and *semaset* classes are denied access to the private member functions of those classes.

Now, let's examine the code for the reader program:

Listing 9-18. The shared memory log buffer reader program: *reader.c*

```
/* reader.c test shared memory log reader routine */

#include <stream.h>
#include <string.h>
#include <sys/types.h>
#include <sys/ipc.h>
#include <sys/shm.h>
#include <signal.h>
#include "shlog.h"
#include "semaset.h"
#include "logmem.h"

extern int sleep(int naptime);
extern int sigcatch(int sig);

int gotsig = FALSE;                // set by signal catcher routine

logmem logmem(LOG_READER);

main( )
{
    signal(SIGTERM, sigcatch);

    char    myline[SHLINE_SIZE+1];
    myline[SHLINE_SIZE] = '\0';   // make sure null-terminated

    while (!gotsig)
    {
        sleep(5);                 // sleep arbitrary amount

        // get monitor and wait until non-empty
    (void)logmem.monnempty();
```

```
                    /* read all the news that's fit in buffer */
                    while (logmem.read(myline) != FAILURE)
                        cout << "\nreader " << "\"" << myline << "\"\n";

    (void)logmem.postmon();              // give up monitor
        }
}



int sigcatch(int sig)
{
    cerr << "\ncaught signal " << sig << "; exiting\n";
    gotsig = TRUE;                       // got signal; break out of loop

    exit(0);
}
```

Note that the reader continues to run until it receives a UNIX *terminate* signal. With the process *exit()* in the interrupt-handling routine, will the destructor for *logmem* be correctly called? (Yes, the C++ translator inserts constructors for global objects in the program prologue, and it inserts destructors for those objects before the system exit routine.) Notice that the reader reads *all* the lines in the shared buffer when it gets control.

The writer program is more straightforward:

Listing 9-19.   The shared memory log buffer writer program:
**   *writer.c***

```
/* writer.c test shared memory log writer routine */

#include <stream.h>
#include <string.h>
#include <sys/types.h>
#include <sys/ipc.h>
#include <sys/shm.h>
#include "shlog.h"
#include "semaset.h"
#include "logmem.h"


extern int sleep(int naptime);
```

continued

```
main(int argc, char * argv[])
{
    sleep(2);                          // wait for reader to initialize

    logmem logmem(0);

    char    myline[SHLINE_SIZE+1];

    int     mypid = getpid();      // designate writer process

    for (int i = 0; i < 10; i++)
    {
        sleep(2);                          // sleep arbitrary amount

        logmem.monnfull(); // get monitor; wait until non-full

        /* write a line in buffer */
        strcpy(myline, form("%d string %d to buffer",
            mypid, i));
        logmem.write(myline);

        cout << "\nwriter " << myline << "\n";

        logmem.postmon();  // give up monitor
    }
    cerr << "\ndetach from shmem log " << logmem.detach()
        << " errno " << errno << "\n";
}
```

The *sleep()* system calls are used to force writers to surrender the
CPU to let other writers and the reader execute, thus allowing a better
mix of messages from different programs on the terminal screen (and
providing a better test of the routines). (The *sleep()* UNIX library routine
delays a process for a specified number of seconds.) The processes
display their output at the terminal (standard output), but you can easily
divert output to a file on the UNIX system. If you type:

```
reader &
writer &
writer &
writer &
writer &
```

from your UNIX terminal, you will see messages from the writers (num-
bered from one to ten) and the reader interleaved on your terminal
screen. Note that when the reader obtains the monitor, it reads all the
messages posted by the different writers to that point. (The & notation
tells UNIX to run the programs in the background, or, more correctly,
it returns control to the user's *shell* after it starts the processes.)

One final note—using the UNIX system *make* facility, you can re-
build all of the changed programs by typing:

```
make
```

with the following *makefile*:

Listing 9-20.   The reader/writer test *makefile*

```
LIBS = logmem.o semaset.o
HEADERS = shlog.h semaset.h logmem.h
DEBUG = +i
CFLAGS = $(DEBUG) -g

all:    reader writer
        @echo "reader and writer are up to date"

reader: reader.o $(LIBS)
        CC -o reader $(CFLAGS) reader.o $(LIBS)

reader.o: reader.c $(HEADERS)
        CC -c $(CFLAGS) reader.c

writer: writer.o $(LIBS)
        CC -o writer $(CFLAGS) writer.o $(LIBS)

writer.o: writer.c $(HEADERS)
        CC -c $(CFLAGS) writer.c

logmem.o: logmem.c $(HEADERS)
        CC -c $(CFLAGS) logmem.c

semaset.o: semaset.c $(HEADERS)
        CC -c $(CFLAGS) semaset.c
```

Similar *make* utilities are also available under MS-DOS.

Summary

This chapter discussed the use of C++ with UNIX, highlighting its data abstraction and object-oriented capabilities for clearly specifying interfaces between objects. After examining the problems of correctly programming multitasking, cooperating-process systems, you saw how to define C++ classes to neatly encapsulate safe solutions to those difficult problems.

The main example demonstrated how a reader and several writers can share a memory buffer that can hold many log messages. The solution used System V shared memory and semaphores and hid the complex implementation details in abstract data classes, so that the client reader and writer processes could use a simple, safe interface.

Programming projects

The following exercises, given without answers in this book, suggest other variations for this example:

1. Implement the example using messages instead of shared memory and semaphores; use the early example as the basis of your efforts. Is your UNIX implementation fair regarding multiple blocked writers? Which implementation is more efficient?

2. Use named pipes instead of shared memory and semaphores; base your solution on the early partial example. How did you handle inter-record marks in the pipeline? How did you guarantee record boundaries? If the reader ever loses track of the start of a message due to buffer overflow by a writer, how can you get the reader synchronized again?

3. Use counting semaphores, not binary ones. This might require fewer system calls, but be careful of "livelock" situations and the "undo" semaphore operation flag.

4. Make the dump routines use *stream I/O*; use overloaded *ostream& operator<<() (logmem&)* functions, so that *cout << logmem* or *cout << semas* works.

5. Rewrite the program for multiple readers. Did you need a "demon" shared memory segment creator? Or did you use the first reader/writer? What if the creator is not the last one alive? Can you start the demon or first process from UNIX's */etc/inittab*?

6. Use inheritance when coding semaphores, shared memory, or both. Can you use *friends* instead of "top-down" refinement?

7. Use operator overloading rather than named functions for the semaphore operations. Is this a good idea? (Some programmers see only "arithmetic" when they see + signs, not "post semaphore.")

8. Map the shared memory section to the terminal screen. How can you alter it when memory changes?

9. Use the shared memory idea to develop a screen controller for multiple processes. Use *curses*. In this example, the reader would be passive. How did you change the access routines (class member functions) to permit multiple *concurrent* readers?

10. Expand the previous exercise to allow each writer a window on a dumb terminal.

Index